American Colonization Society

Memorial of the semi-centennial Anniversary of the American Colonization Society

American Colonization Society

Memorial of the semi-centennial Anniversary of the American Colonization Society

ISBN/EAN: 9783337151270

Printed in Europe, USA, Canada, Australia, Japan

Cover: Foto ©ninafisch / pixelio.de

More available books at **www.hansebooks.com**

MEMORIAL

OF THE

SEMI-CENTENNIAL ANNIVERSARY

OF THE

AMERICAN COLONIZATION SOCIETY,

CELEBRATED AT WASHINGTON,

JANUARY 15, 1867.

WITH DOCUMENTS CONCERNING LIBERIA.

WASHINGTON:
COLONIZATION SOCIETY BUILDING.
MDCCCLXVII.

PREFACE.

The Board of Directors of the American Colonization Society, at their meeting holden at Washington, Jan. 17, 1866, appointed William V. Pettit, Esq., of Philadelphia, the Hon. D. S. Gregory, of New Jersey, the Rev. John Orcutt, D.D., one of the Secretaries of the Society, and William Tracy, Esq., of New York, "to act in co-operation with the Executive Committee, in making arrangements for the semi-centennial anniversary of the Society." In consultation with them, the Executive Committee made the arrangements according to which the exercises of the Fiftieth Annual Meeting of the Society, Jan. 15, 1867, were conducted.

At their meeting the next day, Jan. 16, 1867, the Board of Directors adopted resolutions, tendering their thanks to the several speakers who had addressed the Society the previous evening, and requesting copies of their addresses for publication; tendering thanks to the authors of the communications received from Liberia; directing that the proceedings of that evening be published in a volume, in suitable style, as a memorial of the Fiftieth Anniversary of the Society; and requesting the Rev. Joseph Tracy, D.D., to take charge of and superintend the publication.

For the satisfaction of those who would understand Liberian mind and character, the editor has subjoined, in an appendix, the Declaration of Independence and Constitution of the Republic of Liberia, the Address of the Convention that formed the Constitution, the first Inaugural Address of its first President, and the last Annual Message of President Warner. The reader will readily perceive, in these documents, the results of much careful and successful study, but no servile imitation, of American State Papers of similar character. No candid man, after reading them, can doubt the capacity of colored men, with suitable training and experience, for the management of public affairs. The reader will notice with interest the difference in style, as the different occasions required, between President Warner's Address at the Annual Meeting and his Annual Message. That Address is printed from the author's elegant manuscript, with no correction except two or three evident slips of the pen. The others are reprints from Liberian printed copies.

There is also appended a list, complete so far as is known, of the names of all persons who have been authorized to act as chief magistrates in any of the colonies which now constitute the Republic of Liberia. Their dates have been given, so far as they could be ascertained. In the earlier stages of the enterprise, changes and vacancies from death, disease, and other causes, were frequent; communications were infrequent, and information, coming from agents worn down by sickness and labor, often imperfect and indefinite. Hence, appointments were sometimes made hypothetically, and the time of one agent is partially or wholly included within that of another. Agents of the Government of the United States for the care of recaptured Africans had no authority, from that appointment, to act as agents of the Society, or magistrates of the Colony. Yet, by a mutual understanding, the agents of the Government and the Society appear to have performed each other's duties when necessary, and often the same person was appointed to both offices. The names of the Government's agents are therefore included in the list, but are distinguished by a different type. For similar reasons, the names of most of the physicians appointed and sent out in the earlier years of the Colony have been included.

And, finally, there is appended a table of emigrants settled in Liberia by the Society, with the year, month, and name of the vessel in which they sailed, and the State from which they emigrated. Were it desirable, this table might be enlarged, by giving the name, age, occupation, previous condition as bond or free, education, and religious profession, if any, of every emigrant; but the particulars given seem to be enough.

It will be observed that this table does not include Africans recaptured from slave-traders and sent to Liberia at the expense of the United States, though many of them were delivered into the care of the Society in American ports, and conveyed to Liberia in the Society's vessels.

In a work like this, a complete account, historical and statistical, of the Society and its Colony, could not be given. It is hoped, however, that the selection and treatment of topics is such, that the careful and friendly reader will be able to understand and appreciate the general character of the enterprise in which the Society is engaged.

Thanks are due, and are cordially tendered, to the Hon. J. H. B. Latrobe, President of the Society, and to the Hon. G. Washington Warren, of the Board of Directors, for valuable suggestions and advice, and to William Coppinger, Esq., Corresponding and Recording Secretary, for facts ascertained by careful and laborious researches among ancient records and correspondence.

CONTENTS.

	PAGE.
MINUTES OF THE FIFTIETH ANNUAL MEETING	11
ADDRESS OF PRESIDENT LATROBE	15
SELECTIONS FROM THE ANNUAL REPORT	21
ADDRESS OF PRESIDENT WARNER	37
DR. TRACY'S HISTORICAL DISCOURSE	61
ADDRESS OF BISHOP CLARK	105

APPENDIX.

DECLARATION OF INDEPENDENCE	129
CONSTITUTION OF LIBERIA	133
INAUGURAL ADDRESS OF PRESIDENT ROBERTS	149
ANNUAL MESSAGE OF PRESIDENT WARNER	162

CONTENTS.

	PAGE.
CHIEF MAGISTRATES OF LIBERIA	177
TABLE OF EMIGRANTS	182
COST OF COLONIZATION	191
ORIGINAL MEMBERS OF THE SOCIETY	192

MEMORIAL

OF THE

SEMI-CENTENNIAL ANNIVERSARY

OF THE

AMERICAN COLONIZATION SOCIETY.

MEMORIAL.

The Fiftieth Annual Meeting of the American Colonization Society was holden in Trinity Church, Washington, D.C., on Tuesday, January 15, 1867.

The Hon. J. H. B. Latrobe, of Maryland, President, called the meeting to order at thirty minutes past seven o'clock, P.M. At his request, the Rev. R. R. Gurley, Honorary Secretary, invoked the divine blessing.

The President, after a brief address, called for the Annual Report.

The Corresponding Secretary, William Coppinger, Esq., read portions of the Annual Report. He then presented an address, prepared for the occasion by His Excellency, Daniel B. Warner, President of the Republic of Liberia, and "Reflections on the Return of the Anniversary of the American Colonization Society," by Henry W. Johnson, Attorney and Counsellor at Law in that republic. These could not be read for want of time.

The Rev. Joseph Tracy, D.D., of Massachusetts, presented and read portions of a Historical Discourse on the Rise and Progress of the Society.

The Rt. Rev. Thomas M. Clark, D.D., of Rhode Island, delivered the Semi-centennial Address.

The Rev. John Maclean, D.D., of New Jersey, then pronounced the benediction, and the Society adjourned.

The addresses at the Annual Meeting are given in their order on the subsequent pages.

ADDRESS

OF

HON. JOHN H. B. LATROBE.

ADDRESS OF HON. JOHN H. B. LATROBE,

PRESIDENT OF THE AMERICAN COLONIZATION SOCIETY.

Members of the American Colonization Society,
  Ladies and Gentlemen:

IN calling the meeting to order, the Chair has not forgotten that the Fiftieth Anniversary of the American Colonization Society has been reached.

The Fiftieth Anniversary! Half a century of existence! And yet it seems but a few years since the speaker, then a mere schoolboy, attracted by the lights of a church in Georgetown, peered at nightfall upon a meeting which Francis S. Key was addressing, and where, in all probability, Mercer and Clay and Randolph and Harper and Caldwell and Worthington were present. Dim candles, it is recollected, in tin sconces, lighted up the assembly. To the schoolboy's intelligence, the only interest of the scene was in the familiar voice and the gathered crowd. Of the subject of discussion, nothing was understood, save, as reported at home, that Mr. Key, a well-known friend, was talking about Africa. Circumstances fix this incident in 1816, half a century ago. How idly would the schoolboy not have regarded any promise then made to him, that he would live to preside at the semi-centennial anniversary of the Society whose feeble beginnings he had just witnessed without comprehending them! And now, how profoundly grateful should not the recipient of so high an honor be, not only to those whose choice gave him the seat which he occupies tonight, but most especially to HIM by whose mercy, while others younger and better have fallen, he has been spared to witness the seed, planted in 1816, germinate, and send forth a tree, which, through winters of discouragement and summers of prosperity, has grown until it has attracted the attention of the nations, and has a nation sheltered beneath its branches!

Fifty years! And *such* years! Of what other fifty years has history told the same wondrous tale? They commenced while the thunder of European wars and of our second contest with Great Britain still echoed in our ears. Wearied with the march of battle, the world was resting and gaining strength for a yet grander march,— the march of progress. How astonishing the facts of these fifty years! How extraordinary their developments!

In 1816, there were but three steamboats on the Hudson, and but three west of the Alleghanies. In 1867, where are they not? In 1816, the postage of a letter from Washington to Baltimore was ten cents; to Philadelphia, twelve; to New York, eighteen; and to

New Orleans, twenty-five. Now the postage to San Francisco is but three cents; and the telegraph has made communication with these places as instantaneous as the thoughts to be communicated.

In 1816, if the winds favored, a letter from America reached Europe in three weeks; if adverse, in six. Now, the Secretary of State sends to our minister in Paris what the Emperor of the French receives within the hour that saw it written in Washington. In 1816, it was the labor of days to travel from the capital to New York. Impatient at the nine hours now occupied, the public desire a still more rapid transit. Railroads cover the land as with a net, and are already penetrating the wilderness at the rate of a mile of construction daily, on their route to the Pacific. In 1816, we were staggering under a war-debt of but a few millions. Now we are paying off a war-debt of more than two thousand millions, at the rate of two hundred millions annually.

If to these comparisons were to be added the improvements in science and the arts, hours would be required for the enumeration.

Progress in science, progress in art, progress in all the appliances of human comfort, have signalized the half century whose close we this night commemorate.

But, of all that has been referred to, nothing has been more grand in conception, more wonderful in execution, or of more promising results, than African colonization. Grand in conception, because it solves the problem presented by the presence in the same land of two races, both free, that cannot amalgamate by intermarriage. Wonderful in execution, because with the humblest means, without the patronage of Government, and with few better materials than ignorant free negroes and emancipated slaves, it has built up a republic holding an honorable rank in the family of nations, with churches and schools, with free institutions modelled after our own, and already attracting to it the descendants of those who, brought naked and helpless from Africa, acquired here the religion and civilization with which their children are returning, clothed as with bright raiment, to their ancestral home. More promising of results, because its agencies are at work, not for the welfare of one people only, but for two quarters of the globe itself, benefiting America, blessing Africa; obviating in the one an otherwise inevitable strife, securing in the other the fulfilment of prophecy; illuminating the latter, without diminishing the lustre of the former; blessed of the Almighty in its progress, and finding, in an almost miraculous success, encouragement in the belief that his hand will support it to the end.

PORTIONS

OF THE

FIFTIETH ANNUAL REPORT.

PORTIONS OF THE FIFTIETH ANNUAL REPORT,

READ AT THE ANNUAL MEETING.

The American Colonization Society commemorates the Semi-Centennial Anniversary of its formation. Profound thanks are offered to God for marked progress in its noble work, and for the wider field of activity opened, and that its labors during the year just closed have been more extended and beneficial than for many years past.

Since the last meeting, seven more of the Vice-Presidents of the Society have been removed. The first who was called away was JAMES BOORMAN, Esq., of New York, a liberal giver to promote the benevolent enterprises of the times, and a model of Christian integrity and judgment. Following him, in rapid succession, were Lieut.-Gen. WINFIELD SCOTT, whose goodness of heart and humanity shone not less brightly than his military genius and love of country; Dr. THOMAS HODGKIN, of London, who spent his life in the service of his fellow-creatures of all races, and was universally esteemed for his consistency of character and the utter unselfishness of his devotion to this and every good cause; WILLIAM W. SEATON, Esq., long an active and highly-prized member of the Executive Committee of this Society, and its public advocate and defender, who has left behind him a bright example of disinterested benevolence; Gen. JOHN H. COCKE, of Virginia, for many years spared as the senior Vice-President of the Society, and who had fervently labored for his servants by furnishing the facilities for their spiritual improvement, and the settlement of some, and the preparation of others to enjoy their freedom in Liberia; DANIEL CHANDLER, Esq., of Alabama, justly held in high esteem for his piety and philanthropic character; and Commodore ROBERT F. STOCKTON, of New Jersey, eminent for civic acquirements and naval renown, and for intrepidity in meeting and successfully surmounting the bitter opposition of the natives, and in securing the territory upon which has arisen Monrovia, the capital city of the Liberian Republic.

It is fitting here to notice the great loss sustained by the Society in the decease of JOHN P. CROZER, Esq., of Pennsylvania, a man of rare generous sympathies and abounding liberality, long identified with the religious and charitable institutions of the country. Bound to our cause by the heroic dedication and sacrifice of a younger brother, — Dr. Samuel A. Crozer, who was the first agent and physician appointed by the Society, and who sailed with the first company of emigrants despatched to Western Africa, — he was always much interested in our labors and progress, and frequently attended and participated in the deliberations of the Board of Directors, where he was distinguished by a sound judgment, catholic disposition, uniform courtesy, and genuine kindness. By his will, he made provision for the promotion of the purposes of our organization to the extent of five thousand dollars.

Death has also removed from the ranks of the patrons and efficient friends of the Society, FRANCIS HALL, Esq., of New York; WILLIAM CRANE, Esq., of Baltimore; and Hon. ABRAHAM HANSON, the first Commissioner and Consul-General of the United States to Liberia, whose address at our last annual meeting was full of interest and encouragement.

In the departure of these constant and able advocates of the cause of African colonization, the members and friends of the Society are admonished of the uncertainty of all human supports, and of the necessity of arousing themselves to higher efforts in the light of the ever-shining glory of these excellent and lamented men.

To accommodate the numerous applicants for passage and settlement in Liberia, and in view of the great economy and pressing necessity of having a vessel of our own, adapted to our wants, it was determined to purchase, in September last, the ship "Golconda," 1016 tons, or 303 tons larger than the packet "Mary Caroline Stevens," whose place she takes in the service of the Society between this country and Liberia.

The purchase was not effected until after a thorough examination of the markets for vessels on charter or for sale. She was secured at a very reasonable price for cash. To Dr. James Hall is the Society indebted for the selection, purchase, and fitting out of this ship.

The "Golconda" was purchased and provisioned at Boston, and sailed thence, on Saturday, Oct. 20, for Charleston, S.C., as the nearest and most convenient port for the embarkation of the expected emigrants. On the afternoon of Wednesday, Nov. 21, being the first day of high water on the bar after her arrival at Charleston, she was towed safely out to sea and set sail for Liberia.

She started with exactly six hundred emigrants on board, of whom 194 were from Macon, Ga.; 167 from Newberry, S.C.; 144 from Knoxville, Tenn.; 52 from Charleston, S.C.; and 43 from Columbia, S.C. Of these, 206 are to settle at Sinou, 181 at Carysburg, 155 at Cape Mount, and 58 at Cape Palmas.

A large proportion of the emigrants are professors of religion; of whom it is known that 70 are Methodists, 56 are Baptists, 13 are Presbyterians, and 2 are Episcopalians. Among them is a regularly organized church, — "THE MACON BAPTIST CHURCH OF SINOU COUNTY, LIBERIA," — consisting of pastor, two deacons, and twenty-six members.

A high degree of intelligence is shown, in that 77 can

read, 20 can both read and write, and 2 have had the advantages of a collegiate education.

The trades or occupations are represented by 78 farmers, 33 laborers, 15 carpenters, 13 shoemakers, 9 bricklayers, 9 blacksmiths, 4 wheelwrights, 3 coopers, 3 tailors, 2 millers, 2 cooks, 1 iron-moulder, 1 silversmith, 1 ginmaker, 1 waterman, 1 gunsmith, 1 engineer, 1 goldsmith, 1 dentist, and 1 photographer.

The "Golconda" had five cabin passengers, among whom are the venerable Rev. John Seys, for the past thirty years identified with the interests of Liberia and of the cause of African colonization, now returning as Minister-Resident and Consul-General of the United States to that Republic; and Rev. H. W. Erskine, son of one of the most estimable colored ministers who ever went to the African coast, who was educated in Liberia, entered the ministry, and is now Attorney-General of that rising State. This was his first visit to the land of his birth, made in part to take with him an aged sister and her husband, with their children, grandchildren, and great-grandchildren lately made free, and now joyfully accompanying him.

Since the departure of the "Golconda" from Boston, applications have been received with the names of 78 persons at Winnesboro', S.C.; 25 at Lagrange, Ga.; 78 at Columbus, Ga.; 178 at Newberry, S.C.; and 291 at Mullins Depot, S.C.: in all, 642 for passage to Liberia. Companies are known to be forming, each promising to be at least 150 strong, at Macon, Ga.; at

Florence, S.C.; at Apalachicola, Fla.; and at Newbern, N.C.; while smaller parties have applied from other places, among which may be named Edenton, N.C., and Albemarle County, Va., all hoping to set sail the coming spring for " Fatherland."

Inquiries for information about Liberia, and how to get there, continue to reach the office of the Society, showing that multitudes are using the means, which they never had before, of learning the actual condition and real promise of a country which appeals to them with its ancestral claims, and offers them such advantages as they can hope to obtain nowhere else on the face of the earth.

It is to be distinctly understood that each and all of the movements which resulted in the unusually large emigration by the "Golconda," and those just referred to, were, and are, purely local and spontaneous. The people sought the Society in each and every instance.

Ought not these people also to be helped? Shall we close our hands against those who prefer a home in Liberia, and seek of us the needful aid? If they desire and choose to go to Africa, is it not our duty to aid and encourage them to do so? Can we, in any better way, repay them for their services, or make amends for the past, than by restoring them to their long-lost heritage in their fatherland? And shall we fail to supply Africa with intelligent Christian industry in the persons of her own offspring?

"As teachers, missionaries, and colonies, they will go self-moved; and the waves of the Atlantic, that heard the wail and the groans from the hold of the slave-ship, will yet resound with the song, the psalm, and the prayer, from the lips of colored people returning to found empire and Christian civilization in Africa. How vast, then, are the results of the problem of the colored people in America! They involve all sections and populations here, and extend their influence over two continents. Such a problem may well claim the sympathy and thought of the nation."

In his last annual message, President Warner thus dwells upon the advantages which Liberia is offering to the people of color: —

"On the subject of immigration, we cannot but feel a deep interest. Our need of population is immediate and urgent. Our immense resources cannot be developed; the fruits of the earth, spontaneously produced, cannot be gathered; the fat of the land cannot be made available, — simply for the want of minds and hands to engage in the necessary operations. Surely, with the vast latent capabilities of this country, we have the ability to become a power by no means to be despised in the agricultural and commercial world.

"We have again and again invited our friends in the United States to come over and help us to fill up the vast solitudes, which for centuries have remained uninhabited; while they, in exile in the Western Hemisphere, are jostled and elbowed and trampled upon by an oppressive race. But my hopes are as strong as ever, and my confidence remains unshaken in the destiny of Liberia. She is yet to be the asylum for the oppressed American negro, and a beacon for the guidance of the benighted tribes of this continent. I may not be able to predict the methods by which Africa's exiled sons are to be restored to her bosom; but I feel certain such an occurrence will in some way or other take place."

Rev. Edward W. Blyden, lately Secretary of State of Liberia, and now Fulton Professor of Languages in Liberia College, on a recent occasion said: —

"Any one who has travelled at all in Western Africa, especially in the interior of Liberia, and has seen how extensive and beautiful a country, marvellously fertile, lies uninhabited, with its attractive and perennial verdure overspreading the hills and valleys, cannot but come to the conclusion that this beauteous domain is in reserve for a people who are to come and cultivate it; and we can see no people so well prepared and adapted for this work as the negroes of the United States.

"Africa will, without doubt, be the final home and field of operation for thousands if not millions of them. And the powerful agency that will thus be brought into that land, — of family influences, and the diversified appliances of civilized life in the various mechanical, agricultural, commercial, and civil operations, will rapidly renovate the spirit and character of the African communities; and whole tribes, brought under the pervading influence of Christian principles, will be incorporated among us. And then Anglo-American Christianity, liberty, and law, under the protection of the Liberian flag, will have nothing to impede their indefinite spread over that immense continent."

Liberia is gradually growing in the elements of national stability. The natural riches of that region are enormous, and are such as, sooner or later, will support a commerce to which that at present existing on the coast is merely fractional. The Liberians own and run a fleet of "coasters," collecting palm-oil, cam-wood, ivory, gold-dust, and other commodities. A schooner of eighty tons was built, costing $11,000, and loaded last fall at New York, from money and the proceeds of African produce sent for that purpose by an enterprising merchant of Grand Bassa County. A firm at Monrovia are having a vessel built in one of the ship-yards of New York, to cost $15,000, which it is expected will be ready to sail about the middle of February next.

Bishop Payne, for the past thirty years connected with the Episcopal Mission on the West Coast of Africa, and now temporarily in this country, thus describes what he witnessed at Monrovia on his recent homeward voyage:—

"We enter Monrovia Roads, and find two vessels at anchor. One, a brigantine of 137 tons, English built, is owned by Dr. S. F. McGill and brothers. She is commanded by Captain Kelly, Liberian, and a navigator. The other is a regular English brig, just out, consigned to the firm just named, with a full cargo, and to be loaded entirely by them. Boats are passing rapidly to and from the shore, loaded with palm-oil and sugar. Her "lay days," or days for loading, are forty, but she will be freighted in thirty days. Dr. McGill ships on board of her thirty thousand gallons palm-oil and twenty-five thousand pounds of sugar, from the St. Paul's River.

"Just as we come to anchor, several boats come alongside the bark 'Thomas Pope,' loaded with sugar. It is freight from Mr. Jesse Sharp, one of the prosperous sugar-planters on the St. Paul's. Mr. Sharp judiciously purchased a small steam sugar-mill for $2,500, and paid for it the first year. For fourteen days we are receiving cargo, all from Monrovia. We ship thirty-six thousand gallons palm-oil, sixty-two thousand pounds of sugar, near fourteen thousand pounds of coffee, seven hundred pounds of ivory, besides sundry smaller amounts of freight."

The same devoted laborer for the redemption of Africa affords the following cheering account of what he saw of the thrift, comfort, and progress along the St. Paul's River, during a trip made Friday, April 20, 1866: —

"Emerging from Stockton Creek, we feel we are in a civilized country. On the right, in Lower Caldwell, is the neat establishment of Mr. Powers. Here, too, is a modest frame building, with quite as modest a congregation, called St. Peter's Episcopal Church. Proceeding up the river, we saw two Baptist and Methodist churches, each of brick, on either side of the river. Just opposite to Mr. Powers's, on the Virginia side of the river, is the neat, home-like residence of Rev. John W. Roberts, Bishop of the Liberia Methodist Church. The settlement of Virginia here extends back three or four miles from the river. Above Mr. Roberts's, we soon see the fine brick houses of Mr. William Blackledge and Rev. A. F. Russell. Presently we come to Clay-Ashland, where, besides Grace (Episcopal) Church, are three others. Here are many fine brick houses, the township of Clay-Ashland extending back four or five miles; and now we never lose sight again of cultivated fields and comfortable brick houses. Best amongst these are those of the Messrs. Cooper, DeCoursey, Anderson, Howland, and Washington, sugar-planters. By the time we reach the Gaudilla farm, we have passed four steam-mills, all hard at work. There are many wooden mills, besides those propelled by steam. An intelligent friend has given us the following, as an approximate estimate of the sugar crop on the St. Paul's, in 1866: Sharp, 120,000 lbs.; Cooper, 30,000 lbs.; Anderson, 35,000 lbs.; Howland, 40,000 lbs.; Roe, 30,000 lbs.; sundry smaller farmers, 150,000; total, 575,000 lbs. The coffee crop also is considerable, though we are not able to state how much."

Several of the leading powers of the world have recently given evidence of their regard for Liberia. By order of the Emperor of Russia, a first-class Russian frigate made a complimentary visit in January to Monrovia. Sweden and Norway also sent a national vessel on a similar errand, — the first arrivals of the armed representatives of these two northern European nations in the waters of the African Republic. The celebrated ship "Kearsarge" lately called on her way home from the Mediterranean, — the first American cruiser ordered there since the beginning of the war. The highest diplomatic representative accredited to Liberia is from the United States, — the title being lately changed to that of Minister-Resident and Consul-General. Holland, and Sweden and Norway, have created consulate officers to reside at Monrovia; and it is expected that a treaty of amity and commerce will soon be concluded between Russia and Liberia.

As we close this annual record, we turn our eyes to survey the way in which the Lord hath led us this fifty years.

The American Colonization Society was founded in Washington, D.C., Dec. 21, 1816, by eminent individuals from the several States, memorably prominent among whom was the Rev. Robert Finley, D.D. A Constitution was adopted at an adjourned meeting held in the Hall of the House of Representatives on the "following Saturday," Dec. 28, and officers elected Jan. 1, 1817. Not one, it is believed, of those who took part in these proceedings, or of the officers chosen at the first meeting, is living to witness its Semi-Centennial Anniversary!

The Society has had five Presidents, viz.:—

Jan. 1, 1817, Hon. Bushrod Washington.

Jan. 18, 1830, Hon. Charles Carroll, of Carrollton.

Jan. 20, 1833, Ex-President James Madison.

Dec. 15, 1836, Hon. Henry Clay.

Jan. 19, 1853, Hon. J. H. B. Latrobe.

The whole amount of its receipts during the fifty years has been $2,141,507.77; and the State Colonization Societies received, while acting in an independent capacity, as nearly as we can arrive at it, $417,399.33; making a grand total of $2,558,907.10.

The Society has given passage to 11,909 persons of color, sent in 147 vessels or voyages; and, what is a remarkable providence, not one of the vessels with emigrants on board has been permitted to bew recked or lost! Of these people, 4,541 were born free, 344 purchased their freedom, 5,957 were emancipated for the purpose of going to Liberia, the status of 68 is unknown, 346 were sent, in 1865, from Barbadoes, W.I., and 753 of the class popularly known as "freedmen" have left this country since the termination of the war. Besides these, 1,227 have been settled at "Maryland in Liberia," by the Maryland State Colonization Society. The total emigration, therefore, under colonization auspices and expense, has been 13,136.

The Government of the United States has made the

settlements founded by the Society the asylum of 5,722 recaptured Africans, mostly taken on the high seas by its men-of-war.

The Society has strictly confined its labors to the "colonizing, with their own consent, the free people of color residing in our country, in Africa."

Rev. Samuel J. Mills and Rev. Ebenezer Burgess went on board the "Electra," at Philadelphia, for London, Nov. 16, 1817. They set sail in the "Mary," from London, Feb. 3, 1818, and arrived at Sierra Leone March 22, following. They selected Sherbro Island, about 120 miles from that celebrated British colony, and left thence for the United States May 22, having passed just two months on the west coast of Africa. Mr. Mills died on the homeward voyage. His worthy colleague still lives in a good old age.

The ship "Elizabeth," the "Mayflower" of Liberia, sailed from New York Feb. 6, 1820, with 86 emigrants, and arrived at Sierra Leone March 9. These pioneers were landed at Campelar, Sherbro Island, March 20, 1820. This place was soon abandoned, and the survivors removed to Fourah Bay.

A treaty was signed at and for Mesurado Dec. 15, 1821, the colonists removed, and the American flag raised there, April 25, 1822.

The several settlements, with one exception, were formed into a Commonwealth, the Legislature of which began its first session Aug. 30, 1839.

The people, in Convention assembled, July 26, 1847,

constituted and declared themselves a "free, sovereign, and independent State, by the name and title of the Republic of Liberia."

The flag of the new Republic was raised Aug. 24, 1847, with demonstrations of joy and gratitude.

The territory owned by the Liberian Government extends some six hundred miles along the West-African coast, and reaches back indefinitely toward the interior, the native title to which has been fairly purchased.

It has brought within its elevating influence at least 200,000 of the native inhabitants, who are gradually acquiring the arts, comforts, and conveniences of civilized life. It has a regularly organized government, modelled after our own, with all the departments in successful operation. Schools, seminaries, a college, and some fifty churches, belonging to seven different denominations, are in a hopeful condition. Towns and cities are being built where once the slave-trade flourished with all its untold cruelty, bloodshed, and carnage. Agriculture is extending, and commerce is increasing.

Liberia has exercised, for nigh twenty years, all the powers and attributes of an independent Government, and has been recognized as such by the leading powers of the world.

ADDRESS

OF

HIS EXCELLENCY D. B. WARNER,

PRESIDENT OF LIBERIA.

ADDRESS OF PRESIDENT WARNER.

Mr. President, and Gentlemen of the American Colonization Society:

DOUBTLESS the occasion on which you have come together to-day is one of thrilling interest to every philanthropist present. It dates the semi-centennial existence of an institution, which, fifty years ago, entered upon the prosecution of an enterprise which has already achieved much, and is destined to revolutionize for good an entire continent. A period of fifty years in the age of a nation just beginning its career is short, when compared with the object it has in view and the length of time such an organization is expected to exist; but when viewed in connection with a private association, such as your Society is, it occupies in the catalogue of dates a high and prominent place.

Among the circumstances which led to the founding of your Society, there may be enumerated the frightful proportions to which slavery had grown in the United States of America; the deep moral and physical degradation and immense suffering of its victims; the wide-spreading demoralizing effects it was producing upon the morality, civilization, and Christianity of the country; and the awful sense of the great guilt and immeasurable responsibilities the country was incurring by allowing an institution so reproachful to continue in it and to receive aid and comfort under its flag. The former of these circumstances had produced in some of the States very distressing alarm, causing them to give the question of slavery a serious consideration; and the sufferings of the slave had appealed with powerful effect to the justice, humanity, and benevolence of all the States.

Respecting the first and chief object of the Society at its founding, there have been made various statements; some of which, if true, attribute to it a selfishness which finds a parallel only in that which clinches the hands and petrifies the heart of the most detested and abandoned miser. But such a selfishness as that could not, I think, have continued so long, and been productive of such great and good results as we see flowing from the operations of the scheme of African colonization. But whether it was self-interest, or any thing akin thereto, which prompted the founding of the institution, and has ever since been the mainspring of all its operations, the signs of the times seem to favor the opinion of *many*, that an enterprise was set on foot, which, in process of time, will become a standing wonder of the world; and, in eternity, millions will remember it as the door through which they entered the church militant, and thence the church triumphant.

Perhaps the pages of modern history contain a record

of no beginnings so small, instruments so weak, and wielded by a power so feeble, that have, in the same time, accomplished more than the Society has through its African colonization scheme. This remark should be regarded as neither boastful and extravagant on the part of Liberia, nor enthusiastic and exaggerative in favor of the Society. It is rather an expression given to convictions which are daily being strengthened and confirmed by the progressive movements, both of the Society and of Liberia, and in which the world itself will concur, when the objects and operations, achievements and prospects of both shall have been thoroughly understood by it.

The Society was no sooner formed, than its object and operations became an offence to the hardened slaveholder. By him they were said to be in antagonism to his interest, and the interest of those he held in bondage. He, therefore, hurled against them all the formidable weapons he could command; calling, at the same time, for the curse of Heaven to fall upon them, and blast them forever.

There seems, however, to have been, in the earlier stages of slavery in the United States, some little just and humane consideration for the slave and man of color; but, when this feeling assumed the form of protection and stern justice, the creed of the pro-slavery man was made to run thus: "Go, therefore, now, and work, for there shall no straw be given you, yet ye shall deliver the tale of bricks."

As friends to the Society and African colonization multiplied, the opposition of the pro-slavery men grew stronger, seconded even by some of those for whose especial benefit the association was founded. It was fierce and malicious and formidable enough to discourage and even check a movement much more popular than African colonization.

That there may be brought under view something more of the greatness of the task which the Society imposed upon itself, — or will it be as correct to say, that was imposed upon the Society? — when it assumed to found a colony of the American blacks on the West Coast of Africa, — this dreaded land, — we must take into the account the very limited geographical knowledge it possessed of the country about to be occupied, of the character of the people inhabiting it, the distance of three thousand miles emigrants would have to be transported who were to be the colonists, and the protection which would have to be afforded these from the violence and depredations of the natives in the country. Here, too, in active operation, was a powerful branch of that great laboratory — the slave-trade — that was furnishing the Western World with its victims of cruelty, suffering, and death. It was being carried on by civilized and Christian governments, who made their navies sentinels to watch and repel the approaches of any one that would have the temerity to come to molest them in their infamous work of blood. Long had the horrid flag of this nefarious traffic waved over the land, supported and worshipped by its kings and its princes.

Against this array of might and power, a handful of men, comprising the American Colonization Society,— an association of very limited means, and equally so in point of skill in the management of African affairs,— set out to contend, relying for success upon the pureness of their intention, the justice of their cause, and the hope of receiving aid from Him by whom "kings reign and princes decree righteousness;" and who had said, "Ethiopia shall stretch forth her hand unto God." How they began and succeeded, we will narrate presently.

For more than three centuries previous to the founding of your Society, the African slave-trade had been crossing the Atlantic Ocean to the Western Hemisphere. Annually, it had torn away from their native homes and beloved country, thousands and thousands of the children of Africa, burying thousands of them in the sea, as they expired in the middle passage, and transporting the remainder of them, sick, feeble, and distressed, to foreign countries; there subjecting them to a servitude and to brutalities to which a speedy and violent death is preferable. For years this wicked and unjust traffic had been passing from East to West, attended with sufferings, cruelties, and barbarities, which torture the mind to reflect upon. The Western World had been made black with the shrivelled forms of its victims, and their oppressors drunk with their blood.

But, from the beginning of the foul monster's career,

there was an eye, which never sleeps, looking on upon his work. It took cognizance of all his deeds; of each of his victims that fell in the middle passage, and now lies on the bed of ocean; of all that breathed out their souls on the bloody plantation, whose bones have no resting place but in the open air, exposed to the foot of the impious and the ravages of the night beasts.

True, the American people, as a nation, retired from the trade, declaring it piracy, and those of themselves engaged in it worthy of death; but this declaration was, in effect, like the decrees of King Ahasuerus, and its hypocrisy has received a terrible reward. But the time in the purpose of this All-seeing One having come, when a counter current should set in,— when there should be, at least, a beginning of a returning to their father-land of the suffering African captives, a star appeared to guide them to the spot:—

> "It was their guide, their light, their all;
> It bade their dark forebodings cease;
> And through the storm, and danger's thrall,
> It led them to the port of peace."

Purposely inspired, as I very believe they were, by Omnipotence, with his will to that end, a few philanthropic individuals banded themselves together, and, in the year 1816, founded the American Colonization Society. This is the star which appeared to shed light on the surrounding darkness of American slavery, and to point out to the bondmen the way from the "House of Bondage" to the "Land of Promise." This was the more earnest beginning by those devoted philanthropists, to do that *will* of Heaven with which they had been so impressively inspired.

Still pressing towards their object, the Society, in 1818, employed, commissioned, and sent to the coast of Africa, two commissioners. The honored forerunners of the heaven-blessed scheme, and bearers of credentials sealed with an impress deeper and broader than that which mortals use, were Messrs. Samuel J. Mills and Ebenezer Burgess, — names honored in Liberia by all who hear them. Theirs was the duty to "spy out the land," and to select and purchase a suitable site for the location of a colony. This was to be an asylum, — a peaceful retreat from slavery and oppression — for as many of the African exiles in America as could and would avail themselves of the provisions made by the Society for reaching it. It was to be the foundation of a Christian negro nationality, and a beacon to the countless thousands and millions of Africa's sons who are sitting in darkness and in the region and shadow of death.

Promptly did those agents fulfil their mission, the many obstacles which lay in their way notwithstanding. In treating with the owners of the land selected, they were brought in contact with all that duplicity and treachery for which the natives connected with the slave-trade are so signally famous. This rendered their negotiations both irksome and perplexing. But all these difficulties were heroically encountered and overcome; and then the commissioners turned their faces homeward.

On the return of Mr. Burgess to America (Mr. Mills, his co-adjutor, having resigned his gentle spirit to Him who gave it, while on his way to those who had sent him), and the communication to the Society of his report, the Society determined at once to give their novel enterprise a thorough and practical trial, so soon as circumstances would allow it to do so. After the lapse of two years, matters being favorable, the undertaking was resumed; when in February, 1820, the ship "Elizabeth" was chartered, and sent to the Sherbro Island with a company of eighty-eight emigrants, under the care and superintendence of the Society's new agent, Dr. S. A. Crozer. This was the forming germ of a subsequent growth; and who at that time, judging from its formation and tenderness, could determine the size of the tree it would produce? Who could estimate the number of other happy events depending upon its success? Or who, even now, at its advanced age and growth of only forty-six years, will undertake to figure up the good which has already accrued from it to civilization and Christianity? And what circle less than that which bounds eternity will be sufficiently great to enclose the influence it is now exerting upon the world? Had the opportunity afforded the Society at that time for planting a settlement in Africa been lost, a second one would probably have never occurred.

The location selected for the colony being, as it subsequently and sadly proved to be, one of extreme unhealthiness, the emigrants were early stricken down by its pestilential fevers. Great suffering followed; and death did his work so fast and terribly, that it was found necessary to abandon the island, and remove the surviving colonists to the colony of Sierra-Leone. Here they remained until they were re-enforced by a company by the brig "Nautilus;" and here both companies located until a second and permanent place was found for them in 1821, at Cape Mesurado. At this place the care-worn wanderers utterly demolished the *tent*, substituting it with the more substantial and firmly-fixed lodge, composed of brick, wood, and the durable granite. Here a remnant of that pioneer band and their offspring are resting, having stood the shock of war, endured intense suffering, and undergone and lived through most of the trials and vicissitudes peculiar to newly-founded countries. And here are thousands of others who have come after them, enjoying, in the fullest sense of the word, "liberty and equality." Here no "public sentiment frowns them down," so long as they obey their country's laws.

It was to be out of the "house of bondage," that those way-faring and self-sacrificing men, stooping under the weight of weary years of slavery, launched upon the tumultuous ocean, crossed it, and became the subjects of suffering and privation which put to the test all of human and divine virtues they possessed. And the fortitude and heroism displayed by those founders of Liberia, during their day of trial, were indeed worthy the cause calling them into action; and the names of the veterans themselves, with that of the illustrious Ashmun, and those of your numerous other self-sacrificing agents, and that of the Gordons who fell in the cause of African colonization,—died here that Liberia might live,—will descend in radiance of glory, gathering brightness as years roll on, to generations yet unborn.

All this was done to reclaim from slavery, superstition, and idolatry, and to prepare and garnish *the* home of the millions of Africa's descendants in America, and to bring within the range of morality, civilization, and Christianity, the untold millions of her sons and daughters dwelling in darkness on her soil, and in gross darkness which can be felt.

What a fabric of "civil and religious liberty" was begun at the laying of the corner-stone of the Colony of Liberia! What a monument of God's favor and loving-kindness to the sons of Ham was then being created! What an achievement was being effected in favor of the gospel of peace! And what tongue will refuse to speak His glories forth, who put it into the hearts of those who undertook the work, and, until their death, devoted themselves to its execution, to go forth and build up the waste places in Africa which sin had made!

Thus far I have attempted very little in detail. I have already passed over, unnoticed, hundreds of incidents which occurred between the arrival at Sherbro of the ship "Elizabeth" with the first emigrants, and the formal occupation by the colonists of Cape Mesurado; and there are hundreds of others strewed between that period and the time I am occupying in addressing you.

Some of those incidents were truly afflicting and distressing; and a recollection of them, even at this distant period of time, produces in the mind very sad and painful reflections. Others were cheering and gratifying, and in their more happy effects are still looming up before us in the most flattering prospects of success, both to the Society and to the Republic of Liberia.

In my last inaugural address, I have already noticed what I think should be regarded by us all as very remarkable in the enterprise of your Society, viz.: the exemption from those more sad and distressing casualties or disasters, so common to the maritime world, of all its vessels but one, I think, transporting emigrants to Liberia.* Are not such remarkable instances of the preservation of ships very rare? And have we another such instance given, as in the case of the Society, in which a company has sent its vessels across the ocean for forty-six years, consecutively, and has lost but one of them? Were I certain that the case of the Society

---

* In that single instance of wreck, no emigrant was lost.—[ED.]

furnished the only instance of the kind, I would seize upon it with the greater tenacity, as an incontrovertible proof of God's special favor towards the returning bondmen of America, and of his pre-determined purpose that they should once more visit, and permanently settle in, their country, — long lost and disgraced though it may have been, — driving out the Canaanite, and breaking down and trampling under foot the power of the slaver.

Granting that some vessel and her company of emigrants shall be lost, — sunk in the depths of the sea, — will that be sufficient to break down the opinion, that the Supreme Being has willed and fore-ordained that there shall be an exodus of the colored population of America to their own land? No more so, I think, than the falling in the wilderness of all the Jews, except two, over twenty-one years of age, that left Egypt for Canaan, before they reached that place, was sufficient to prove that it had not been pre-ordained that they should leave Egypt, and go into Canaan. If any of the descendants of Africa in America start hither, despising the country — their sacredly reserved inheritance — to which they are coming, should it be thought strange if they do not reach it?

The late war in America, — that terrible "uprising of a great people," — if it could be viewed in all its phases and connections, would probably furnish an exact key to the question, "Shall the people go to their own place?" The very *watch-word* of that war was, "Let my people go, that they may serve me in the wilderness." The burden of President Lincoln's administration was, Loose the shackles, and let the oppressed go free! And President Johnson, extending the order, says to the people, "Go to Liberia."

All the propositions, from 1777 to the present time, made by various Governments, the Government of the United States of America not excepted, for the settlement of the people elsewhere than their own country, have failed, — failed, may we not say, like the building of Babel, because they were in direct opposition to that plan for settling them, designed by Him who is the Great Designer of the universe itself. He saith, "Surely, as I have thought, so shall it come to pass; and as I have purposed, so shall it stand." *

It would seem, then, that it is no wilderness in Mississippi, in any of the north-western Territories, nor in Central America, to which the people should remove or be removed, but to the wilderness of Western and of Central Africa. These, doubtless, are the localities ordained of old to be the future dwelling-places of the returning captives of Africa, and the deep solitudes requiring the melody of their songs, that the solitary places may be glad; and the people themselves should be constantly pleading, "Send me away, that I may go unto mine own place."

On being invited to come to Liberia, the colored

---

* Isaiah xiv. 24

people of America should not regard the invitation in the light of a request made of them to surrender their own country, and come to one belonging to others. The contrary is the true state of the case. Africa, and not America, is their country. It was made theirs when

> "God drave asunder, and assigned their lot
> To all the nations."

It has been for centuries, and is still being, kept in sacred reserve for them, and none shall inherit their portion until they come. And they ought to come; and come they will, when it shall be said to them, — and it will be said to them in a manner they shall not be able to resist, — "Get thee out from this land, and return to the land of thy kindred."

Here is ample room to receive them, bread enough to feed them, wealth to enrich them, and a way open before them to the object of their highest aspirations.

"Can the Ethiopian change his skin, or the leopard his spots?" So neither can finite minds change or frustrate the mind and purposes of the Infinite. "For the Lord of hosts hath purposed, and who shall disannul it? His hand is stretched out, and who shall turn it back?"

But, you ask me, What is that purpose? The sum total of the answer is with Him whose "thoughts are not as our thoughts;" but the opinion entertained by many respecting it is, that, in the course of time, the two races — the black and white races — must separate; and the deep blue Atlantic Ocean will be the dividing — the Mason and Dixon — line between them. Besides this, there seems yet to be solved but one other question remaining; viz., Can the blacks be absorbed by the whites? That is, can there or will there be, through the means of a spontaneous amalgamation, a gradual passing away of the former into mulattoes, and these again into the dominant race, so that, in a few centuries, the whole of the present negro population of America will have been changed into the white element? This is not probable; neither should it be thought desirable.

It will be but increasing the difficulty (perhaps I am too dogmatical in my opinion on this, and some of the foregoing subjects), the settling of the people by themselves in any part of America, where they and the whites can have easy and frequent intercourse with each other. This opinion is based on the probability, that, under such circumstances, one or the other people will invade the rights of his neighbor. This will gender into an unpleasant altercation between them; and, if the cause of offence proceed from the side of the blacks, will there not always be found among the whites those who will shoot down a score of blacks for an injury done, nay, even for an insult offered, to one of the whites? If such an occurrence were to take place near or at the allotted home of the four millions of blacks, would it not be resented? And, if resented, the consequences would probably be such as I need not, if I could, describe. If it was not resented, I can think of but two things to which such an enlightened and successful restraint upon depraved human nature would be attributable. First, that the blacks, in separating from the whites, solemnly vowed never to quarrel with them (the whites), except in a *legal* way, under any circumstance whatever; and, secondly, that they felt themselves numerically too weak to contend successfully with their white neighbors in a quarrel in which deadly weapons would be used. If the latter conclusion should be the barrier to their protecting and defending themselves when they *should* do so, then the blacks would not be living in the enjoyment of that social and political ease and equality for which they are, but vainly, contending in America.

But to return. If I could be less commendatory in my remarks while I address you, I would prefer it; but I cannot well be so, and give utterance to what I feel to be genuine convictions relative to your Society and the Republic of Liberia. The life-long interests of millions of the African race in the Western Hemisphere are involved in the question. Shall those millions remain where they are, and let Africa go down, and sink yet lower; or should they return to their fatherland, and redeem it from the stigma and reproach which have rested upon it for ages, dishonoring its name, and throwing a darker shade over its ancient glory? The salvation of an entire continent of many millions of inhabitants is at stake; and it is but just, that every laudable means should be called into requisition to secure it; and that those means should be regarded with a proper appreciation, and their operations promoted; and every thing ought to be said and done that will have, upon the whole subject, a wholesome and profitable bearing.

But for the inauguration of your Society, and the subsequent founding of Liberia, and the emigrating to it from American slavery of a few of the civilized descendants of Africa, what a fund of native, but rare and brilliant, talent would have lain hidden in the minds of thousands who are now employing it in diffusing useful and saving knowledge among thousands of thousands, who, but for receiving it through this channel, would have gone without it from the cradle to the grave!

History, in all probability, never would have had impressed on its pages, as men of great common sense, unflagging fortitude, and dauntless courage, the names of Elijah Johnson, Lot Cary, Daniel Hawkins, Allen James, Richmond Sampson, Thomas Spencer, John Lawrence, and the names of numbers of others who emigrated to Liberia in the darkness of the night of African slavery, fought here, and died in the work of laying the foundation of a negro Christian empire, and erecting the standard of freedom and of the cross of the Saviour. They toiled hard and long at this, praying, at the same time, that the sun of righteousness would shine on this benighted land, and chase hence, forever, the thick darkness in which it has been enveloped for thousands of years.

The oratorial powers of the lamented Hilary Teage, the diplomatic abilities of Joseph J. Roberts, the statesmanship of the late President Benson, the legal abilities of Chief-Justice John Day, and the ecclesiastic endowments of James S. Payne, and the admirable acquirements and abilities of many others in Liberia, would have been so many gifts vainly bestowed, but for a place for their display, and opportunities for their improvement; and these places and opportunities were not to be found in a land of slavery and proscription.

The banks of the St. Paul's, St. John's, Sinoe, and Farmington River, and of the River Cavalla, now teeming with civilized life and industry, presenting to view comfortable Christian homes, inviting school-houses and imposing church edifices, but for the founding of Liberia would have remained until this day studded with slave barracoons, the theatres of indescribable sufferings, wickedness, and shocking deaths. And what is to be said of the site on which is erected Liberia College? And have we, in truth, lived to see a college in Liberia? Its site is now no more a place of concealment for the subtile and sinewy boar, and the stealthy leopard. Its former forest echoes no longer the horrifying yell of the perfidious and murderous Dey, invading Monrovia; it is no longer made vocal with the doleful noise of the night-bird. An edifice, dedicated to the arts and sciences, stands there; and its halls are thronged with Liberia's youthful aspirants, preparing themselves to assert the rights of Africa, and to redeem her from her present thraldom.

And what can I say more! From every stand-point

I have yet been able to occupy, I can see nothing in the founding of the American Colonization Society, and its subsequent operations, but a lofty philanthropy engaged in the prosecution of a purpose which can be appreciated justly only by the mind that can grasp eternity. And yet we have the mortification to hear the Society pronounced a cheat; its agents, knaves; emigration, a gross injustice; the Republic of Liberia, a sham and a grave-yard; and the whole enterprise a deception! But all these pitiful indulgences and unjust criminations fail most shamefully to disprove the *fact*, that this day the sun, in the brightness of his glory, shines most majestically upon a palpable contradiction of *all* of them, in the real form of the highly respected and extensively recognized Republic of Liberia. Let its traducers come and see it. While they, on their side of the wall, are pouring water on the flame to extinguish it, on the opposite side there is a Hand, secretly, and as constantly, keeping it alive by feeding it with grateful oil.

With all her faults and failings, her poverty and weakness, Liberia is endeavoring to prove herself grateful to those who founded her, and have watched over her, cared for and fostered her for forty-six years, and so render herself worthy of the relations she sustains to Africa, and to the civilized nations with whom she has treaties.

Your offspring, Mr. President, and gentlemen of the society, is yet existing, and, withal, is growing, — growing in that which is of "good report." Her growth may be tardy; so may it be of long continuance. But, if our colored brethren would come over and help us, we should get on faster, and our prosperity would be much more abundant. They have been so frequently invited to come, and the advantages they would have in this country have been so clearly and repeatedly set before them, that I deem it unnecessary to say any thing further to encourage them to come than I have already said. If they will persist in building Babels in the land of Shinar, and pyramids in Egypt, which will eventually be to *them* only so many eye-sores whenever they look at them from this side of the waters, we have only to say to them, *build on.*

Since your founding, you have been called to lament the death of many of your once active and efficient members, whose presence in your meetings was so animating and cheering. In the far-off land of Africa, repose the dust of some of them. But there are yet remaining among you faces that have been familiar with each other, perhaps for fifty years. Doubtless there is among you your venerable and superannuated corresponding secretary, whom you sent to Liberia in 1824, to reconnoitre the colony, and to inspect the Agency of the great Ashmun, your then Colonial Agent, whose intrinsic worth, as a person for the times, the Society did not at that time know. There are also yet in Liberia, among the living, a few of the Crozer band, and a remnant of the Ashmun contemporaries. But Liberia, as well as the Society, has had her bereavements. Her great men passed away just at the time, in human calculations, when their services were most wanted. They are gone from their labor and toil, and their works follow them.

Notwithstanding many evil reports have gone abroad against our "land of promise," deterring many in America, and perhaps elsewhere, from coming to help us possess it — and there are yet being uttered predictions that we must "eventually fail and come to naught," — yet both you and we have abundant reasons to rejoice, and to believe that He who has begun the work of Africa's redemption will carry it on to a glorious completion. That great Architect of the universe has given us already too many assurances of his good will towards us — and he is able to make that good will abundantly effectual — to allow us to doubt one moment his faithfulness in all things pertaining to his creatures, or to believe he will abandon us while we are yet trusting in him. The sure and immutable word is, "Righteousness exalteth a nation; but sin is a reproach to any people." By securing the first, the second may be avoided.

In conclusion, Mr. President and gentlemen, I have only to remark, that, thus far, through the vicissitudes of fifty years, amidst the sneers and scoffs of those who would scoff and sneer at your undertaking, against the spiteful and virulent opposition of anti-colonizationists, with a determination of purpose, having a sanctified reference to the glory of God, you have steadily held on your way, using your best endeavors for the redemption of Africa, and the salvation of her millions of souls. Were I permitted to speak a word in behalf of myself, in your presence, I would say, I shall never be able to command language to express my gratitude to God for guiding my infant feet to the Colony of Liberia. My time in Liberia is almost coeval with the existence of the place, and I have yet to *feel* the slightest regret at my being here.

And now, to Him who hath sustained you, and given you of his free Spirit to guide you in all your acts and deliberations, be ascribed might, majesty, and dominion, now and forever.

HISTORICAL DISCOURSE.

HISTORICAL DISCOURSE.

Mr. President:

A PUBLIC notice has promised " An Historical Discourse on the Rise and Progress of the Society " which now celebrates its fiftieth anniversary. The treatment of the first topic — the Rise — may, perhaps, be aided by an illustration. It shall be drawn from the practice of the ancients, mentioned by Seneca, of building altars and offering worship at the sources of rivers. Remains of such temples, evidently Grecian, are still seen at the two sources of the Jordan; and substructions, older than Grecian, at that of the Chrysorrhoas, esteemed by the people of Damascus "better than all the waters of Israel." In both these instances, however, the water from these sources soon unites with less pretentious streams, coming from a much greater distance. But what if there be no vast flood bursting forth at any one point? What if we find only here the bubbling fountain, at which the wild bird scarce slakes her thirst; there, the drops trickling from the face of a cliff; yonder, the superfluous moisture escaping from a bed of moss; and moisture from a thousand other places, in varied forms, all collected by the slopes and channels which the Great Creator has provided for that purpose, into one vast Father of Waters, fertilizing the plains and bearing the commerce of half a continent? Plainly, you can erect your altar in no one place. You can worship only the Beneficent Wisdom which is everywhere, and which has so made the world that kindred good influences naturally flow together, and combine into broad streams of blessing to mankind.

So of the origin of our Society, and of our work. The sentiment out of which it grew, more or less definitely formed into specific plans, was everywhere, tending to realize itself in beneficent action for the colored race. This sentiment gushed forth at many points; so that many persons have been named as the originators of our enterprise. And there is some ground for each of these claims, and, doubtless, for many others that might have been advanced. They were originators, as truly as if there had been no others. Their relative merits cannot be settled by chronology, for the thought was often as fresh and original in the later projector as in any that had preceded him.

The earliest movement known to have any historical connection with our Society was the visit of the Rev. Samuel Hopkins of Newport, R.I. to his neighbor, the Rev. Ezra Stiles, April 7, 1773. The diary of Dr. Stiles has preserved the record. Dr. Hopkins proposed to educate two pious negro youths for the ministry, and send them to Africa as missionaries; hoping, evidently, to send more in time. He needed assistance to meet the expense. The more practical mind of Dr. Stiles suggested that the enterprise would not succeed in that form; that thirty or forty suitable persons must be sent out, and the whole conducted by a society formed for the purpose. This idea of a purely missionary settlement grew, in a few years, into a definite plan for a colony, with its agricultural, mechanical, and commercial interests. Aug. 31, 1773, Drs. Stiles and Hopkins issued a circular, inviting contributions to their enterprise. Feb. 7, 1774, a society of ladies in Newport had just made their first contribution; and aid had been received from several parts of Massachusetts and Connecticut. Nov. 21, two of the young men sailed for New York, on their way to Princeton, N.J. to be educated under Dr. Witherspoon, president of the college. Three days later, bills were drawn on London for amounts collected in aid of their enterprise in England and in Scotland. April 10, 1776, another circular was issued. They then thought their colony would be on the Gold Coast, near Annamaboe, where one of their young men had influential relatives, who were anxious for his return, as had been learned by letters from Africa, confirming his own account.

The war of Independence suspended these labors; but the plan and the purpose survived it. In 1784, and again in 1787, Dr. Hopkins endeavored to induce merchants to send out a vessel with a few emigrants, to procure lands and make a beginning, and with goods, the profits on which would, of course, diminish the expense. In March, 1789, he had consultations with Dr. William Thornton, "a young man from the West Indies," who proposed to take out a company of free blacks, and found a colony in Africa. A number volunteered to go with him, but the enterprise failed for want of funds. Dr. Thornton was afterwards a member of the first Board of Managers of the American Colonization Society.

A month later, Granville Sharpe and others sent the first colonists from London to Sierra Leone. This design was already known to Hopkins. Perhaps, too, Sharpe had heard of the plans of Hopkins, as they had been well known in England for some years; but they had no direct intercourse with each other till Hopkins wrote to Sharpe, Jan. 15, 1789, inquiring whether, and on what terms, and with what prospects, blacks from America could join the colony. There were then "Christian Blacks" desirous to emigrate, enough to form a church; and one of them was fit to be its pastor.

Unsuccessful in this, he continued his labors. In 1791, he wished the Connecticut Emancipation Society to be incorporated, with power to act as an education and colonization society. In 1793, he preached a sermon before a kindred society at Providence, which was published with an appendix, in which he advocated almost the exact course of action afterward adopted by this Society, and urged its execution by the United-States

Government, the several State Governments, and by voluntary societies.

Hopkins died Dec. 20, 1803; but the influence of these labors still lived. They must have been well known to Capt. Paul Cuffee of New Bedford, and the thirty emigrants whom he took to Sierra Leone in his own vessel, early in 1815; and in 1826, two of his " hopeful young men," Newport Gardner, aged seventy-five, and John Nubia,* aged seventy, hoping to move their brethren by their example, sailed from Boston in the brig " Vine," the eighth vessel sent out by this Society.

The next movement having any historical result was in Virginia. Dec. 31, 1800, the Legislature, in secret session,—

"*Resolved*, That the Governor be requested to correspond with the President of the United States, on the subject of purchasing lands without the limits of this State, whither persons obnoxious to the laws or dangerous to the peace of society may be removed."

The Governor, Monroe, in communicating this Resolution to the President, stated that it was passed in consequence of a conspiracy of slaves in and around Richmond, for which the conspirators, under existing laws, might be doomed to death. It was deemed more humane, and it was hoped not less expedient, to transport

---

* Known in Hopkins's correspondence as Salmur Nubia, and familiarly in Newport as Jack Mason.

such offenders beyond the limits of the State. President Jefferson favored the idea, discussed the objections to several locations, said that "Africa would offer a last and undoubted resort," and promised his assistance. The Legislature, Jan. 16, 1802, directed a continuance of the correspondence, "for the purpose of obtaining a place without the limits of" the United States, " to which free negroes or mulattoes, and such negroes or mulattoes as may be emancipated, may be sent or choose to remove as a place of asylum;" requesting the President "to prefer Africa, or any of the Spanish or Portuguese settlements in South America." This resolution differs from the former, in that it does not contemplate a penal colony, and does contemplate increased facilities for emancipation, in a mode which the State did not esteem dangerous. The President corresponded with the British Government concerning Sierra Leone, and with the Portuguese concerning their possessions in South America, but without success. In 1805, Jan. 22, a resolution was passed, instructing the senators and requesting the representatves from that State to endeavor to procure a suitable territory in Louisiana. No action followed, and the matter slept ten years. Yet the proposition of Ann Mifflin, and the correspondence of John Lynd with Thomas Jefferson in 1811, showed that the idea was still alive and at work.

Another of these numerous origins must be noticed. In the spring of 1808, a few undergraduates of Williams College, Mass., formed themselves into a society, whose object was, "to effect, in the persons of its members, a mission or missions to the heathen." In about two years, this society was transferred to the Theological Seminary at Andover, of which most of them had become members. Here they procured the formation of a "Society of Inquiry respecting Missions;" and there was thenceforth the chief seat of their labors. With becoming modesty, they regarded themselves as little else than mere school-boys, competent, indeed, to make inquiries, collect information, and discover wants that ought to be supplied, but needing the guidance of older and wiser men to mature judicious plans and execute them successfully. The proposal of four of them to go on a mission to the heathen in foreign lands, led directly to the formation of the American Board of Commissioners for Foreign Missions. Suggestions from these young men, or some of them, also led to the formation of the American Bible Society, and, though in some cases less directly, several other kindred institutions, for which the state of feeling in the religious world was prepared.

Samuel J. Mills has been commonly regarded as the leader of these inquirers. With a companion, he made a journey of inquiry through large parts of the new settlements in the United States, especially the south-western part. He came back with the knowledge of many wants to be supplied, and fully convinced, that, to use his own words, "We must save the negroes, or the negroes will ruin us;" and that there was so much at the South of right feeling towards the negroes, that something might be done towards saving them. The matter was abundantly discussed. A colony was proposed, somewhere in the vast wilderness between the Ohio and the great lakes. But one of them at length objected to that location. "Whether any of us live to see it or not," said he, "the time will come when white men will want all that region, and will have it, and our colony will be overwhelmed by them." So they concluded that the colony must be in Africa.

Mills went to New Jersey, to study theology with Dr. Griffin at Newark, and still more, as Dr. Griffin soon thought, to engage him and other leading men in that region in considering whether certain good objects could be accomplished, and how. While there, he originated the school for the education of pious blacks at Parsippany, some thirty miles from Princeton. It was placed under the care and patronage of the Synod of New Jersey; and thus the Presbyterian clergy of that State were brought into active connection with Mills, and his idea of saving the negro. His project of a colony north of the Ohio, or somewhere else, was well known to Dr. Alexander of Princeton, and doubtless to others.

Among the most eminent of that clergy was the Rev. Dr. Robert Finley. No record has been found of any direct intercourse between him and Mills; and there is no reason to suspect that Mills furnished him with a plan of a society, to be formed at Washington, for colonizing free blacks in Africa. That plan seems to have developed itself in his own mind, while contemplating that class of facts to which Mills was so busily calling attention; and it is certain that he had it under consideration as early as February, 1815. From about that time, he was industrious in recommending it to his friends; but they, while admitting that its object was good, generally distrusted its success. After probably nearly two years of such labor, he called a public meeting at Princeton, to consider the subject; but few besides the Faculties of the College and the Theological Seminary attended, and only Dr. Alexander appears to have aided him in commending it. Still he persevered; and when Congress assembled, early in December, 1816, repaired to Washington, to attempt the formation of his proposed society. On his arrival, he went at once to his brother-in-law, Elias B. Caldwell. That these brothers had previously corresponded on the subject, is a probable conjecture, but not a known fact. Yet the idea of colonization was not then new to Mr. Caldwell. It had already been suggested from another source.

Late in February, 1816, the Virginia secret resolutions and correspondence of 1801–05 first became known to Charles Fenton Mercer, a member of the Legislature of that State. Not being under the obligation of secrecy, he at once made them known extensively in the State, and pledged himself to renew them at the next session of the Legislature. Being at Washington,—it must have been in March or April,— he made known the facts and his intentions to two friends. One was his old schoolmate at Princeton, Elias B. Caldwell, who approved his object, and promised to use his influence with his Presbyterian friends in New Jersey in favor of it. The other was Francis S. Key, who would attempt a similar movement in Maryland. Gen. Mercer redeemed his pledge. His proposed resolution passed the House of Delegates, Dec. 14, by a vote of 132 to 14, and the Senate, Dec. 23, with one dissenting vote. This was done without any knowledge of the plans and movements of Dr. Finley for forming a society, and indeed without any expectation that a society would be formed. His idea was, that colonization would be carried by the State Governments, under the sanction and protection of the National Government. Still, this expression of Virginia's mind rendered important and perhaps indispensable aid to the formation and success of the Society; for the action of the House of Delegates was known in Washington before Gen. Mercer's resolution had passed the Senate, and before any public meeting was holden to form a society.

To arrange that meeting, and secure attendance upon it, cost Dr. Finley no slight labor. The goodness of the object was generally admitted; but, at the preliminary consultations, those invited and expected were generally absent. Charles Marsh, member of Congress from Vermont, noticed this disposition of almost everybody to leave this good work to others; and, as this was the only project that he had ever heard of, promising great good to the black race, he determined that it should not be allowed to die in that way. He decided that those who knew the plan to be a good one should attend the meetings. Of course, as all who ever knew his inexhaustible adroitness and persistency will easily understand, "a very respectable mumber" of them attended the first public meeting, Dec. 21, 1816. Henry Clay, in the necessary absence of Judge Washington, was called to the chair. Elias B. Caldwell, the brother-in-law of Dr. Finley and the schoolmate and friend of Gen. Mercer, perfectly informed of the plans and movements of both, made the leading argument in favor of forming a society. He stated that public attention had been called to the subject in New Jersey, New York, Indiana, Tennessee, Virginia, and perhaps other places. He was supported by remarks from John Randolph of Virginia, and Robert Wright of Maryland. A committee was appointed to prepare a constitution, and the meeting adjourned for one week.

At the adjourned meeting, Dec. 28, the committee reported a constitution, which was adopted. Fifty gentlemen affixed their names to it as members. The twenty-third name on the list is Samuel J. Mills. What brought him there at that time, and what he was about while there, we can only infer from other parts of his history.

Jan. 1, 1817, the day fixed by the Constitution, the Society met for the election of officers. Hon. Bushrod Washington, of Virginia, was chosen President, with twelve Vice-Presidents, from nine States, including Georgia, Kentucky and Massachusetts, and one from the District of Columbia. Dr. William Thornton, whose visit to Dr. Hopkins in 1787 has already been mentioned, was a member of the Board of Managers.

Thus the Society was formed and organized, not by the labors of any one projector, or by the influence of a movement in any one part of the country, but by the union of the tendencies which, remote from each other and independent of each other, had been working towards that result for more than forty years. That the Virginia movement, or the New-Jersey movement, or the New-England movements, would have accomplished any thing without the union of all, some may perhaps believe, but facts have not proved. Its true origin was, in the desire of good men everywhere to do the best thing then practicable for the black race, in this country and in Africa; that desire prompting all these movements, and sustaining them when providentially united in one.

Gen. Mercer was not present at the formation of the Society. His plan was, colonization by the National and State Governments; and, late in life, he expressed a doubt whether more good would not have been done by such action, if no Society had been formed; as the movement would then have had the united support of the South, which was lost by bringing Northern men into the movement, and thus throwing important Southern interests " open to the public discussions and acts of a Society spread through the United States, and to the interference of other counsellors and agents than their own Government." At the time, however, he made no such objection. His confidential friends took a leading part in the formation of the Society, and he himself became one of its most active and efficient supporters. In a few weeks, he procured the formation of several auxiliaries in Virginia. He procured, by personal solicitation, large donations to its funds. He wrote several of its earlier Reports. He rendered various services, without which it is not easy to see how the Society could ever have become active.

The first step towards planting a colony in Africa was, to find and procure a location where it might be planted and prosper. For this purpose, Africa must be visited, and preliminary arrangements made. Samuel J. Mills offered himself for that service, was accepted, and authorized to select his companion. He selected his friend, Ebenezer Burgess, now Rev. Dr. Burgess, of Dedham, Mass., the man who, years before, had opposed the plan for colonizing north the Ohio, because white men would want that country, and argued that the colony must be in Africa. Their letter of instructions was dated Nov. 5, 1817. Money to repay the expense of the expedition was borrowed, and the loan repaid from funds raised by Gen. Mercer and Rev. William Meade, afterwards Bishop Meade of Virginia.

They sailed Nov. 16; Mills remarking to one of his associates in these movements, as he was about to embark, "This is the most important enterprise in which I have ever been engaged." Arriving in England in

December, they were courteously received by His Royal Highness the Duke of Gloucester, Patron and President, and by the other officers of the African Institution. Mr. Wilberforce introduced them to Lord Bathurst, Secretary of State for the Colonies, who gave them letters to the Governor and other officers at Sierra Leone, directing them to aid the explorers in their explorations. Having touched at the Gambia, they arrived at Sierra Leone, March 22, 1818. The Governor and other officers received them with great personal kindness, and very literally obeyed the instructions of the Home Government, as to furnishing facilities for inquiry, but did not conceal their unwillingness that an American Colony should be established in their vicinity. The principal merchants felt the same unwillingness.

They were more cordially received by the members of the "Friendly Society," instituted among the colonists at the suggestion of Paul Cuffee in 1811. Its President, John Kizell, who had been a slave in the West Indies and the United States, entered heartily into their plans, accompanied them on some of their explorations, and introduced them to native chiefs over whom he possessed much influence. They examined the coast as far as Sherbro, obtained promises, that, on the arrival of colonists, suitable land should be furnished for their settlement, and being unable, for want of time and funds, to visit the Bassa Country, Cape Palmas, Accra, and the Bight of Benin, as they desired, returned to Sierra

Leone, and, May 22, embarked for England on their homeward voyage.

When they left home, Mills was suffering from a pulmonary disease. The climate of England aggravated it. That of Africa suspended its operation, as it often does. A few days after leaving Sierra Leone it returned, aided by a severe cold; and on the 16th of June, he gently expired, and at sunset his body was committed to the ocean. Nearly thirty years ago, I wrote, "It was fitting that the remains of such a man, whose character no monument could suitably represent, should rest where none could be attempted." Now, it has been made my duty to say, that, if the Society will cause a monument to his memory to be erected in Liberia, the funds are ready to defray the expense. Liberia has recorded her debt to both explorers, by uniting their names in the name of Millsburgh, which, as the record states, was devised for that purpose.

Their report established the fact, that territory might be procured and a colony planted. But how was the Society to plant a colony, with less than three thousand dollars in its treasury, and its receipts less than one hundred dollars a month? "A great political necessity" furnished the means.

The Act of Congress of March 2, 1807, had prohibited the importation of slaves after the end of that year, and provided for punishing the importer; but the slave so imported became subject, like all other persons, to the laws of the State in which he was found. In several of the States, laws were enacted and legal proceedings devised, under which it was still found profitable to import slaves, and incur the penalty, if it could not be evaded, as it often was. The first attempt to interfere with this policy of the slave-traders was made by the legislature of Georgia. That legislature enacted, Dec. 19, 1817, that the Governor should take all such imported slaves out of the hands of private speculators into his own custody, and sell them at auction for the benefit of the State treasury; provided, however, that if the Colonization Society would undertake to transport them to Africa, and would pay all expenses incurred by the State, the Governor was requested to aid the Society as he might deem expedient. This was the first official movement, if not the first suggestion, for the return of recaptured slaves to Africa.

The Act of Congress of April 20, 1818, increased the penalties of importation, but still left the slaves imported subject to the laws of the several States, and the work still went on.

While Gen. Mercer was preparing the Second Annual Report, to be presented in January, 1819, his attention was drawn to these laws, and the practice under them. The Report discussed the subject, and about forty pages of its appendix were filled with documents showing the facts. In Congress, Gen. Mercer procured the drafting of a bill to remedy the evil, which passed both Houses, and was approved by the President, Monroe, March 3, 1819. By this Act, all slaves illegally imported, or taken at sea, were to be kept in the custody of the United-States Government till removed beyond the limits of the United States; and the President was to appoint an agent or agents on the coast of Africa to receive them, and the sum of one hundred thousand dollars was appropriated to meet the expense.

About six weeks after this Act was passed, the Hon. W. H. Crawford of Georgia, Secretary of the Treasury, found, in a Georgia newspaper, an advertisement of illegally imported slaves, to be sold at auction under the State law of 1817. He immediately informed the Society; and the Rev. William Meade was sent to Georgia as its agent, to receive them in behalf of the Society. Litigation with Spanish claimants prevented immediate success; but, some years afterwards, they were delivered to the Society, and sent to Africa. There was then about fifty thousand dollars in the State treasury, as the proceeds of such sales. This the Society hoped to obtain; but there was no law authorizing the Governor to pay it over, and it was not done.

President Monroe, as appears by his Message of Dec. 17, 1819, understood the law of March 3 to mean, that a suitable residence must be provided, on the coast of Africa, for the agents and those intrusted to their care. For this purpose he determined to send a ship to the coast, with two agents, and the necessary men and means to procure a place and make it habitable.

Evidently, this work of the Government and the enterprise of the Society might best be prosecuted by their united action in establishing one settlement, where the agents of both should reside, and to which emigrants and recaptured slaves should be sent. The Government appointed the Rev. Samuel Bacon, already in the service of the Society, as its agent, with whom Mr. John P. Bankson was afterwards associated. The Society appointed Dr. Samuel A. Crozer its sole agent. The Government chartered the ship "Elizabeth," of three hundred tons, and "agreed to receive on board such free blacks, recommended by the Society, as might be required for the purposes of the agency." Dr. Crozer took out goods and stores for the purchase of land and the use of the emigrants. The emigrants were all considered as attached to this joint agency of the Government, and were to be entirely subjected to its control till regularly discharged. They were to erect cottages for at least three hundred recaptured Africans, and cultivate land for their own subsistence. For the expenses of the expedition, the Government placed more than thirty thousand dollars in the hands of Mr. Bacon, and sent a ship of war to co-operate. Thus provided, the "Elizabeth" sailed from New York, Feb. 6, 1820, with eighty-eight emigrants from Virginia, Maryland, Pennsylvania, and New York.

And in this co-operation, to which the Government found itself forced by its own necessities, the Society first found the power to go forward and accomplish its work. And if the ancients were right in considering the immense fountain which bursts forth by the side of a streamlet and transforms it into a river, the true source of the river, to be honored by altars and worship, with equal propriety may your monuments distinguish this point in the stream of your history.

President Monroe appears to have been a constant friend of colonization ever since 1801, when, as Governor of Virginia, he corresponded with Jefferson on the subject. He gave an attentive ear to the Annual Reports of the Society, showing the condition of the slave-trade, and the need of action for its suppression. His known sentiments encouraged Gen. Mercer to prepare and procure the enactment of the law of 1819. His interpretation and execution of that law furnished the means by which the work was begun. And the then youthful and ardent friend, whose presence forbids fit eulogy now, was right, when he first suggested that the metropolis of the nascent State should, by its name, commemorate his merits.

The first emigrants were to erect houses for three hundred recaptured slaves. The whole number of such, for whom the Government has found it necessary to provide through the Society, has been five thousand seven hundred and twenty-two. The resident agency of the United States for recaptured Africans continued, though occasionally vacant, till the declaration of Liberian independence. All this could not have been done, and well done, without a colony large and strong enough to live by its own vitality; and, therefore, the substantial success of our enterprise was a national necessity.

Such, as we have seen, were the forces which caused this Society to be formed; such the process of its formation; such the national need of its aid, which procured for it the means of successful activity. Having seen these, let us pass rapidly over events, the exciting and tragic interest of which have caused them to be abundantly recorded elsewhere, — the arrival of the "Elizabeth" at Sierra Leone; the cordial reception of the emigrants by Kizell, at Campelar, his own place on Sherbro Island; the discouraging attempts to purchase land for a permanent settlement, defeated, — not by the treachery of Kizell, for he was no traitor, — but by secret influences from those at Sierra Leone, who wished the colony all success, but at a much greater distance from themselves; the hardships, sickness, and deaths heroically endured; the removal from Campelar to Fourah Bay; the purchase of Cape Mesurado by Capt. Stockton and Dr. Ayres, at the risk of their lives; the arrival of the colonists, and their lodgment on an island, Jan. 7, 1822; the occupation of the Cape, April 25; the return of the agents, and the proposal that the emigrants also should return, and the enterprise be abandoned; the heroic reply of Elijah Johnson, "No: I have been two years searching for a home in Africa, and I have found it; and I shall stay here;" the heroic determinatiom of the others to remain with him; his appointment as sole agent; the troubles and dangers from the first, and then, and afterwards, from a host of native kings, who regretted the sale of the Cape, and determined to expel or exterminate the colony, lest it should interfere with the slave-trade; the offer of a force of marines from a British man-of-war, if Johnson would only cede a few feet of ground on which to erect a British flag; his prompt reply, " We want no flag-staff put up here, that will cost more to get it down again than it will to whip the natives;" the arrival of Ashmun, and his assumption of the agency, Aug. 9, 1822; his energetic labors, both diplomatic and military, for the protection of the colony; the assault on the settlement on the morning of Nov. 11, by about eight hundred natives, and their repulse by the thirty-five colonists, capable of bearing arms; the second assault, by perhaps twice their former number, Dec. 2, and their final defeat. Passing by all these, let us examine a crisis in the affairs of the colony, involving and elucidating a principle, and itself needing elucidation.

There had been complaints against the colonists of turbulence and insubordination. They, in turn, accused the Agents of oppression and other offences. The trouble grew into what was called "mutiny" and "sedition." Numbers utterly refused obedience to the Agent, and proceeded to take forcibly their supply of food from the public store. How can we account for the fact, that such men as Lot Cary, and others, were betrayed into such conduct? True, there had been complaints about the distribution of lands, and other acts of the several Agents, and representations had been sent to the Society; but these are insufficient to explain it.

The explanation must be found in the fact, that the colony had really no civil government. What occupied the place of a civil government was a pure despotism of an agent, resting on no legal basis, and possessing no physical force with which to compel obedience. Of course, the colonists, though they appear to have been far from comprehending the difficulty, felt that something was wanting, something out of order, something wrong; and were " insubordinate."

That such an assertion may be received, it needs to be proved. Consider, then, that the " Elizabeth " and her company were sent out by the United States, and not by the Society. Ship, money, and men were under the direction of the government's agents, with instructions to build houses for three hundred recaptured slaves. Their instructions said, " You are not to exercise any power or authority founded on the principles of colonization, but to confine yourselves to that of performing the benevolent intentions of the Act of Congress of March 3, 1819." And the President, in his message of Dec. 20, 1819, said that they would receive " an express injunction to exercise no power founded on the principle of colonization, or other power than that of performing the benevolent offices above recited, by the permission and sanction of the existing government under which they may establish themselves." There is not only no authority given to the agents to establish a government, but an express assumption that the place selected would be under a government existing independently of them, "by the permission and sanction" of which they would act. Evidently the colonists had no civil government derived from this source.

Does the deed of cession by which the territory was holden throw any light on the subject? That deed

> "Witnesseth, That whereas certain persons, citizens of the United States of America, are desirous to establish themselves on the western coast of Africa, and have invested Capt. Robert F. Stockton and Eli Ayres with full powers to treat with and purchase from us, the said kings, princes and headmen, certain lands [which are described], we do hereby, in consideration of [certain specified articles of merchandise], forever cede and relinquish the above-described lands to Capt. Robert F. Stockton and Eli Ayres, To Have and To Hold the said premises for the use of these said citizens of America."

We must carefully observe that Capt. Stockton and Dr. Ayres do not appear in this transaction as agents of the United States, or of the Colonization Society, but as agents of "certain persons" who were "desirous of establishing *themselves* on the western coast of Africa," that is, of the colonists. The colonists, the deed says, had invested them with full powers to treat with kings for the cession of territory. Certainly, land bought by their authorized agents for their use, and ceded for their use "forever," was their land. It never became the property of the United States, or of the Society. The next paragraph confirms this view:—

"The contracting parties pledge themselves to live in peace and friendship forever; and do further contract not to make war, or otherwise molest or disturb each other."

The "contracting parties" who thus mutually pledge themselves are evidently the kings, princes and headmen, on the one part, and the colonists on the other.

With the right of soil, the right of jurisdiction passed from the kings to the other contracting party, — the colonists. They were the supreme lords of the soil, and had a natural right to organize and establish a government for it. But they had not exercised that right. There was no existing civil government resting on that basis.

The Society had acted on this subject seasonably. Its Board of Managers, June 26, 1820, while the emigrants were still at Campelar, adopted a "Constitution for the Government of the African Settlement at ——." Of course, it could not go into operation as a civil government "at ——," or at all, while they were living within the jurisdiction of some other government already established. Its first article, as amended Dec. 20, was, —

"All persons born within the limits of the territory held by the American Colonization Society in ——, or remaining there to reside, shall be free, and entitled to all such rights and privileges as are enjoyed by the citizens of the United States."

By its own terms, it applied only to territory held by

the Society; and Cape Mesurado, as has been shown, was not held by the Society, but by Capt. Stockton and Dr. Ayres, as agents of the emigrants; that is, by the emigrants themselves. What authority had a constitution, formed by an unincorporated association of private individuals in another country, three thousand miles off, over a territory which was not their property, but the property of its inhabitants, who, acting as a sovereign people, had procured it by a treaty of cession and peace with sovereign princes? The seventh article however, provides that "every settler coming to the age of twenty-one years, and those now of age, shall take an oath or affirmation to support the constitution." Mr. Ashmun, in his address to the colonists, March 22, 1824, reminded them that they had taken that oath. By that oath, the individuals who took it certainly placed themselves under a moral obligation to obey the constitution thus made for them by others, though they had never adopted it, as a body, by any public act. Let us look, then, at its provisions.

The first article, as we have seen, provides that all the colonists should be entitled to "all such rights and privileges as are enjoyed by the citizens of the United States." The word "citizens," having been substituted by amendment for "free people," must be taken to secure all the rights and privileges by which citizens are distinguished from "people" merely "free." The oath bound them to support this article as much as any other.

"Art. 2. — The Colonization Society shall, from time to time, make all such rules as they may think fit for the government of the settlement, until they shall withdraw their agents, and leave the settlers to govern themselves."

This expressly takes from these "citizens" the "right and privilege" of making any law or "rule" for their own government, and subjects them to whatever rules the Society shall "see fit" to make for them; and, taken in connection with the tenth article, restrains them from the "right and privilege" of altering or amending their own constitution, and confers that right on the Managers of the Society. The eighth article confers unlimited legislative power on the Society's resident Agents, subject only to repeal by the Board of Managers.

The third article invests the Agents with all judicial power, except such as they should delegate to Justices of the Peace of their own appointment, if they should choose to appoint any.

The fourth article gives the Agents the appointment of all officers not appointed by the Board of Managers, and of judging for themselves what officers are needed.

The "settlers" being thus deprived of all voice in their own government, either in the making of laws or the choice of officers to administer them, it is not easy to see what rights and privileges enjoyed by citizens of the United States, in distinction from people merely free, were left to them.

It does not appear from any published record, that the colonists understood those legal difficulties; but it is evident from their conduct that they did not feel that reverence for laws thus made for them, which American "citizens" usually feel for laws in the making of which they have borne their part. There was "insubordination." Ashmun, faithful to the Society and to his own convictions, did his best to repress it, but in vain. Complaints were sent to the Society against his administration; and the evil increased, till, in utter discouragement, he put the government into the hands of Elijah Johnson, and embarked for the Cape Verde Islands. He had already informed the Board of Managers, that, in his opinion, "the evil was incurable by any means which fall within their existing provisions."

In this emergency, the Government, on representations of the Society, sent out the armed schooner "Porpoise," with Ralph Randolph Gurley, a young man then unknown to fame, duly commissioned and empowered by the Government and the Society to ascertain the condition of affairs, and "to make such temporary arrangements for the security of the public interests and the government of the establishment, as, upon proper consideration, circumstances might, in his judgment, require." Touching at Porto Praya, he unexpectedly met Mr. Ashmun, who returned with him to Cape Mesurado, where they arrived Aug. 13, 1824.

On their voyage of three weeks to the Cape, they carefully discussed these troubles, their causes, and their remedy. After their arrival, the colonists were heard and consulted, misapprehensions were dispelled, and specific grievances received satisfactory attention. But the chief attention was given to establishing "an efficient government, founded in the approbation of the people, and adaptable not only to their present but future necessities." The probable necessity of such a work had occurred to Mr. Gurley on his voyage from the Cape Verdes, if not before; and facts ascertained after his arrival fully proved it.

In the end, a "Plan for the Civil Government of Liberia" was adopted, according to which there was to be a Vice-agent, appointed by the Agent from three nominated by the people, unless he saw fit to disapprove the choice and order a new election. He was to advise and assist the Agent, and perform his duties in case of absence or disability. Two Councillors, to be associated with the Vice-agent as a council on all public affairs, and several important committees, were to be appointed in like manner. There was to be a judiciary, consisting of the Agent and two Justices of the Peace appointed by him; and he was to appoint the necessary executive officers. The supremacy of the Society, in cases of last resort, was retained and established.

The colonists, now increased to a hundred, were convened "beneath the thatched roof of the first rude house for divine worship ever erected in the colony." The Plan of Government was read and explained to them, and received their unanimous approval, and solemn pledge "to maintain it as the constitution of their choice." Receiving also the assent of the special Agent of the Society and the United States, sent out with full power on their part " to establish a government," no one could deny that it was, from that hour, in force on a legitimate basis; and, with amendments and changes regularly made as occasions have required, it is in force still.

True, the Society had still the ultimate decision of all questions of government; but it henceforth held this power, not by its own assumption, but by the vote of the people, who, by their own act, made the Society a department of their own government.

This change was not the work of Mr. Ashmun. He distrusted the fitness of the colonists to take any part in the government, and only consented to it as an experiment, because some change must be made. He was even alarmed at its ready and unanimous acceptance by the people, fearing that they did not understand it, or reserved the expression of their dissent for a more favorable opportunity.

Neither was it the work of the Board of Managers. When reported to them, they resolved, Dec. 29, 1824, that "such parts as could not well be dispensed with might be tried as an experiment of the Agent," but gave it no further sanction; and in their Annual Report in January, without publishing it, plainly intimated their dissent.

The whole responsibility, therefore, for this Plan of Government, rested on him who proposed it and those who adopted it. Events soon justified their action, even in the judgment of those who at first condemned it. At a meeting held May 18, 1825, it was

"*Resolved*, That the Board of Managers, considering the satisfactory information afforded by recent accounts from the colony of the successful operation of the plan for the civil government thereof, as established by their Agents in August last, and seeing therein reasons to reconsider their instructions to the Agent of the 29th of December, 1824, now approve the principles in that form of government, and give their sanction to the same."

And in their next Annual Report, January, 1826, they say,—

"The new system of government organized in the colony immediately after the return of the present Agent, Mr. Ashmun, from the Cape de Verdes, has resulted in the most beneficial effects. It was deemed important to render, as far as practicable, all the political arrangements of the colony, so many preparatory measures to its independence; and to this end is the government which has been established believed to be particularly adapted. The whole system went into operation with the full sanction of the people. The spirit of restlessness and insubordination ceased from the first day of its operation; indolence, despondency, and distrust were succeeded by industry, enterprise, and confidence; and the experience of more than a year has confirmed the hope, that it will, at least for a considerable time, fulfil all the purposes of its institution."

Mr. Ashmun's distrust, also, soon disappeared. His despatches authorized and compelled the change of opinion in the Board of Managers. He soon disbanded, as useless, the military guard of twelve men, which he at first thought necessary for his own protection amidst the dangers of the experiment. And, early in 1828, the Board received from him a plan of government, the same in principle, and to some extent in language; but drawn out in much greater detail, and placing a much greater amount of power directly in the hands of the people; and at a meeting of the Managers, Oct. 22, 1828, it was adopted by them as the Constitution of Liberia.

The modesty of the principal actor, and his delicate regard for the feelings of others, in his Life of Ashmun and in the Annual Reports prepared by him, have made the part he acted less prominent than its merits deserve. He has even left it doubtful how far he saw the defects and inconsistencies of the original constitution. But it is enough for his glory, that he alone among white men saw the safety of trusting a negro people with some part in the management of their own concerns; and that, by boldly acting on his belief, he placed his name on the not long list of legislators whose wisdom organized States on principles that secured peace, permanency, coherence, and a healthy growth.

The second decade, and the first half of the third, — from 1830 to 1845,—were distinguished by the independent action of State societies; of Maryland first, purchasing and settling Cape Palmas; then of New York; then of Pennsylvania; then of Pennsylvania and New York united, and the planting of the settlements on the St. John's River by their united action; the setting apart, by the parent Society, of lands for the Kentucky, Mississippi, and Louisiana Societies, on which, however, separate colonies were never organized; the plan for uniting all these colonies, planted and projected, in one federal republic; all these things leading naturally to changes in the constitution of the Parent Society, making its supreme Board of Directors mainly a Board of Delegates from the State Societies. A proper discussion of this period would require a laborious examination of the published and unpublished documents of the Parent and the several State Societies, and of the often conflicting recollections and opinions of living witnesses. Its discussion is the less important, because those arrangements, however expedient or even necessary they may have been or appeared to be at the time, have passed away. Those colonies are now only parts of a single republic, "one and indivisible;" and though most of the State Societies still retain the power of separate action, they find little occasion to use it. Let us, therefore, pass on to the next topic involving a crisis.

January, 1845, the Legislature of Liberia was in session; for, by successive amendments of her constitution, she now had a legislature, with power to make all necessary laws, subject, however, to the veto of the Society. She had a governor, — Joseph J. Roberts, — first elected lieutenant-governor by the people, and appointed governor by the Society after the death of Governor Buchanan, in 1841. Her government was authorized to make treaties with the neighboring tribes; but these, also, were subject to the veto of the Society. For several years, however, the Society had found no occasion demanding the exercise of its veto power. By treaties with the native powers, several valuable tracts of territory had been acquired, including some important points for trade; and settlements had been made upon them, and regular government established. Laws had been enacted, regulating commerce, and imposing duties on imported goods.

For several centuries, British subjects had been accustomed to trade on this coast for slaves and other African commodities. Even after the act of Parliament of 1807 prohibiting the slave-trade, they continued the traffic as they could. Some of them dealt in slaves, at least till June, 1813, when His Majesty's ship "Thais" landed forty men at Cape Mesurado, and after a battle, in which they lost one man killed, stormed the barracoons of Bostock and McQuinn, British subjects, and captured their owners. When direct participation in the slave-trade had become too dangerous to be continued, they still carried on a lucrative commerce with the natives, and with slave-traders of other nations, who were glad to find on the coast a supply of such English goods as were necessary for their business. Very naturally, such men were unwilling that a regular government, with law, civilization, and Christianity, should take possession of their old haunts of trade. They refused to obey the laws. They landed goods without paying duties; and when the goods were seized by the collector, and sold according to law, they applied to the British Government for redress.

That Government seems to have been, at first, somewhat embarrassed. It opened a correspondence with ours, to ascertain whether Liberia was a colony of the United States. Our government replied, through Mr. Everett at London and Mr. Upshur at Washington, that Liberia was not a colony of the United States, but " an independent political community," founded for benevolent purposes, in which all nations ought to desire its success; and that, as such, it needed and had a right to acquire territory and govern it, which right all nations ought to respect.

Having ascertained this, the British Government at once proceeded to sustain the claims of the British traders, denying the right of the Liberians to acquire territory by treaty, or to govern that lately acquired; though, for more than twenty years, they had been allowed, without objection, to acquire and govern Cape Mesurado and other important places; and they were made to understand that the British navy would enforce this decision of the British Government.

These difficulties were now before the legislature. What could be done? A treaty must be negotiated with Great Britain. The Liberian Constitution made no provision for negotiating treaties, except with the neighboring tribes, and those subject to the veto of the

Society. The Society was not a sovereign power, with whom Great Britain could negotiate; nor had it, under its own constitution or that of Liberia, any power concerning treaties, except that of veto. A crisis had come, to which the structure of the Liberian Government was not adapted. The legislature informed the Society of the difficulties and dangers growing out of their alleged want of national sovereignty, and requested its consideration and advice.

When the Directors of the Society met in January, 1846, these matters had been before their minds for months, and they were prepared to act. The constitution of the Society was amended in several respects, and especially by striking out whatever related to the government of the colonies. It was then

Resolved, That, in the opinion of this Board, the time has arrived when it is expedient for the people of the Commonwealth of Liberia to take into their own hands the whole work of self-government, including the management of all their foreign relations; and that this Society should cease to exercise any part of the same.

Resolved, That we recommend to them so to amend their constitution, as is necessary for the accomplishment of this object.

Resolved, That we recommend to them to publish to the world a declaration of their true character, as a sovereign and independent State.

The resolutions took this shape for the sake of avoiding all appearance of conferring rights of sovereignty on the people of Liberia. Those rights were theirs already, and had been ever since they were a people. They were advised, not to make themselves into a new sovereign State not before existing, but to publish a declaration of their true character, as being one already. It was not for the Society to give them a new constitution. It was their right and their duty, as a sovereign people, to make one for themselves. The Society did not relinquish to them its power in their government. What it had, they had conferred upon it by their constitution, and they were advised to take it away.

On the reception of this advice in Liberia, the legislature, at a special session, instructed the governor to submit the question to the people in their primary assemblies. The people voted, Oct. 27, 1846, in favor of assuming the entire responsibility of their government. The legislature, at its next session, ordered a convention of delegates to form a new constitution. The convention assembled, and, after twenty-one days of deliberation, adopted, on the twenty-sixth day of July, 1847, their new Constitution and Declaration of Independence. In September, the Constitution was ratified by the almost unanimous vote of the people in their primary assemblies. The Governor, Joseph J. Roberts, was elected President. On the third day of January, 1848, he delivered his inaugural address; and the new government went into operation. In the course of that year, the independence of the Republic was formally acknowledged by the governments of Great Britain and

France. It has since been acknowledged by nearly all the leading States of Europe and America.

Nor is the young Republic without influence in the family of nations. In 1853, agents of the British Government were endeavoring to prosecute the coolie-trade in the vicinity, and even within the legal jurisdiction, of the Republic. The vigorous and decided measures of President Roberts checked it; and, after a few words in Parliament, the attempt was abandoned. A few years afterwards, agents of the French Government engaged in a similar attempt so pertinaciously, that President Benson was obliged to send his predecessor as ambassador to Paris on the subject. The result was the entire abolition of that traffic on the whole coast of Africa, east as well as west.

It was a remark of one of the wisest men who ever acted as agent for a colonization society, that Divine Providence intends Liberia as a proof to all nations, that free institutions are adapted to the wants and capacities of every race of men. To prove it, God has taken a portion of the race that the wisdom of this world would pronounce — indeed, had pronounced — the most incapable of successful self-government, and has placed the duty and burden of self-government upon them; and they have borne it, and they are bearing it, with complete success. The whole history of Liberia corroborates this remark, — from the first years of Ashmun, when affairs went badly for want of self-government; from Gurley's first visit, when the introduction of the principle, and a little of the practice, gave peace and prosperity; down to the present time, when that little young republic is not only recognized as one in the family of nations, but commands a degree of respect, and exerts an amount of influence, among the nations, altogether out of proportion to her population or her resources.

The principles and designs from which she originated, and the whole course of her history, and of God's dealings with her, authorize us to offer with confidence the prayer for her perpetuity, *Esto perpetua.*

A few words are demanded by a topic which could not be introduced in its chronological place without disturbing the continuity of the narrative.

It will be remembered that when Dr. Hopkins visited Dr. Stiles, in 1773, it was to consult about educating two young men as missionaries to Africa, and their plan for a colony grew out of their conviction of the necessity of such a basis for missionary labors; and that, of the young men educated through their exertions, two, in 1826, when they were old, actually sailed to Liberia, not expecting to live and labor, but to set an example of Christian enterprise for the land of their fathers. The missionary element, it is well known, was strong in the minds of Mills and his associates at Andover, and of Finley and his brethren in New Jersey. However strong it may have been in the minds of individuals in Virginia, it could not well show itself in their legislative action, and does not, therefore, appear on the record. But it was actively alive among the colored people in that State. They, even as early as 1815, before our Society was formed, organized an African Missionary Society in Richmond, which contributed from a hundred to a hundred and fifty dollars annually. This might be, and probably was, expended in the support of English missions at or near Sierra Leone. In 1818, a similar society was formed in Petersburg, which, in April, 1819, proposed to our Society that some of its members should be sent out as colonists for missionary purposes. The Richmond Society sent out its most able and zealous member, the Rev. Lot Cary, who went out in our second company, by the "Nautilus," arriving at Sierra Leone in March, 1821, and was among the first who took possession of Cape Mesurado. The Richmond Society is understood to have made remittances to him for several years, and perhaps to the close of his life, in 1828. Besides his labors at and near his home, he commenced a mission, fifty miles distant, among the Vey people at Cape Mount; employing John Revey, afterwards Secretary of the Maryland Colony at Cape Palmas, as a schoolmaster. It was of short continuance; but its influence on the mind of one of the pupils led to the invention, years afterwards, of the syllabic alphabet for the Vey language, the discovery of which by a German missionary, after it had been long in use, excited much interest in the literary world.

This opening for missions attracted attention in

Europe. In October, 1825, the Rev. Dr. Blumhardt, Principal of the Missionary College at Basle in Switzerland, wrote to Mr. Ashmun, requesting information on the subject. Mr. Ashmun replied favorably the next April. Four young men were sent out as missionaries. The climate did not allow this mission to be permanent. Some died, and the health of others failed; but, before its dispersion, it exerted a beneficial influence, especially on the minds of some young Liberians, which is felt to this day.

The first white missionary from the United States appears to have been the Rev. Calvin Holton, a Baptist, who sailed from Boston in the "Vine," in 1826. "He was not suffered to continue, by reason of death." He was followed by a noble army of martyrs, Baptist, Methodist, Presbyterian, and Episcopalian; but their usefulness has consisted mostly in the support and direction given to pious Liberians who have labored under them or with them, and who often well supplied their places when vacant. As a result, nearly all the churches in the Republic contain native communicants, who are converts from heathenism.

In February, March, and April, 1819, two missionary explorers from Sierra Leone, with an interpreter, carefully examined the whole coast from Sherbro to the St. John's River. They suffered repeatedly from theft, detected and defeated two conspiracies to rob and murder them, and returned, having found no place where a mission could be hopefully attempted. Our first emigrants sailed in February, 1820.

Now, that whole line of coast, with as much more beyond it to the south and east, some five hundred and twenty miles in all, is under the jurisdiction of a Christian State, with Christian laws and institutions; with its common schools, high schools, and college; with a nominally Christian population of some fifteen to twenty thousand, and a native population of some hundreds of thousands, among whom heathenism has lost much of its power, and is fast losing the remainder; among whom missionary stations are numerous, both on the coast and in the interior; the line of apparent danger, or even difficulty, silently and quietly receding before them as they advance. And Liberian Christians are planning and acting very intelligently for their advancement.

Attorney-General Erskine, of Liberia, emigrated from East Tennessee with his father in his boyhood. He has been, for many years, one of the most able and influential Presbyterian missionaries there. If our ship, the "Golconda," has made a successful voyage, she has just landed at Cape Mount a hundred and forty-four emigrants, selected by him in his native region, to strengthen the settlement at Cape Mount, so as make it a better base for missionary operations among the Veys.

The Vey people are intimately connected with the Mandingoes, the great trading-people of Western Africa, who read, write, and keep accounts in the Arabic language, and whose commercial intercourse extends to the comparatively civilized nations of Central Africa, where the Arabic is vernacular. To those nations, European missionary societies have been in vain seeking access through Egypt and Abessinia for half a century. Liberia College has already begun to distribute Arabic books, from the press of the American mission at Beirût in Syria, among the Mandingoes; and that mission has furnished books for further distribution, containing a Circular Letter "from the learned men of Mount Lebanon to the learned men of Moghreb," that is, of the West, inviting correspondence, and offering a supply of books through Liberia College, the geographical position of which, and its objects, are described. As things move slowly in Africa, the desired result, though confidently expected, must be distant. But the planting of those hundred and forty-four missionary colonists at Cape Mount is exactly the right thing, at the right place, to hasten it; and it is only one of many instances showing the care and thought of Liberian Christians for their brethren still in the darkness of heathenism.

Thus the early missionary plans of Hopkins and Stiles, of Mills and Burgess, and Finley and Caldwell, and of Lot Cary and his society at Richmond, are more than executed already; and of their ultimate hope, the Christian civilization of Africa, the dawn distinctly appears.

ADDRESS

OF THE

RT. REV. THOMAS M. CLARK, D.D.

ADDRESS OF RT. REV. THOMAS M. CLARK, D.D.

BISHOP OF PROTESTANT EPISCOPAL CHURCH, RHODE ISLAND.

We celebrate the present anniversary of the American Colonization Society under peculiar and interesting auspices. Fifty years ago a few far-sighted Christian men, actuated by a pure and earnest faith, and having in view simply the elevation of the African and the rescue of Africa from barbarism, laid the foundation of an enterprise which has ever since pursued its quiet and unobtrusive way, gradually gaining favor and influence, and commending itself more and more to the favor of the judicious and the good. It has not failed to encounter some opposition, and this has come from very different quarters. On the one hand, it has been objected that the policy of the Society tended to rivet the chains of African slavery, and, on the other, that it must result in disturbing and making insecure the relations of the master and the slave. Both of these objections could hardly be valid; and now that, in the providence of God, the institution of slavery in this Republic no longer exists, both have ceased to have any pertinence, as indeed neither ever had any foundation.

The cause of African colonization stands before the nation to-day in a new and most important aspect. By a process which, ten years ago, no one dreamed of or thought possible, four millions of slaves have been suddenly emancipated. The freedom of the African has been purchased at a terrible price; and the wrongs which our fathers inflicted upon these people when they tore them from their native homes, and brought them here to labor and die on a foreign shore, we have been made to expiate in tears and blood. Neither has this great end been accomplished without the endurance of terrible suffering on the part of the slaves themselves. Thousands upon thousands have perished by the highway, of cold and hunger; and, in this bleak January night, tens of thousands are wanderers without a roof to shelter them.

What is to be done for this great multitude of human beings, thus suddenly cast upon their own resources? How are the new relations in which they stand to society to be adjusted? What is to be their social condition and their final destiny? These are questions involving one of the most delicate, difficult, and solemn problems ever presented to the consideration of man. They demand the broadest, profoundest, and most impartial judgment. It is unfortunate for the country, and unpropitious to the liberated slave, that they have become so intimately identified with political controversy, and, therefore, so much in danger of being handled mainly with a view to political and party ends. The call is all the more imperative upon those who really have at heart the welfare of the African, and honestly desire his elevation, to rally in his behalf, and, if possible, save him from being crushed between the Northern and the Southern mill-stone.

The opinions of men as to the probable future of the African in this country are various and discordant. The remark most common upon the lips of those whom you meet in ordinary intercourse is, that the race will, sooner or later, fade away and become extinct. All history, we are told, shows that it is impossible for two distinct races to dwell together on terms of equality in the same land; and the inferior must yield either to the process of absorption or extermination.

The statistics of our Northern cities are cited in confirmation of this theory. When the census of 1860 was taken in Philadelphia, it was found that, during a period of six months, there were among this people only one hundred and forty-eight births to three hundred and six deaths; the deaths being more than double the births. In Boston, from the years 1855 to 1862, there were three hundred and four births and five hundred deaths. This ratio, of course, is very much affected by the laws of climate. The North is not the natural home of the African, and he can hardly be expected to thrive there; but the returns from the whole United States show that while the rate of annual deaths among the whites is less than two and three-quarters per cent, or about one in every thirty-seven of the living, among the colored, it is about three and a half per cent, or one in every twenty-eight.

In rejoinder to this theory, it is argued, that inasmuch as labor is the great want of our land, and there are departments of work which this race can supply to better advantage than any other people, it will be for our interest to save them from decay and extermination. Unlike the original Indian, they are a laboring people, and they will, therefore, always continue to live amongst us, and increase and multiply, although it may be that their social position in many respects will be, as it has been, inferior and subordinate.

There are others who take much higher ground as to the future of the Republic. They affirm that we have only to give him all his political rights, and place him on precisely the same ground of political equality with other American citizens, and he will soon become competent to use those rights wisely and intelligently. The social bar which has thus far impeded his elevation will in time give way before the fact that he is endowed with all the privileges and immunities which belong to every other member of the Republic, and all distinctions of caste will gradually cease to exist.

I do not feel qualified to cast the horoscope of the African; neither do I think that any man living, with the material now on hand, is able to do it. The argument upon which I base the claims of this Society does not require that we should penetrate the secrets of the future. That the great body of this people are needed here, and that at present no other class is competent to take their place; that they are capable of education, and have a claim upon us to give them this great boon without stint or measure; that they possess such qualities as may, with proper training, make them useful members of society; that every protection should be thrown around them which the most impartial law can provide; that full political rights should be conferred upon them, just as soon and just as far as they become capable of exercising those rights intelligently, — on these points I do not think there is room for debate.

But, supposing all this to be done, and all the benefits to accrue which might reasonably be expected, still in this land the African will always be an exotic. It is not the region for which the Almighty endowed him. He cannot thrive here as he will under his native skies. He will have difficulties to overcome peculiar to his race and condition. He will have to fight against obstructions which are not shared by the white man. No legislation, no change or improvement in public sentiment, can avert this result; and these embarrassments he will feel all the more as he rises in rank and culture. They are experienced at the North, where slavery has been long abolished, and where no distinction of color is recognized by law, just as keenly and painfully as ever; and, therefore, there will always be a class of men and women of African descent, and this of the higher order, who will desire to extricate themselves from these unpropitious circumstances, and find a home for themselves and for their children in that land where their race are supreme, independent of protection or patronage, and where they may become the architects of their own destiny.

I have the same respect for God's image, whether it stands before me blanched or bronzed. It is *the man* whom I regard; and intelligence and virtue make the man, not the pigment under his skin. But, if African blood ran in my veins, I would not live here, to be kicked about like a foot-ball from pillar to post, while politicians play their game; to be insulted by the very patronage of those who assume to be my special advocates; to be made a public spectacle of wonder if I happened to excel in any great thing, and to be charged with natural and invincible infirmity if I could not break through the iron walls which encompass me. I would go to the land of my fathers, where I could feel that my soul is my own; where I should be called to make no apology for the impertinence of having been born; where I could rule, instead of being ruled; where the highest posts of honor and influence are open to me and my children; where no white man is to say whether I shall vote or not; and, if none would help me to go, I would live on a crust and grind my bones with labor, till I had earned enough to carry me there. And yet there are those, calling themselves the exclusive friends of the African, who are exerting all their efforts to hinder him from doing this very thing. Here let me quote the words of Edward Everett: " Suppose any one had gone among that little company of persecuted Christians in England, in the year 1608, who afterward became the Pilgrim Church at Leyden; or suppose any one had gone in 1630 to the more important company of Gov. Winthrop, the great founder of Massachusetts; had tried to excite their feelings against the projected emigration; had told them that England belonged to them as much as it did to their oppressors; had led them to stand upon their rights, and, if necessary, bleed and die for them; had depicted the hardships and sufferings of the passage; had painted in the darkest colors the terrors of the wilderness into which they were about to venture. Would that have been true friendship? Would it have been kindness? Would it have been humanity? Or to come nearer home: suppose, at the present day, one should go into Ireland, or France, or Switzerland, or Germany, or Norway, or any of the countries from which hundreds of thousands of men, in a depressed, destitute, and unhappy condition, are emigrating to the United States to find a refuge, a home, a social position, and employment; suppose any one should go to them, and try to stimulate a morbid patriotism, a bitter nationality, telling them the country where they were born belonged as much to them as to the more favored classes; inducing them to stay where they were born; telling them that it was doubtful whether they would get employment in the new country; talking of the expense, the diseases, the hardships of the poor emigrants, and in this way endeavor to deter them from this great adventure, which is to end in procuring a home and a position in the world and an education for themselves and their children. Would this be friendship? Would this be kindness? Would this be humanity? But these are the appeals which are made to the free colored population of this country; and it is by appeals like this that the Society and the colony have become, as I am sorry to believe is the case, highly unpopular among them."

There is a ground upon which the American Colonization Society rests its claims to sympathy and support, that is lifted above the level of all the discordant views at which I have briefly glanced, and which seems to be impregnable. One of the great continents of the earth, up to the present time, has remained, for the past, undeveloped. Until very recently, its vast interior was known upon the map only as a blank, and was supposed to be a sterile, uninhabited desert. The explorations of travellers have just revealed to us, in that unknown region, navigable rivers, a prolific soil, and a swarming population. The multitudinous tribes of Africa are not, like the inhabitants of the East, a worn-out, effete, debilitated people. The experiment of culture has not been tested with them, and it remains to be seen of what they are capable.

Is Africa never to be redeemed? Is that magnificent land never to have a history? Is she never to take rank with the empires and peoples? Is the darkness that has brooded over her from the beginning, never to be lifted ? Are her great resources never to be developed ? Will her broad rivers never be traversed by the steamship, and her fertile plains never resound to the thunder of the locomotive ? Is she never to have a literature ? Is the light of the gospel never to shine there ? God made that continent, and he did not make it for nought. This moral wilderness is destined hereafter to blossom with the noblest fruits of civilization and the sweetest flowers of religion. Splendid cities will rise there, her dark jungles will be disinfected by the increase of pure and undefiled religion, and Ethiopia stretch out her hands, not in deprecating supplication before the spirit of infernal wrath and evil, but in grateful songs and thanksgivings to a kind and merciful God.

But now the practical question arises, *How* is Africa to be redeemed ? It is very evident that, *left to herself*, she will make no advance. This land is to-day in substantially the same condition that it has occupied for ages. The tendencies are all stationary. Even the Dutch who settled in the interior of Southern Africa have so far relapsed into barbarism, that they are hardly distinguishable from the Hottentots among whom they live. Without the infusion of some powerful element, strong enough to counteract the native torpor of the land, Africa will probably be the same a thousand years hence that she is to-day.

How is this controlling, counteracting element to be introduced ? Some will say, by opening the continent to the commerce of the world. But there is an important preliminary work to be done, before any extensive trade with this people can be possible. There must be exports, in order that there may be imports; and, when a people raise only what is necessary for their own subsistence, there can be nothing to send away. Thus far, traffic with this portion of the world has been confined to a few articles; and it is a melancholy fact that the first thing which ever stimulated the African to any sort of enterprise was, the discovery that he could find a market abroad for the captives whom he had taken in war. The trade which has been opened with this people has been a curse, and not a blessing. Gunpowder and rum in exchange for slaves are neither a means of civilization nor of grace.

"Throw open this continent to the influences of civilization by conquest. War is a rough and frightful process; but it has been one of the great civilizers of the world. Send fleets and armies, and break the spell of death by the thunder of artillery."

No foreign army will ever subjugate this land. There is an invisible cordon of defence encircling it, against which powder and steel would contend in vain. The pestilence that walketh in darkness is stronger than any forces that can be gathered at noonday.

May we not, then, rely upon the labor of the Christian missionary, armed with the weapons of the gospel of peace, to subdue and regenerate this continent by the power of love, and so bring it into loving sympathy with the civilized world?

What has been the result of his self-denying labors in that benighted land? "The Roman Catholic missionaries labored in Western Africa for two hundred and fourteen years; but every vestige of their influence has been gone for many generations. The Moravians, beginning in 1736, toiled for thirty-four years, making five attempts, at a cost of eleven lives, and accomplished nothing. An English attempt, at Bulama Island, in 1792, partly missionary in its character, was abandoned in two years with the loss of a hundred lives. A mission sent to the Foulahs from England, in 1795, returned without commencing its labors. The London, Edinburgh, and Glasgow societies commenced their stations in 1797, which were extinct in three years, and five or six missionaries dead. Then there are eighteen Protestant missionary attempts, before the settlement of Liberia, all of which failed." There is now an Episcopal mission under the shadow of Liberia, that has done a good work; but it has been at a woful sacrifice of valuable lives.

The fact seems to be demonstrated, that, if Africa is ever to be redeemed, it must be through the instrumentality of the African.

The problem of slavery has always been hard to solve. What was the design of the Almighty in permitting this institution to exist? It certainly was not to benefit the land where these Africans were brought. In any respect our country would have been more prosperous, more peaceful, and more united, if not one of that race had ever set his foot upon our territory.

But if Africa is to be lifted out of barbarism through the agency of the African, and if he could not be reached by the hand of civilization on his native soil; if there were no natural tendencies towards a higher development in the race itself, and if they were inaccessible to any direct influence from without; if neither commerce, or conquests, or peaceful instruction could be brought to bear upon them at home, — we may begin to see why it was permitted that they should be taken from their own country, and placed under such circumstances as would bring them in contact with civilization and Christianity, even though this was to be done in a way which shocks our sense of justice, and was far from favorable to their own highest culture.

The only conceivable process by which the great continent of Africa can ever be civilized and Christianized is, through the system of colonization, and transplanting to her shores all the institutions of civilization and Christianity, under the auspices and supreme control, not of the white man, but of the children of the soil. Every well-conducted and prosperous colony will gradually become a power, before which the ancient structures of idolatry and superstition and barbarism must sooner or later fall. The material for this work has been provided in a rough and strange manner, which is, however, not without striking precedents in history. It was a nation of liberated slaves that colonized and possessed the " promised land."

The opponents of colonization have sometimes asked,

with a sneer, if we consider the plantation negro a competent and fit representative of American culture, qualified to act as a Christian missionary, and to introduce the arts of civilization, science, education, commerce, manufactures, and agriculture into Africa. If it had been the policy of this Society to send out cargo after cargo of the lowest and most degraded class of Africans to be found in the land, there might be some good foundation for this contemptuous question; but it has not been so. Not a few who have emigrated to Liberia have been men of more than ordinary culture; and the great body of colonists have been sufficiently well trained in mechanical and agricultural pursuits to qualify them for the position of useful and productive members of society. It is not the lowest order who are likely to seek a refuge in Liberia. They have the same local attachments which the domestic animal has for its home. They love the quiet nooks and the warm shelter and the abundant food which they find there. They do not care to tempt the perils of an ocean voyage, and to encounter the hardships of a new settlement. They do not care for Africa because it was the home of their ancestors. They do not care for Africa because they may assert their manhood there, and lay the foundation of great things for themselves and their children. They are troubled with no such lofty sentiments as these; and therefore they would rather grind cane in Louisiana, and gather cotton in Carolina, than become the founders of a great nation on the other side of the sea.

But, after all, the great question to be considered on such an occasion as the present is this: What have been the actual results of African colonization? Has Liberia, upon the whole, proved to be a success, or failure? Forty-six years ago, the first band of emigrants landed and established themselves on Cape Mesurado. Nineteen and a half years ago, Liberia ceased to be a colony, and became an independent republic. Have the labors, and the sacrifices, and the means which have been expended upon this enterprise, resulted favorably or not?

The work of colonizing one region of the earth from another and a distant quarter has always been slow and difficult, and liable to peculiar and serious embarrassments.

Seventeen years after the first colony was planted at Jamestown, Va., it appears that about one hundred and fifty thousand pounds sterling had been expended; more than nine thousand persons had been sent from Europe to people it; and yet the population was reduced to eighteen hundred. Seventy-eight years after the settlement of Connecticut, the population amounted to only seventeen thousand. The Maine colony, after the lapse of one hundred and twenty years, numbered ten thousand. Of the original members of the Massachusetts Bay Company, quite a large number soon returned to England, wearied and discouraged.

The Republic of Liberia numbers to-day among its civilized inhabitants about thirty thousand persons, about fifteen thousand of which are American Liberians; that is, those who have emigrated from the United States with their descendants. More than three hundred thousand aborigines reside within the territory of Liberia, and are brought more or less directly under the influence and control of her civilized institutions. There are nearly fifty churches in the Republic, representing five different denominations, with their Sunday schools and Bible classes, and contributing something every week for missionary purposes. The exports last year amounted to about three hundred thousand dollars.

The undeveloped capacities for trade, no one can estimate. With a most prolific soil, and a climate capable of producing almost every variety of tropical fruit, the resources of the land are beyond computation. A sea-coast line six hundred miles in length, and an interior stretching indefinitely into the heart of the country, offer the most splendid facilities for foreign commerce.

For a thousand miles along the coast, and two hundred miles inland, the influence of the government has been brought to bear upon domestic slavery among the natives, and upon the extirpation of the slave-trade, until both have ceased to exist.

A well-ordered and well-governed community has been established on the coast of Africa, with its courts of justice intelligently presided over; with its legislative assemblies wisely constructed and equitably conducted; with its schools and college furnishing a sound and thorough education, and with its Christian churches teaching the people the practical duties which pertain to the present life, and also revealing to them the way of salvation through Jesus Christ.

Has the work of African colonization proved to be a failure? Are these results nothing? All may not have been accomplished that was anticipated by some of the more sanguine friends of the enterprise. The Society has been called to contend with difficulties which could not have been foreseen in the beginning; it has encountered opposition in quarters where it least expected; vigorous efforts have been made to prejudice the colored people against us; but still there stands the Republic of Liberia to-day, free, independent, and prosperous. All nations recognize and salute her flag. She needs no governmental protection from any other land. All that she asks of us is this, — send us people, industrious, moral, intelligent. If they have not the means themselves, aid them to establish themselves on these shores. We will give them land, if for a few months you will only assist them in their preparation to become self-supporting citizens. And this is the simple work which the American Colonization Society proposes to do.

A strange thing occurred in the history of the world on the last twenty-sixth of July. It was the nineteenth anniversary of the independence of Liberia; and on the heights of Lebanon in Syria, at the house of the United-States consul, the Rev. Mr. Blyden, Fulton Professor in Liberia College, was requested to deliver an address appropriate to the day. I do not think that I can do better than to give you a few words taken from his speech: "Most wonderful," he says, "have been the changes, which, within a few years, the moral and religious aspects of that portion of Africa have undergone. Where, a few years ago, stood virgin forests or impenetrable jungles, we now behold churches erected to the living God; we hear the sound of the church-going bell, and regular Sabbath ministrations are enjoyed. If you could see Liberia as she now is, with her six hundred miles of coast snatched from the abominations of the slave-trade, her thriving towns and villages, her spacious streets and fine houses, her happy homes with their varied delights, her churches with their Sabbath schools and their solemn and delightful services; could you contemplate all the diversified means of improvement and enjoyment, and indications on every hand of ease and happiness, and plodding industry of her population, without those feverish and distracting pursuits and rivalries which make large cities so unpleasant; could you behold these things, and contrast the state of things now with what it was forty years ago, when the eighty-eight negro pilgrims first landed on these shores, where the primeval forests stood around them with their awful, unbroken solitudes; could you listen, as they listened, to the rush of the wind through those forests, to the roar of wild beasts, and the savage music of treacherous foes all around them; were you, I say, in a position to make this contrast, you would exclaim, 'What hath God wrought!' You would acknowledge that the spirit of Christianity and civilization has moved upon the face of these turbid waters, and that beauty and order have emerged out of materials rude and unpromising; you would recognize on that coast a germ of moral renovation, which shall at length burst into glorious efflorescence all over the land: the wilderness and the desert shall bloom and blossom as the rose."

What is to be the history of African Colonization during the next fifty years? No one believes it possible that this new nationality is destined to die out; that this people are doomed to show that they are incapable of self-government, and incompetent to hold a place among the kingdoms of the earth. So far from this, I believe that they are destined to draw around them a class of colored men, endowed with a constantly-increasing intelligence, and a more and more advanced manliness. With the broader and higher education which this class are now receiving amongst us, it may be anticipated that, from time to time, large numbers will say, " Let us go back to our own land, and show the world what Africans can do in Africa; let us do for that continent what the Anglo-Saxon has done for America; let us plant the same institutions there which have made these United States such a power in the earth — only, instead of exterminating the aboriginal inhabitants, as has been done here, let us try to civilize and Christianize the millions that now grovel in barbarism there."

I was very much impressed with a thought that was suggested in an address on the future of the African race, which I heard some years since from the lips of the Rev. Professor Crummell, of Liberia. It was substantially as follows: If the Hindoos or the Chinamen, or the common order of people in any of the European States, were to undertake the experiment of self-government, they would labor under a great disadvantage, from the fact that they are familiar with no form of free institutions which would serve as a model and guide in framing and regulating a representative government; whereas the settlers of Liberia, although many of them were born and trained in slavery, could not help becoming, in a degree, familiar with our religious and political habits and principles. They are, therefore, better qualified to establish and conduct a republic of their own, than any other people in a corresponding position.

There is at this moment among the colored population of the United States, such a *spontaneous* tendency towards emigration as has never been known before; and, when they find that they are no longer an important faction in the political struggles of the country, they will see still more clearly than they now do, that it is for their own comfort and interest, as well as for the good of Africa, to make that land their permanent abode. They have, indeed, the same right to dwell here that any of us have; they have a claim to the same just and equitable treatment; and we are bound to see that the freedom which has been suddenly given them shall prove to be a blessing, and not a curse. But certain races seem to have been intended for certain regions; and as the palm-tree could never flourish in our cold valleys, so the African can never develop his best energies, and find his highest level, in any foreign land. And this will always be to him, in some respects, an alien country. He can never forget the wrongs that have been done to him and his ancestors here; and there is nothing in his reminiscences of the past to make him proud of his American citizenship. We may want to keep him here to do the drudgery that we shrink from ourselves; we may be willing to give him the right of suffrage, that we may use it for our own political advantage; but he must either sink his own individuality, or retain it at a cost, which, in the end, will make him suffer.

Why, then, not go to a republic that he can call his own? There are great fortunes to be made in that land, whenever the same industry and skill shall be brought into action there which have made men rich here. There are posts of honor and influence open to him in that land, lofty enough to satisfy one's proudest ambition. There is a magnificent work to be done for a magnificent continent, which he alone is competent to do. A greater field for enterprise, a greater field for the spread of the gospel of Christ and the establishment of a noble civilization, was never opened to man.

It may demand some sacrifice at first; there may be ties which it is hard to sunder, trials to be endured which it will demand a vigorous will to face; but no great work is accomplished without suffering. White men, bred in luxury and affluence, accomplished women, moved by the love of Christ, have gone to that distant land to carry the unsearchable treasures of a pure and holy faith to a people perishing in darkness; and they went forth to encounter perils which the black man has comparatively little cause to fear.

It is not impossible that, in process of time, the work of the Colonization Society may cease any longer to be needed. The citizens of Liberia, in their prosperity, may themselves provide the means for the removal to that land of all who wish to go there, and are unable to pay the cost, as thousands from Great Britain and Europe are brought to our country every year by the voluntary offerings of those who have preceded them.

But, meanwhile, there is likely to be a great demand upon the resources of this Society. If the multitudes of that unhappy and ill-treated people, who are, at this moment, floating about, dependent upon public charity for their support, and over whose future such an impervious and gloomy cloud is suspended, could all be gathered up, and removed to a pleasant home, a section of land be there secured to them, and the implements placed in their hands, with which, by ordinary labor, they would be able to earn for themselves a comfortable livelihood, would not this be an act of real Christian charity?

We owe an enormous debt to the African: how can we best discharge that debt? Our brothers' blood cries to us from the ground. God hears that cry, and holds us accountable. As we would avert further calamity from our own land, as we would protect ourselves from the slow but certain dispensations of justice, let us, as far as we can, redeem and expiate the wrong we have done the African. We have all eaten the fruit of his unrecompensed labor. Let us now give him back some portion of that which we have taken from him. Let your wealth flow by thousands and tens of thousands into the treasury of this National Society. It will be well used, and bring forth abundant fruit.

APPENDIX.

APPENDIX.

DECLARATION OF INDEPENDENCE.

WE, the representatives of the people of the Commonwealth of Liberia, in Convention assembled, invested with authority for forming a new government, relying upon the aid and protection of the Great Arbiter of human events, do hereby, in the name and on behalf of the people of this Commonwealth, publish and declare the said Commonwealth a FREE, SOVEREIGN, AND INDEPENDENT STATE, by the name and title of the REPUBLIC OF LIBERIA.

While announcing to the nations of the world the new position which the people of this Republic have felt themselves called upon to assume, courtesy to their opinion seems to demand a brief accompanying statement of the causes which induced them, first to expatriate themselves from the land of their nativity and to form settlements on this barbarous coast, and now to organize their government by the assumption of a sovereign and independent character. Therefore we respectfully ask their attention to the following facts:—

We recognize in all men certain natural and inalienable rights; among these are life, liberty, and the right to acquire, possess, enjoy, and defend property. By the practice and consent of men in all ages, some system or form of government is proven to be necessary to exercise, enjoy, and secure these rights; and every people has a right to institute a government, and to choose and adopt that system or form of it, which, in their opinion, will most effectually accomplish these objects, and secure their happiness, which does not interfere with the just rights of others. The right, therefore, to institute government, and to all the powers necessary to conduct it, is an inalienable right, and cannot be resisted without the grossest injustice.

We, the people of the Republic of Liberia, were originally the inhabitants of the United States of North America.

In some parts of that country, we were debarred by law, from all the rights and privileges of men; in other parts, public sentiment, more powerful than law, frowned us down.

We were everywhere shut out from all civil office.

We were excluded from all participation in the government.

We were taxed without our consent.

We were compelled to contribute to the resources of a country which gave us no protection.

We were made a separate and distinct class, and against us every avenue to improvement was effectually closed. Strangers from all lands, of a color different from ours, were preferred before us.

We uttered our complaints; but they were unattended to, or only met by alleging the peculiar institutions of the country.

All hope of a favorable change in our country was thus wholly extinguished in our bosoms, and we looked with anxiety abroad for some asylum from the deep degradation.

The western coast of Africa was the place selected by American benevolence and philanthropy for our future home. Removed beyond those influences which depressed us in our native land, it was hoped we would be enabled to enjoy those rights and privileges, and exercise and improve those faculties, which the God of nature has given us in common with the rest of mankind.

Under the auspices of the American Colonization Society, we established ourselves here, on land acquired by purchase from the lords of the soil.

In an original compact with this Society, we, for important reasons, delegated to it certain political powers; while this institution stipulated, that whenever the people should become capable of conducting the government, or whenever the people should desire it, this institution would resign the delegated power, peaceably withdraw its supervision, and leave the people to the government of themselves.

Under the auspices and guidance of this institution, which has nobly and in perfect faith redeemed its pledges to the people, we have grown and prospered.

From time to time, our number has been increased by emigration from America, and by accession from native tribes; and from time to time, as circumstances required it, we have extended our borders by acquisition of land by honorable purchase from the natives of the country.

As our territory has extended, and our population increased, our commerce has also increased. The flags of most of the civilized nations of the earth float in our harbors, and their merchants are opening an honorable and profitable trade. Until recently, these visits have been of a uniformly harmonious character; but as they have become more frequent, and to more numerous points of our extending coast, questions have arisen, which, it is supposed, can be adjusted only by agreement between sovereign powers.

For years past, the American Colonization Society has virtually withdrawn from all direct and active part in the administration of the government, except in the appointment of the governor, who is also a colonist, for the apparent purpose of testing the ability of the people to conduct the affairs of government; and no complaint of crude legislation, nor of mismanagement, nor of mal-administration, has yet been heard.

In view of these facts, this institution, the American Colonization Society, with that good faith which has uniformly marked all its dealings with us, did, by a set of resolutions in January, in the year of our Lord one thousand eight hundred and forty-six, dissolve all political connection with the people of this Republic, return the power with which it was delegated, and left the people to the government of themselves.

The people of the Republic of Liberia, then, are of right, and in fact, a free, sovereign, and independent State, possessed of all the rights, powers, and functions of government.

In assuming the momentous responsibilities of the position they have taken, the people of this Republic feel justified by the necessities of the case; and, with this conviction, they throw themselves with confidence upon the candid consideration of the civilized world.

Liberia is not the offspring of grasping ambition, nor the tool of avaricious speculation.

No desire for territorial aggrandizement brought us to these shores; nor do we believe so sordid a motive entered into the high considerations of those who aided us in providing this asylum.

Liberia is an asylum from the most grinding oppression.

In coming to the shores of Africa, we indulged the pleasing hope that we would be permitted to exercise and improve those faculties which impart to man his dignity, to nourish in our hearts the flame of honorable ambition, to cherish and indulge those aspirations which a beneficent Creator had implanted in every human heart, and to evince to all who despise, ridicule, and oppress our race, that we possess with them a common nature, are with them susceptible of equal refinement, and capable of equal advancement in all that adorns and dignifies man.

We were animated with the hope that here we should be at liberty to train up our children in the way they should go, to inspire them with the love of an honorable fame, to kindle within them the flame of a lofty philanthropy, and to form strong within them the principles of humanity, virtue, and religion.

Among the strongest motives to leave our native land, to abandon forever the scenes of our childhood, and to sever the most endeared connections, was the desire for a retreat, where, free from the agitations of fear and molestation, we could, in composure and security, approach in worship the God of our fathers.

Thus far our highest hopes have been realized.

Liberia is already the happy home of thousands who were once the doomed victims of oppression ; and if left unmolested to go on with her natural and spontaneous growth, if her movements be left free from the paralyzing intrigues of jealous ambition and unscrupulous avarice, she will throw open a wider and yet a wider door for thousands who are now looking with an anxious eye for some land of rest.

Our courts of justice are open equally to the stranger and the citizen for the redress of grievances, for the remedy of injuries, and for the punishment of crime.

Our numerous and well-attended schools attest our efforts and our desire for the improvement of our children.

Our churches for the worship of our Creator, everywhere to be seen, bear testimony to our piety and to our acknowledgment of his providence.

The native African, bowing down with us before the altar of the living God, declare that from us, feeble as we are, the light of Christianity has gone forth; while upon that curse of curses, the slave-trade, a deadly blight has fallen as far as our influence extends.

Therefore, in the name of humanity and virtue and religion, in the name of the Great God, our common Creator and our common Judge, we appeal to the nations of Christendom, and earnestly and respectfully ask of them that they will regard us with the sympathy and friendly considerations to which the peculiarities of our condition entitle us, and to extend to us that comity which marks the friendly intercourse of civilized and independent communities.

CONSTITUTION.

ARTICLE I.

Declaration of Rights.

The end of the institution, maintenance, and administration of government, is to secure the existence of the body politic, to protect it, and to furnish the individuals who compose it with the power of enjoying in safety and tranquillity their natural rights, and the blessings of life; and, whenever these great objects are not obtained, the people have a right to alter the government, and to take measures necessary for their safety, prosperity, and happiness.

Therefore we, the people of the Commonwealth of Liberia, in Africa, acknowledging with devout gratitude the goodness of God in granting to us the blessings of the Christian religion, and political, religious, and civil liberty, do, in order to secure these blessings for ourselves and our posterity, and to establish justice, insure domestic peace, and promote the general welfare, hereby solemnly associate and constitute ourselves a free, sovereign, and independent State, by the name of the Republic of Liberia; and do ordain and establish this constitution for the government of the same.

SECTION 1. All men are born equally free and independent, and have certain natural inherent and inalienable rights,—among which are the rights of enjoying and defending life and liberty, of acquiring, possessing, and protecting property, and of pursuing and obtaining safety and happiness.

SECT. 2. All power is inherent in the people: all free governments are instituted by their authority and for their benefit, and they have a right to alter and reform the same when their safety and happiness require it.

SECT. 3. All men have a natural and inalienable right to worship God according to the dictates of their own consciences, without obstruction or molestation from others. All persons demeaning themselves peaceably, and not obstructing others in their religious worship, are entitled to the protection of law in the free exercise of their own religion; and no sect of Christians shall have exclusive privileges or preference over any other sect, but all shall be alike tolerated; and no religious test whatever shall be required as a qualification for civil office, or the exercise of any civil right.

SECT. 4. There shall be no slavery within this Republic; nor shall any citizen of this Republic, or any person resident therein, deal in slaves, either within or without this Republic, directly or indirectly.

Sect. 5. The people have a right at all times, in an orderly and peaceable manner, to assemble and consult upon the common good, to instruct their representatives, and to petition the government or any public functionaries for the redress of grievances.

Sect. 6. Every person injured shall have remedy therefor by due course of law. Justice shall be done without denial or delay; and in all cases not arising under martial law or upon impeachment, the parties shall have a right to a trial by jury, and to be heard in person or by counsel, or both.

Sect. 7. No person shall be held to answer for a capital or infamous crime, except in cases of impeachment, cases arising in the army and navy, and petty offences, unless upon presentment by a grand jury; and every person criminally charged shall have a right to be seasonably furnished with a copy of the charge, to be confronted with the witnesses against him, to have compulsory process for obtaining witnesses in his favor, and to have a speedy, public, and impartial trial by a jury of the vicinity. He shall not be compelled to furnish or give evidence against himself; and no person shall, for the same offence, be twice put in jeopardy of life or limb.

Sect. 8. No person shall be deprived of life, liberty, property, or privilege, but by the judgment of his peers, or the law of the land.

Sect. 9. No place shall be searched nor person seized on a criminal charge or suspicion, unless upon warrant lawfully issued, upon probable cause supported by oath or solemn affirmation, specially designating the place or person, and the object of the search.

Sect. 10. Excessive bail shall not be required, nor excessive fines imposed, nor excessive punishments inflicted; nor shall the legislature make any law impairing the obligation of contracts, nor any law rendering any act punishable in any manner in which it was not punishable when it was committed.

Sect. 11. All elections shall be by ballot; and every male citizen of twenty-one years of age, possessing real estate, shall have the right of suffrage.

Sect. 12. The people have a right to keep and to bear arms for the common defence. And as, in time of peace, armies are dangerous to liberty, they ought not to be maintained without the consent of the legislature; and the military power shall always be held in exact subordination to the civil authority, and be governed by it.

Sect. 13. Private property shall not be taken for public use without just compensation.

Sect. 14. The powers of this government shall be divided into three distinct departments, the legislative, executive, and judicial; and no person belonging to one of these departments shall exercise any of the powers belonging to either of the others. This section is not to be construed to include Justices of the Peace.

Sect. 15. The liberty of the press is essential to the security of freedom in a State: it ought not, therefore, to be restrained in this Republic.

The press shall be free to every person who undertakes to examine the proceedings of the legislature or any branch of government; and no law shall ever be made to restrain the rights thereof. The free communication of thoughts and opinions is one of the invaluable rights of man; and every citizen may freely speak, write, and print on any subject, being responsible for the abuse of that liberty.

In prosecutions for the publication of papers investigating the official conduct of officers, or men in a public capacity, or where the matter published is proper for public information, the truth thereof may be given in evidence. And in all indictments for libels, the jury shall have a right to determine the law and the facts under the direction of the court, as in other cases.

Sect. 16. No subsidy, charge, impost, or duties ought to be established, fixed, laid, or levied, under any pretext whatsoever, without the consent of the people, or their representatives in the legislature.

Sect. 17. Suits may be brought against the Republic in such manner and in such cases as the legislature may by law direct.

SECT. 18. No person can, in any case, be subjected to the law martial, or to any penalties or pains by virtue of that law (except those employed in the army or navy, and except the militia in actual service), but by the authority of the legislature.

SECT. 19. In order to prevent those who are vested with authority from becoming oppressors, the people have a right, at such periods and in such manner as they shall establish by their frame of government, to cause their public officers to return to private life, and fill up vacant places by certain and regular elections and appointments.

SECT. 20. That all prisoners shall be bailable by sufficient sureties, unless for capital offences when the proof is evident or presumption great; and the privilege and the benefit of the writ of habeas corpus shall be enjoyed in this Republic, in the most free, easy, cheap, expeditious, and ample manner, and shall not be suspended by the legislature, except upon the most urgent and pressing occasions, and for a limited time, not exceeding twelve months.

ARTICLE II.

Legislative Powers.

SECTION 1. The legislative power shall be vested in a Legislature of Liberia, and consist of two separate branches, — a House of Representatives and a Senate, — to be styled the Legislature of Liberia, each of which shall have a negative on the other; and the enacting style of their acts and laws shall be, "It is enacted by the Senate and House of Representatives of the Republic of Liberia in Legislature assembled."

SECT. 2. The representatives shall be elected by and for the inhabitants of the several counties of Liberia, and shall be apportioned among the several counties of Liberia as follows: The County of Montserado shall have four representatives, the County of Grand Bassa shall have three, and the County of Sinoe shall have one; and all counties hereafter which shall be admitted in the

Republic shall have one representative, and for every ten thousand inhabitants one representative shall be added. No person shall be a representative who has not resided in the county two whole years immediately previous to his election, and who shall not, when elected, be an inhabitant of the county, and does not own real estate of not less value than one hundred and fifty dollars in the county in which he resides, and who shall not have attained the age of twenty-three years. The representatives shall be elected biennially, and shall serve two years from the time of their election.

SECT. 3. When a vacancy occurs in the representation of any county by death, resignation, or otherwise, it shall be filled by a new election.

SECT. 4. The House of Representatives shall elect their own speaker and other officers. They shall also have the sole power of impeachment.

SECT. 5. The Senate shall consist of two members from Montserado County, two from Bassa County, two from Sinoe County, and two from each county which may be hereafter incorporated into this Republic. No person shall be a senator who shall not have resided three whole years immediately previous to his election in the Republic of Liberia, and who shall not, when elected, be an inhabitant of the county which he represents, and who does not own real estate of not less value than two hundred dollars in the county which he represents, and who shall not have attained the age of twenty-five years. The senator for each county who shall have the highest number of votes shall retain his seat for four years; and the one who shall have the next highest number of votes, two years; and all who are afterwards elected to fill their seats shall remain in office four years.

SECT. 6. The Senate shall try all impeachments, the senators being first sworn or solemnly affirmed to try the same impartially, and according to law; and no person shall be convicted but by the concurrence of two-thirds of the senators present. Judgment in such cases shall not extend beyond removal from office, and disqualification to hold an office in the Republic; but the party may still be tried at law for the same offence.

When either the President or Vice-President is to be tried, the Chief Justice shall preside.

Sect. 7. It shall be the duty of the Legislature, as soon as conveniently may be after the adoption of this constitution, and once at least in every ten years afterwards, to cause a true census to be taken of each town and county of the Republic of Liberia; and a representative shall be allowed every town having a population of ten thousand inhabitants; and, for every additional ten thousand in the counties after the first census, one representative shall be added to that county, until the number of representatives shall amount to thirty. Afterwards, one representative shall be added for every thirty thousand.

Sect. 8. Each branch of the legislature shall be judge of the election returns and qualifications of its own members. A majority of each shall be necessary to transact business; but a less number may adjourn from day to day, and compel the attendance of absent members. Each house may adopt its own rules of proceeding, enforce order, and, with the concurrence of two-thirds, may expel a member.

Sect. 9. Neither house shall adjourn for more than two days without the consent of the other; and both houses shall sit in the same town.

Sect. 10. Every bill or resolution which shall have passed both branches of the Legislature, shall, before it becomes a law, be laid before the President for his approval. If he approves, he shall shall sign it; if not, he shall return it to the Legislature with his objections: if the Legislature shall afterwards pass the bill or resolution by a vote of two-thirds in each branch, it shall become a law. If the President shall neglect to return such bill or resolution to the Legislature, with his objection, for five days after the same shall have been so laid before him,—the Legislature remaining in session during that time, such neglect shall be equivalent to his signature.

Sect. 11. The Senators and Representatives shall receive from the Republic a compensation for their services, to be ascertained by law; and shall be privileged from arrest except for treason, felony, or breach of the peace, while attending at, going to, or returning from, the session of the Legislature.

ARTICLE III.

Executive Power.

Section 1. The Supreme Executive power shall be vested in a President, who shall be elected by the people, and shall hold his office for the term of two years. He shall be commander-in-chief of the army and navy. He shall, in the recess of the legislature, have power to call out the militia, or any portion thereof, into actual service in defence of the Republic. He shall have power to make treaties, provided the Senate concur therein by a vote of two-thirds of the senators present. He shall nominate, and, with the advice and consent of the Senate, appoint and commission, all ambassadors and other public ministers and consuls, secretaries of state, of war, of the navy, and of the treasury, attorney-general, all judges of courts, sheriffs, coroners, marshals, justices of the peace, clerks of courts, registers, notaries public, and all other officers of State, civil and military, whose appointment may not be otherwise provided for by the constitution, or by standing laws. And, in the recess of the Senate, he may fill any vacancy in those offices, until the next session of the Senate. He shall receive all ambassadors and other public ministers. He shall take care that the laws be faithfully executed; he shall inform the Legislature, from time to time, of the condition of the Republic, and recommend any public measures for their adoption which he may think expedient. He may, after conviction, remit any public forfeitures and penalties, and grant reprieves and pardons for public offences, except in cases of impeachment. He may require information and advice from any public officer, touching matters pertaining to his office. He may, on extraordinary occasions, convene the Legislature, and may adjourn the two houses whenever they cannot agree as to the time of adjournment.

SECT. 2. There shall be a Vice-President, who shall be elected in the same manner and for the same term as that of the President, and whose qualifications shall be the same. He shall be President of the Senate, and give the casting vote when the house is equally divided on any subject. And in case of the removal of the President from office, or his death, resignation, or inability to discharge the powers and duties of the said office, the same shall devolve on the Vice-President; and the Legislature may by law provide for the case of removal, death, resignation, or inability, both of the President and Vice-President, declaring what officer shall then act as President; and such officer shall act accordingly, until the disability be removed, or a President shall be elected.

SECT. 3. The Secretary of State shall keep the records of the State, and all the records and papers of the legislative body, and all other public records and documents not belonging to any other department, and shall lay the same, when required, before the President or Legislature. He shall attend upon them when required, and perform such other duties as may be enjoined by law.

SECT. 4. The Secretary of the Treasury, or other persons who may by law be charged with the custody of the public moneys, shall, before he receive such moneys, give bonds to the State, with sufficient sureties to the acceptance of the Legislature, for the faithful discharge of his trust. He shall exhibit a true account of such moneys when required by the President or Legislature; and no moneys shall be drawn from the treasury but by warrant from the President, in consequence of appropriation made by law.

SECT. 5. All ambassadors and other public ministers and consuls, the Secretary of State, of War, of the Treasury, and of the Navy, the Attorney-general, and Postmaster-general, shall hold their offices during the pleasure of the President. All justices of the peace, sheriffs, marshals, clerks of courts, registers, and notaries public, shall hold their office for the term of two years from the date of their respective commissions, but may be removed from office within that time by the President, at his pleasure; and all other officers whose term of office may not be otherwise limited by law, shall hold their office during the pleasure of the President.

Sect. 6. Every civil officer may be removed from office, by impeachment, for official misconduct. Every such officer may also be removed by the President, upon the address of both branches of the Legislature, stating the particular reasons for his removal.

Sect. 7. No person shall be eligible to the office of President who has not been a citizen of this Republic for at least five years, and shall not have attained the age of thirty-five years; and who shall not be possessed of unincumbered real estate, of not less value than six hundred dollars.

Sect. 8. The President shall at stated times receive for his services a compensation, which shall neither be increased nor diminished during the period for which he shall have been elected. And, before he enters on the execution of his office, he shall take the following oath or affirmation: —

I do solemnly swear (or affirm) that I will faithfully execute the office of the President of the Republic of Liberia, and will to the best of my ability preserve, protect, and defend the constitution, and enforce the laws, of the Republic of Liberia.

ARTICLE IV.

Judicial Department.

Section 1. The judicial power of this Republic shall be vested in one Supreme Court, and such subordinate courts as the Legislature may from time to time establish. The judges of the Supreme Court, and all other judges of courts, shall hold their office during good behavior, but may be removed by the President on the address of two-thirds of both houses for that purpose, or by impeachment and conviction thereon. The judges shall have salaries established by law, which may be increased, but not diminished, during their continuance in office. They shall not receive any other perquisite or emoluments whatever, from parties or others on account of any duty required of them.

SECT. 2. The Supreme Court shall have original jurisdiction in all cases affecting ambassadors or other public ministers and consuls, and those to which the Republic shall be a party. In all other cases, the Supreme Court shall have appellate jurisdiction, both as to law and fact, with such exceptions, and under such regulations, as the legislature shall from time to time make.

ARTICLE V.

Miscellaneous Provisions.

SECTION 1. All laws now in force in the Commonwealth of Liberia, and not repugnant to this constitution, shall be in force as the laws of the Republic of Liberia, until they shall be repealed by the Legislature.

SECT. 2. All judges, magistrates, and other officers now concerned in the administration of justice in the Commonwealth of Liberia, and all other existing civil and military officers therein, shall continue to hold and discharge their respective offices in the name and by the authority of the Republic, until others shall be appointed and commissioned in their stead pursuant to this Constitution.

SECT. 3. All towns and municipal corporations within this Republic, constituted under the laws of the Commonwealth of Liberia, shall retain their existing organizations and privileges; and the respective officers thereof shall remain in office, and act under the authority of this Republic, in the same manner and with the like powers as they now possess under the laws of said Commonwealth.

Sect. 4. The first election of President, Vice-President, Senators and Representatives, shall be held on the first Tuesday in October in the year of our Lord eighteen hundred and forty-seven, in the same manner as elections of members of the council are chosen in the Commonwealth of Liberia; and the votes shall be certified and returned to the Colonial Secretary; and the result of the election shall be ascertained, posted, and notified by him as it is now by law provided in case of such members of council.

Sect. 5. All other elections of President, Vice-President, Senators and Representatives, shall be held in the respective towns on the first Tuesday in May, in every two years, to be held and regulated in such manner as the Legislature may by law prescribe. The returns of votes shall be made to the Secretary of State, who shall open the same, and forthwith issue notice of the election to the persons apparently so elected Senators and Representatives; and all such returns shall be by him laid before the Legislature at its next ensuing session, together with a list of the names of the persons who appear by such returns to have been duly elected Senators and Representatives; and the persons appearing by said returns to be duly elected shall proceed to organize themselves accordingly as the Senate and House of Representatives. The votes for President shall be sorted, counted, and declared by the House of Representatives; and, if no person shall appear to have a majority of such votes, the Senators and Representatives present shall in convention, by joint ballot, elect from among the persons having the three highest numbers of votes a person to act as President for the ensuing term.

Sect. 6. The Legislature shall assemble once at least in every year, and such meeting shall be on the first Monday in January, unless a different day shall be appointed by law.

Sect. 7. Every legislator and other officer appointed under this constitution, shall, before he enters upon the duties of his office, take and subscribe a solemn oath or affirmation to support the Constitution of this Republic, and faithfully and impartially discharge the duties of such office. The presiding officer of the Senate shall administer such oath or affirmation to the President, in convention of both houses; and the President shall administer the same to the Vice-President, to the Senators and to the Representatives in like manner. If the President is unable to attend, the Chief Justice of the Supreme Court may administer the oath or affirmation to him at any place, and also to the Vice-President, Senators and Representatives in convention. Other officers may take such oath or affirmation before the President, Chief Justice, or any other person who may be designated by law.

SECT. 8. All elections of public officers shall be made by a majority of the votes, except in cases otherwise regulated by the constitution or by law.

SECT. 9. Officers created by this constitution which the circumstances of the Republic do not require that they shall be filled, shall not be filled until the Legislature shall deem it necessary.

SECT. 10. The property of which a woman may be possessed at the time of her marriage, and also that of which she may afterwards become possessed, otherwise than by her husband, shall not be held responsible for his debts, whether contracted before or after marriage.

Nor shall the property thus intended to be secured to the woman be alienated otherwise than by her free and voluntary consent; and such alienation may be made by her either by sale, devise, or otherwise.

SECT. 11. In all cases in which estates are insolvent, the widow shall be entitled to one-third of the real estate during her natural life, and to one-third of the personal estate, which she shall hold in her own right, subject to alienation by her by devise or otherwise.

SECT. 12. No person shall be entitled to hold real estate in this Republic unless he be a citizen of the same. Nevertheless, this article shall not be construed to apply to colonization, missionary, educational, or other benevolent institutions, so long as the property or estate is applied to its legitimate purposes.

Sect. 13. The great object of forming these colonies being to provide a home for the dispersed and oppressed children of Africa, and to regenerate and enlighten this benighted continent, none but persons of color shall be admitted to citizenship in this Republic.

Sect. 14. The purchase of any land by any citizen or citizens from the aborigines of this country, for his or their own use, or for the benefit of others, as estate or estates in fee simple, shall be considered null and void to all intents and purposes.

Sect. 15. The improvement of the native tribes and their advancement in the arts of agriculture and husbandry being a cherished object of this government, it shall be the duty of the President to appoint in each county some discreet person, whose duty it shall be to make regular and periodical tours through the country, for the purpose of calling the attention of the natives to these wholesome branches of industry, and of instructing them in the same; and the legislature shall, as soon as can conveniently be done, make provision for these purposes by the appropriation of money.

Sect. 16. The existing regulations of the American Colonization Society, in the Commonwealth, relative to emigrants, shall remain the same in the Republic, until regulated by compact between the Society and the Republic: nevertheless, the Legislature shall make no law prohibiting emigration; and it shall be among the first duties of the legislature to take measures to arrange the future relations between the American Colonization Society and this Republic.

Sect. 17. This Constitution may be altered whenever two-thirds of both branches of the legislature shall deem it necessary; in which case the alterations or amendments shall first be considered and approved by the legislature, by the concurrence of two-thirds of the members of each branch, and afterwards by them submitted to the people, and adopted by two-thirds of all the electors at the next biennial meeting for the election of senators and representatives.

Done in Convention at Monrovia, in the County of Montserado, by the unanimous consent of the people of the Commonwealth of Liberia, this twenty-sixth day of July, in the year of our Lord one thousand eight hundred and forty-seven, and of the Republic the first.

In witness whereof we have hereto set our names.

S. BENEDICT, *President,*
J. N. LEWIS,
H. TEAGE,
BEVERLY R. WILSON, } Montserado County.
ELIJAH JOHNSON,
J. B. GRIPON,

JOHN DAY,
A. W. GARDNER,
AMÓS HERRING, } Grand Bassa County.
EPHRAIM TILLER,

R. E. MURRAY, County of Sinoe.

J. W. PROUT, *Secretary of Convention.*

Monrovia, July 29, 1847.

Fellow-Citizens, — Having finished our labors, we now have the honor of submitting to your consideration, through the Governor, that Constitution which, in our opinion, will best suit the peculiar circumstances of the people of this infant Republic. That our labors will meet the full approbation of every individual citizen is scarcely to be expected. We trust, however, that a large majority of our fellow-citizens will approve our doings, and adopt the constitution herewith submitted.

In our deliberations, we endeavored to keep our minds steadily fixed upon the great objects of civil government, and have done what we conceived to be best for the general interest of this rising Republic. We endeavored carefully to arrange every subject that might possibly arise, calculated to disturb in the least the friendly feeling which now so happily subsists between the different counties of this Republic. We felt deeply the importance and magnitude of the work submitted to our hands, and have done the very best we could in order to afford general satisfaction.

In view of the peculiarity of our circumstances, the new position we have assumed is indeed a gigantic one; and the government now calls to its support every citizen who is at all concerned for the safety and future prosperity of this our only home.

Knowing, however, that our cause is just, we feel encouraged, and believe that under God, by a speedy perseverance, we shall fully succeed.

In publishing to the world our *Independence*, we have thought proper to accompany that document with a declaration of the causes which induced us to leave the land of our nativity, and to form settlements on this coast; and also an appeal to the sympathies of all civilized nations, soliciting their aid and protection, and especially that they would, notwithstanding our peculiar circumstances, speedily recognize our *Independence*.

And that the flag of this Republic at no distant day may be seen floating upon every breeze, and in every land respected.

It is our earnest desire that the affairs of this government may be so conducted as to merit the approbation of all Christendom, and restore to Africa her long-lost glory; and that Liberia, under the guidance of Heaven, may continue a happy asylum for our long-oppressed race, and a blessing to the benighted and degraded natives of this vast peninsula: to secure which is our ardent wish and prayer.

With great respect, we have the honor of being
           Your obedient and humble servants.
By the unanimous order of the convention,

                       SAMUEL BENEDICT,
                                President.

FLAG AND SEAL OF THE REPUBLIC OF LIBERIA.

THE following flag and seal were adopted by the Convention as the insignia of the Republic of Liberia, and ordered to be employed to mark its nationality:—

Flag. — Six red stripes with five white stripes, alternately displayed longitudinally. In the upper angle of the flag, next to the spear, a square blue ground covering in depth five stripes. In the centre of the blue, one white star.

Seal. — A dove on the wing, with an open scroll in its claws. A view of the ocean, with a ship under sail. The sun, just emerging from the waters. A palm-tree, and at its base a plough and spade. Beneath the emblems, the words REPUBLIC OF LIBERIA, and above the emblems, the national motto, THE LOVE OF LIBERTY BROUGHT US HERE.

The former seal of the Commonwealth is ordered to be used until that for the Republic shall be engraved.

By order of the convention.

S. BENEDICT,
President.

INAUGURAL ADDRESS

OF HIS EXCELLENCY J. J. ROBERTS, PRESIDENT OF THE REPUBLIC OF LIBERIA.

Delivered at the first meeting of the Legislature of the Republic, Jan. 3, 1848.

FELLOW-CITIZENS, — Before I proceed to add the solemnity of an oath to the obligations imposed on me, it is with great pleasure I avail myself of the occasion, now presented, to express the profound impressions made on me by the call of my fellow-citizens to the station and the duties to which I am now about to pledge myself. So distinguished a mark of confidence, proceeding from the deliberate suffrage of my fellow-citizens, would, under any circumstances, have commanded my gratitude and devotion, as well as filled me with an awful sense of the trust to be assumed. But I feel particularly gratified at this evidence of the confidence of my fellow-citizens, inasmuch as it strengthens the impression on me, that my endeavors to discharge faithfully the duties which devolved on me as Chief Executive officer of the Commonwealth, during the last six years of our political connection with the American Colonization Society, have been favorably estimated. I nevertheless meet the responsibilities of this day with feelings of the deepest solicitude. I feel, fellow-citizens, that the present is a momentous period in the history of Liberia; and I assure you, under the various circumstances which give peculiar solemnity to the crisis, I am sensible that both the honor and the responsibility alloted to me are inexpressibly enhanced.

We have just entered upon a new and important career. To

give effect to all the measures and powers of the government, we have found it necessary to remodel our Constitution and to erect ourselves into an independent State, which, in its infancy, is exposed to numberless hazards and perils, and which can never attain to maturity or ripen into firmness, unless it is managed with affectionate assiduity and guarded by great abilities. I therefore deeply deplore my want of talents, and feel my mind filled with anxiety and uneasiness to find myself so unequal to the duties of the important station to which I am called. When I reflect upon the weight and magnitude now belonging to the station, and the many difficulties which, in the nature of things, must necessarily attend it, I feel more like retreating from the responsible position, than attempting to go forward in the discharge of the duties of my office.

Indeed, gentlemen of the Legislature, if I had less reliance upon your co-operation and the indulgence and support of a reflecting people, and felt less deeply a consciousness of the duty I owe my country, and a conviction of the guidance of an all-wise Providence in the management of our political affairs, I should be compelled to shrink from the task. I, however, enter upon the duties assigned me, relying upon your wisdom and virtue to supply my defects, and under the full conviction that my fellow-citizens at large, who, on the most trying occasions, have always manifested a degree of patriotism, perseverance, and fidelity, that would reflect credit upon the citizens of any country, will support the government established by their voluntary consent, and appointed by their own free choice.

While I congratulate my fellow-citizens on the dawn of a new and more perfect government, I would also remind them of the increased responsibility they too have assumed.

Indeed, if there ever was a period in the annals of Liberia, for popular jealousy to be awakened, and popular virtue to exert itself, it is the present. Other eras, I know, have been marked by dangers and difficulties which "tried men's souls;" but, whatever was their measure, disappointment and overthrow have generally been their fate. That patriotism and virtue which distinguish men of every age, clime, and color, who are determined to be free, never forsook that little band of patriots — the pioneers in this noble enterprise — in the hour of important trial. At a time when they were almost without arms, ammunition, discipline, or government, — a mere handful of isolated Christian pilgrims in pursuit of civil and religious liberty, surrounded by savage and warlike tribes bent upon their ruin and total annihilation, — with "a staff and a sling" only, as it were, they determined, in the name of the "Lord of Hosts," to stand their ground, and defend themselves to the last extremity against their powerful adversary. And need I remind you, fellow-citizens, how signally Almighty God delivered them, and how he has hitherto prospered and crowned all our efforts with success?

These first adventurers, inspired by the love of liberty and equal rights, supported by industry and protected by Heaven, became inured to toil, to hardships, and to war. In spite, however, of every obstacle, they obtained a settlement, and happily, under God, succeeded in laying here the foundation of a free government. Their attention, of course, was then turned to the security of those rights for which they had encountered so many perils and inconveniencies. For this purpose, a constitution, or form of government, anomalous, it is true, was adopted.

Under the circumstances, expediency required that certain powers of the government should be delegated to the American Colonization Society, their patrons and benefactors, with the understanding, that, whenever the colonies should feel themselves capable of assuming the whole responsibility of the government, that institution would resign the delegated power, and leave the people to the government of themselves.

At that time it was scarcely supposed, I presume, that the colonies would advance so rapidly as to make it necessary, or even desirable, on the part of the colonists, to dissolve that connection within the short space of twenty-five years. Such, however, is the case. Necessity has demanded it.

Under the fostering care of the American Colonization Society, these infant settlements soon began to prosper and flourish; and a profitable trade, in a few years, opened an intercourse between them and the subjects and citizens of foreign countries. This intercourse eventually involved us in difficulties with British traders, and, of consequence, with the British Government, which could not be settled, for the want of certain powers in the government here, not provided for in the Constitution. Nor, indeed, would the British Government recognize in the people of Liberia the rights of sovereignty — "such as imposing custom dues and levying taxes upon British commerce" — so long as their political connection with the Colonization Society continued. Under these circumstances, a change in our relations with the Society, and the adoption of a new constitution, were deemed, by a large majority of the citizens of the Commonwealth, absolutely necessary. Such also was the opinion of the Board of Directors of the American Colonization Society, who recommended the measure as the only means of relieving the government from these embarrassments, and the citizens from innumerable inconveniences.

In view of these facts, to have shrunk from the responsibility, notwithstanding weighty reasons adverse to the measure suggested themselves, would have betrayed a weakness and timidity unbecoming freemen.

Therefore, on full consideration of all the circumstances, it appeared that the period had arrived when it became the duty of the people of Liberia to assume a new position, — such a one that foreign powers would consider them an independent nation.

As you are aware, fellow-citizens, the independence of Liberia has been the subject of much speculation and some animadversion, both at home and abroad.

1st. We are told that the pecuniary assistance the government here has hitherto received from the Colonization Society will now cease; and that in a few years we will find ourselves groaning under enormous taxes, or the affairs of the government will be exceedingly embarrassed, if not totally paralyzed.

I am persuaded, however, that this conclusion by no means follows. To what extent, if at all, the Society contemplates withdrawing the pecuniary aid hitherto granted to the Commonwealth, from the new government, I am not advised; nor have I any data upon which to form even an opinion in regard to it. We have this assurance, however, from Rev. Mr. McLain, Secretary of the Society, "that the interest of the Board of Directors, in all that concerns the people of Liberia, will not be diminished, but rather increased, by the alteration in the present relations subsisting between them and the American Colonization Society; and that it is the intention of the Society to prosecute its work as vigorously as heretofore, and on the same high and liberal principles."

We are truly, fellow-citizens, under many obligations to the Colonization Society. Indeed, it is impossible for one people to have stronger ties upon the gratitude of another than that Society has upon the people of Liberia.

To the wisdom, philanthropy, and magnanimity of the members of the Colonization Society, who, for more than a quarter of a century, have watched with the deepest solicitude the progress of these colonies, and have devoted much of their time and substance to support them, we owe, under God, the political, civil, and religious liberty and independence we this day enjoy; and I have no doubt in my own mind, but that they will continue to aid us in every way the circumstances of the Society will admit of.

The necessity of imposing additional taxes upon the people to meet the additional expenses of the government consequent upon the new order of things, is very evident; but I confess, fellow-citizens, I can see no just grounds of fear that they will be enormous or oppressive.

It is true, that for the first few years, in the absence of any foreign assistance, we may find our finances somewhat limited, perhaps barely sufficient to defray the ordinary expenses of the government; but in a country like ours, abounding in a sufficiency of natural resources, which are so easily developed, it is scarcely probable that the government at any time will be greatly embarrassed, certainly not totally paralyzed.

2d. It has been urged that the numerical strength of the government is yet too small; and that we have not sufficient intelligence, experience, or wealth, to command respect abroad; and that, in the event foreign powers should refuse to acknowledge our independence, the embarrassments of the government and its citizens will be increased, rather than diminished.

Now, according to the best computation I am at present able to make, and which I believe is pretty nearly correct, the population of Liberia Proper — including, of course, the aboriginal inhabitants who have incorporated themselves with us, and subscribed to the constitution and laws of the Republic — is now upwards of eighty thousand; and we may reasonably suppose that the inhabitants will increase almost in the ratio of compound interest. I have no doubt that the natural population of the Republic, in the course of twenty years, will be doubled; and we have great reason to believe that the number of immigrants arriving from America, and perhaps other countries, will be very considerable. The free people of color in the United States, wearied with beating the air to advance themselves to equal immunities with the whites in that country, and tired of the oppression which weighs them down *there*, are seriously turning their attention to Liberia as the only asylum they can flee to and be happy.

While we exceedingly lament the want of greater intelligence and more experience to fit us for the proper or more perfect management of our public affairs, we flatter ourselves that the adverse circumstances under which we so long labored in the land of our birth, and the integrity of our motives, will plead our excuse for our want of abilities; and that, in the candor and charity of an impartial world, our well-meant, however feeble, efforts will find an apology. I am also persuaded that no magnanimous nation will seek to abridge our rights, or withhold from the Republic those civilities and "that comity which marks the friendly intercourse between civilized and independent communities," in consequence of our weakness and present poverty.

And, with respect to the independence of Liberia, I know it to be a favorable object with many great and good men, both in Europe and the United States, and, I have great reason to believe, with several European powers, who entertain commercial views.

3d. We are gravely accused, fellow-citizens, of acting prematurely, and without due reflection, in this whole matter, with regard to the probable consequences of taking into our own hands the whole work of self-government, including the management of our foreign relations; and I have also heard it remarked, that fears are entertained by some persons abroad, that the citizens of Liberia, when thrown upon their own resources, will probably not sustain the government, and that anarchy and its attendant ruins will be the result of their independence.

The impression, however, that the people have acted prematurely, and without regard to consequences, is evidently erroneous. And, to judge of the future from the past, I have no hesitancy in asserting that the fears entertained respecting the disposition of the people here to insubordination are totally groundless. No people, perhaps, have exhibited greater devotion for their government and institutions, and have submitted more readily to lawful authority, than the citizens of Liberia; which, indeed, must be obvious to every one at all familiar with the past history of these colonies. But to return. It is well known that the object of independence has been agitating the public mind for more than five years, and that every consideration for and against it, has been warmly discussed.

I am sensible, however, it is no uncommon thing for men to be warm in a cause, and yet not know why it is they are warm. In such cases, the passion of one is lighted up by the passion of another, and the whole circle is in a flame; but the mind in the mean time is like a dark chamber, without a single ray of light to pervade it. In this case it will happen, that, when the hasty passion shall have spent its force, all virtuous and patriotic resolutions which it kindled up will also die with it; as, in the great affairs of religion, a strong flash of ideas on the fancy may excite a combustion of devotion; but, unless the reason is engaged to feed and supply the burning, it will die away, and neither light nor heat will be found remaining in it.

It was the commendation of a certain people of whom we read in the Bible, that, when the gospel was first preached to them, " they searched the Scriptures daily, whether these things were so." Those who, without examination, had received it, without examination might also give it up: but this more "honorable" people had maturely weighed the doctrine; and, embracing it, they gave ground to believe, that as they were rational, so they would be persevering Christians.

The political concerns of Liberia have been equally the objects of attentive consideration. And it affords the most pleasing reflection, that the people of these colonies have not acted rashly or unadvisedly with respect to their independence, but all the measures which have been adopted in regard to it are strongly marked with great caution and matured deliberation, and will bear the strictest scrutiny of reason and conscience.

The time has been, I admit, when men, without being chargeable with timidity, or with a disposition to undervalue the capacities of the African race, might have doubted the success of the colonization enterprise and the feasibility of establishing an independent Christian State on this coast, composed of and conducted wholly by colored men; but, fellow-citizens, that time has passed. The American Colonization Society has redeemed its pledge, and I believe in my soul, that the permanency of the government of the Republic of Liberia is now fixed upon as firm a basis as human wisdom is capable of devising. Nor is there any reason to apprehend that the divine Disposer of human events, after having separated us from the house of bondage, and led us safely through so many dangers, towards the land of liberty and promise, will leave the work of our political redemption and consequent happiness unfinished, and either permit us to perish in a wilderness of difficulties, or suffer us to be carried back in chains to that country of prejudices, from whose oppression he has mercifully delivered us with his outstretched arm.

And, fellow-citizens, it must afford the most heartfelt pleasure and satisfaction to every friend of Liberia, and real lover of liberty in general, to observe by what a fortunate train of circumstances and incidents the people of these colonies have arrived at absolute freedom and independence. When we look abroad and see by what slow and painful steps, marked with blood and ills of every kind, other States of the world have advanced to liberty and independence, we cannot but admire and praise that all-gracious Providence, who, by his unerring ways, has, with so few sufferings on our part compared with other States, led us to this happy stage in our progress toward those great and important objects. And that it is the will of Heaven that mankind should be free, is clearly evidenced by the wealth, vigor, virtue, and consequent happiness of all free States. But the idea that Providence will establish such governments as he shall deem most fit for his creatures, and will give them wealth, influence, and happiness without their efforts, is palpably absurd. In short, God's moral government of the earth is always performed by the intervention of second causes. Therefore, fellow-citizens, while with pious gratitude we survey the frequent interpositions of Heaven in our behalf, we ought to remember, that as the disbelief of an overruling Providence is atheism, so an absolute confidence of having our government relieved from every embarrassment, and its citizens made respectable and happy by the immediate hand of God, without our own exertions, is the most culpable presumption. Nor have we any reason to expect that he will miraculously make Liberia a paradise, and deliver us in a moment of time from all the ills and inconveniences consequent upon the peculiar circumstances under which we are placed, merely to convince us that he favors our cause and government.

Sufficient notifications of his will are always given, and those who will not then believe, neither would they believe though one should rise from the dead to inform them. Who can trace the progress of these colonies, and mark the incidents of the wars in which they have been engaged, without seeing evident tokens of providential favor? Let us, therefore, inflexibly persevere in exerting our most strenuous efforts in an humble and rational dependence on the great Governor of all the world, and we have the fairest prospects of surmounting all the difficulties which may be thrown in our way. And that we may expect, and that we shall have, difficulties, sore difficulties, yet to contend against in our progress to maturity, is certain. And as the political happiness or wretchedness of ourselves and our children, and of generations yet unborn, is in our hands, nay more, the redemption of Africa from the deep degradation, superstition, and idolatry in which she has so long been involved, it becomes us to lay our shoulders to the wheel, and manfully resist every obstacle which may oppose our progress in the great work which lies before us. The gospel, fellow-citizens, is yet to be preached to vast numbers inhabiting this dark continent; and I have the highest reason to believe that it was one of the great objects of the Almighty in establishing these colonies, that they might be the means of introducing civilization and religion among the barbarous nations of this country. And to what work more noble could our powers be applied, than that of bringing up from darkness, debasement, and misery, our fellow-men, and shedding abroad over them the light of science and Christianity? The means of doing so, fellow-citizens, are in our reach, and if we neglect, or do not make use of them, what excuse shall we make to our Creator and final Judge? This is a question of the deepest concern to us all, and which, in my opinion, will materially affect our happiness in the world to come. And surely, if it ever has been incumbent on the people of Liberia to know truth and to follow it, it is now. Rouse, therefore, fellow-citizens, and do your duty like men; and be persuaded that Divine Providence, as heretofore, will continue to bless all your virtuous efforts.

But if there be any among us dead to all sense of honor and love of their country; if deaf to all the calls of liberty, virtue, and religion; if forgetful of the benevolence and magnanimity of those who have procured this asylum for them, and the future happiness of their children; if neither the examples nor the success of other nations, the dictates of reason and of nature, or the great duties they owe to their God, themselves, and their posterity, have any effect upon them; if neither the injuries they received in the land whence they came, the prize they are contending for, the future blessings or curses of their children, the applause or reproach of all mankind, the approbation or displeasure of the great Judge, or the happiness or misery consequent upon their conduct in this and a future state, can move them, — then let them be assured that they deserve to be slaves, and are entitled to nothing but anguish and tribulation. Let them banish forever from their minds the hope of obtaining that freedom, reputation, and happiness, which, as men, they are entitled to. Let them forget every duty, human and divine, remember not that they have children, and beware how they call to mind the justice of the Supreme Being. Let them return into slavery, and hug their chains, and be a reproach and a by-word among all nations.

But I am persuaded, fellow-citizens, that we have none such among us; that every citizen will do his duty, and exert himself to the utmost of his abilities to sustain the honor of his country, promote her interests, and the interests of his fellow-citizens, and to hand down unimpaired to future generations the freedom and independence we this day enjoy.

As to myself, fellow-citizens, I assure you I never have been indifferent to what concerns the interests of Liberia, my adopted country; and I am sensible of no passion which could seduce me knowingly from the path of duty or of justice. The weakness of human nature, and the limits of my own understanding, may, no doubt will, produce errors of judgment. I repeat, therefore, that I shall need all the indulgence I have hitherto received at your hands. I shall need, too, the favor of that Being in whose hands we are, who has led us, as Israel of old, from our native land, and planted us in a country abounding in all the necessaries and comforts of life; who has covered our infancy with his Providence, and to whose goodness I ask you to join with me in supplications, that he will so enlighten the minds of your servants, guide their councils, and prosper their measures, that whatsoever they do shall result in your good, and shall secure to you the peace, friendship, and approbation of all nations.

ANNUAL MESSAGE OF PRESIDENT WARNER,

DECEMBER, 1866.

Fellow-Citizens of the Senate and House of Representatives of the Republic of Liberia:

The expiration of another twelve months has brought around the period when it becomes my duty to lay before you a statement of the affairs of the Republic, and to recommend such measures as appear to me calculated to enhance the welfare of the nation. In discharging this duty, I have to invite you to unite with me in rendering unfeigned thanks to our heavenly Father for the blessings with which the past year has been crowned. The immunity we have enjoyed from those epidemic diseases which have been the scourge of other lands, the bountiful harvests that have blessed the labors of the husbandman, the peace that has prevailed, to a great extent, within our borders, are unmistakable marks of divine favor; and for these mercies we should show ourselves grateful by pursuing such a course of conduct as will meet the approbation of the Almighty.

Foreign Relations. — Our relations with foreign nations are satisfactory, with the exception of the North-western boundary dispute. This question, which has been pending for the last five years without having yet come to a solution, must be settled before it can be determined which of the two governments — this or Her Britannic Majesty's — is responsible for the numerous atrocities which have been committed, as well as for those which are daily being committed, by the natives in the territories in dispute. The predatory wars waged by the natives in those parts of the country against the peaceful natives living in close proximity to our settlement at Grand Cape Mount, and to the great detriment of that settlement; the vast amount of merchandise introduced from adjoining provinces without bringing a revenue to this Government; the open rebellion of the natives, instigated by unprincipled traders living within the territories claimed by this Government, — are evils which are likely to continue for a long time, and to affect most injuriously the interests of the Republic, unless this question of boundary be at once set at rest.

The finances of the Government have not been in such a condition as to allow us to occupy those windward territories with civilized settlements, or we might long since have availed ourselves of the surest method of confirming the claim which we have rightfully acquired by fair and honorable purchase.

On this subject, the Government has renewed the correspondence which two years ago was broken off by the brief reply of the British Government to the last requisition of the Liberian Government. And it is to be hoped that the magnanimity and keen sense of justice of the British Government will allow the question to be put at rest speedily and amicably.

I have appointed Monsieur L. Carrance Consul for this Republic, at Bordeaux, in France. I have also granted a commission to Senor Senmartity Brogues as Liberian Consul at Barcelona and Madrid, in Spain. I felt particular gratification in making this latter appointment; and, in a despatch from the Spanish Minister for Foreign Affairs, we are assured that it was hailed by Her Catholic Majesty's Government as the forerunner of the establishment of friendly and commercial relations between the two countries.

During the year, I have granted my exequatur to Samuel F. McGill, Esq., Consul for Sweden and Norway; also to C. T. W. F. Jantzen, Esq., Consul for Hamburg, at Monrovia.

It is with feelings of inexpressible sorrow that I have to announce to you the death of Abraham Hanson, Esq., late United-States Commissioner and Consul-General, which occurred in the month of

July last, at the legation in Monrovia. The death of Mr. Hanson cast a deep gloom over our community. Never has a foreign functionary stood higher in the estimation of a people than Mr. Hanson did in that of the Liberian, nor succeeded in establishing a better understanding than that which subsisted between Mr. Hanson and the Government to which he was accredited. As a gentleman of Christian character, of kind and benevolent disposition, endearing himself to all who knew him, and as a liberal-minded public functionary, Mr. Hanson justly merited every mark of respect shown to him; and his memory claims a prominent place in the affections of this people.

To fill the office made vacant by the death of Mr. Hanson, the Government of the United States has appointed William A. Johnson, Esq., Vice-Consul General at Monrovia; and I have accorded to him my exequatur.

The Government has been invited to participate in the International Exhibition to be held in Paris during the next year. It will be to me a matter of profound regret if, from any consideration, the Government should be compelled to decline the friendly offer. Such exhibitions tend, to a great extent, to bring into notice the products and commodities of different countries; and considering the limited commerce of Liberia, notwithstanding her vast but undeveloped resources, we should put forth a vigorous effort to improve the opportunity now afforded the country of exhibiting to the world its rich products.

In the latter part of 1864, we made application to the Government of the United States for the purchase of a gunboat. The application was generously responded to, and the sale of a vessel on very liberal terms was provided for.

A treaty of amity and commerce has recently been negotiated between this Republic and the Empire of Austria, which I will lay before the Senate for ratification.

THE MAILS. — The postal convention between this government and that of Great Britain continues in operation. Recent arrangements provide that the steamers bearing the monthly mails shall touch at Monrovia as well as Cape Palmas. This gives us increased facilities for communicating with foreign countries. But in order to have regular intercourse between our settlements, and to prevent those serious delays which too often occur in the operations of the Government from want of mail carriage, it is necessary that you provide some sure and economical means for conveying the mails to and from the different settlements along the coast.

INTERNATIONAL HOSPITAL. — A proposition has been made to this government, by a wealthy and influential gentleman in France, to establish in this city, under the patronage of our Government, an International Hospital. He petitions for a grant of land suitable for this benevolent object, and a small appropriation to assist in the enterprise. I hope you will take this subject under favorable consideration. The seaport towns all over the civilized world could not give a stronger expression of their appreciation of the severe toil and abundant services of seamen, than by erecting buildings in their respective localities for their accommodation when distressed either from shipwreck, sickness, or other causes. Travellers, also, to this coast, would experience an inexpressible feeling of relief from a knowledge that such an asylum existed for their reception when assailed or wasted by the diseases of the climate.

THE PUBLIC REVENUE. — It is necessary that vigorous measures be adopted and executed in order to enhance the public revenue. It is true there is in the paper currency a marked improvement, which tends greatly to the advantage of the citizens generally; but it cannot be of material benefit to the Government, unless the receipts of the treasury constantly exceed, or at least equal, the expenditures it may be necessary to make to carry on the Government. While I admit that all unnecessary expenditures should be abolished, I am not inclined to favor the opinion that the expenses generally of the Government are a waste, because they make no return in kind for the capital invested. The citizens need protection in the prosecution of their various interests; and this the Government should not only have the ability to give, but its ability should be so fully known and seen as to render it unnecessary, except in extraordinary cases, to put it to the test.

THE NATIVE TRIBES. — I have for a long time thought that the native tribes residing within the near jurisdiction of the Republic could be brought into closer relationship with us, by being required to contribute to the support of the Government, and by being allowed such a representation in our national council as will easily commend itself to their comprehension. Such a measure inaugurated among these, will induce those tribes more remote to seek to sustain similar relations to us. No desire to exterminate these people and aggrandize their territory brought us here. They are our brethren, deluded though they often appear; and our constitution expressly declares that their improvement is a cherished object of this Government. The Government, then, being for mutual advantage, is one that calls for mutual support. The aborigines should assist in the great work we have to perform. Like the civilized population, they should give something in return for the protection and redress which our courts always, and our armies often, are required to render them. And I doubt not that many of them are now willing to assist; and when they shall have been convinced that the civilization of which the Republic is the nucleus must spread far and wide over this continent, enlightening and refining its inhabitants, and raising them in the scale of being; that it is a work designed by the Almighty himself, and cannot be stayed, — I am sure they will become willing coadjutors.

I therefore recommend that the discretionary powers given to the Executive in the fifth section of an act regulating taxes and licenses, passed by the Legislature in 1858, to require our aborigines to contribute to the support of the Government in such a manner as he shall deem best, be made a positive law, to be enforced in common with other revenue laws. There are in these forests men of royal blood, and of minds susceptible of the most exalted ideas of systematic and well-balanced government; and, by a proper appreciation of them, they could be made to sustain to us a much nearer and dearer relation than that of being mere contributors to our treasury.

PASSPORTS. — I have also to suggest that, for each passport issued by the Secretary of State, a fee of two dollars be charged, to go into the treasury; that said passport be issued only on the presentation of the treasurer's receipt acknowledging the payment of the fee; and that the receipts be passed quarterly from the Department of State to the Secretary of the Treasury.

Our passport law needs other important amendments. At all times and under all circumstances, the present law allows persons of all characters to obtain passports, simply by giving ten days' notice of their intention to leave the Republic, and paying a fee of fifty cents for each passport. Taking advantage of these easy circumstances under which they can leave the Republic, many of a wilfully thriftless class, whether long in the country or recent comers to it, go to foreign countries only to find the obstacles to be surmounted by indolent persons more numerous than they are in Liberia. In a short time, they become reduced to extremities in the communities they enter. Did they break off their allegiance to the Government of this Republic, we should be saved all further concern about them; but, to avoid the duties and responsibilities of citizens of the new State to which they may have gone, they retain their passports and their allegiance, and in this way, to say the least of it, occasion this Government considerable anxiety, as it is often called upon to relieve its destitute citizens.

PATENTS. — The patent law in force in the Republic should be so amended, as to require every person filing a *caveat* in the patent-office to pay a small fee for the privilege thus secured to him.

PAY OF MEMBERS. — I am fully aware that most men in the public service are already required to make some sacrifice. Still they should always set examples of patriotism, in order that the citizens generally may be induced to second their efforts the more cheerfully. In this connection, I have again to propose to you a recommendation made during the session of '64,— that each member of the legislature receive for his services a salary, not to exceed the amount to which he would be entitled for a session of a moderate length, at a reasonable pay per diem.

LICENSE-FEES. — I have often considered, that, in the administration of the affairs of a nation, justice requires that burdens imposed should be borne equally by the citizens, or in proportion to each man's ability. In our system of licenses, this principle does not operate. There are only three classes of citizens — merchants, lawyers, and auctioneers — who pay a license-fee for being allowed to follow their various vocations. It is not clear to my mind, upon what principle certain classes of our citizens are taxed for procuring a livelihood, while others are exempt. I have on a previous occasion spoken of the propriety of requiring persons following other trades or professions to pay a reasonable license-fee, and I would again bring this subject to your notice.

MANUFACTURE OF ARDENT SPIRITS. — There is pursued in the country an occupation which, to say the least of it, brings no good either to proprietors or customers. I refer to the distilling of ardent spirits. We are, it is true, under a free government, with a liberal constitution; and while total prohibition may appear to some as an invasion of the rights of citizens, yet I cannot see upon what principle of political economy or justice the trade in distilling ardent spirits has been encumbered with the lightest tax, while wholesome, unobjectionable occupations pay to support a Government which knows that its people are demoralized, and shuts its eyes upon the fact. Each still erected or in operation in the Republic should pay a tax proportioned to the capacity in gallons of the said still.

It would be very far from fulfilling our mission to this country, that we continue to demoralize the natives by the abundant sale to them of ardent spirits. It seems clear to my mind that, as in the case of individuals, God holds men responsible for thus putting into the hands of their fellows materials capable of so much harm, inciting them to rapine, murder, and war. So in our case, as a nation, God will not hold us guiltless of this sin which we have been committing to the destruction of our heathen brethren, as well as ourselves; and surely their blood will he require at our hands, and will hold us chargeable for the evils which these tribes commit under the influence of this destructive drink.

The manufacture of ardent spirits, and the traffic in them by other civilized countries, should not be argued by us in justification of the Republic of Liberia engaging in the same thing. The prosperity of those other countries might have been much more abundant and abiding, and there would have been committed in them a less number of murders, had there been in them a total absence of ardent spirits. And may not the secret of the slow progress we are making, compared with the great advantages we have of a fertile soil, a uniformly favorable climate, and the enormous percentage of the yield of our crops, and the evanescent character which the accumulations we make from time to time assume, be attributed to the sin of manufacturing and selling rum? Ardent spirits had much to do with the kidnapping and forcing of our forefathers from their ancient homes to a land of slavery. It caused the opening in that land of many premature graves, which closed over the mangled bodies and broken hearts of the victims of American bondage. We may not hope to escape similar misfortunes and evils, if we persist in manufacturing and selling ardent spirits.

Besides this, the ease with which these natives procure fire-arms and ammunition increases the hostilities, and protracts those bloody struggles in which they engage, but which is our duty to check. The Government of Liberia is the guardian of the tribes which have placed themselves under its jurisdiction; and we should advise, admonish, and gently coerce them into that subjection to law and order which they sometimes appear reluctant to yield. And when our civilized communities so far forget their duty to these heathen as to place in their hands the instruments of death, encouraging them to lawless and murderous acts, they, too, should be restrained by law. I have, therefore, to recommend the placing of a high duty on the importation of fire-arms, powder, and ardent spirits. These articles are by no means essential to the traffic of the country.

INTERCOURSE WITH THE NATIVES.—There is no subject which more affects the interests of this Government than that of the tribes by whom we are surrounded. It must be admitted that the relation we sustain to these aborigines is very different from that held by any other civilized people to the natives of a barbarous country which they have entered. We often find the circumstances attendant on this relation exceedingly embarrassing. These people are our brethren, and yet we sometimes find them in antagonism to us. And then, again, in their own case, another and very important difficulty arises from the fact, that there are chiefs under our jurisdiction who have laws, which we find it difficult to abrogate at once, conflicting with our statutes; thus keeping their subjects in constant dread of violating our laws on the one hand, and incurring the penalty of their own code on the other.

I have already referred to the propriety of making these tribes understand the necessity of contributing to the maintenance of this government; and I have now to suggest that there be some restriction placed on the intercourse of the civilized settlers with the natives, defining how far that intercourse shall extend, and when and for what purposes it shall be allowed. Many disturbances, and during the present year several of a serious nature, have arisen, resulting from that unlimited intercourse with the natives, which has been continued for years by persons ostensibly engaged in trade, who have gone among these tribes to the demoralizing of themselves and to the great disprofit of the natives.

I am of opinion that persons going among the aborigines to reside should be made to show that they are engaged in some lawful and necessary enterprise, and to give bond and security, to be renewed from time to time, for their conforming to law and conserving the public peace; and, whenever it might appear that such persons are no longer prosecuting lawful business with the natives, they should be required to withdraw from them; and, for being allowed to prosecute trade among the natives, they should obtain a license, for which they ought to pay a tax proportionate to the amount of capital invested in such native trade.

PRINCE BOYER.—I have to inform you that in the month of June last, Prince Boyer, of Tradetown, seized and detained the Hon. J. M. Horace, at said place. By this act of Boyer, the Government was placed in a serious dilemma. To have attempted to force the exasperated chief while Mr. Horace was in his power, would have endangered the life of the latter; and the conditions proposed by Boyer, on which his prisoner could be released, were such as the Government could not accede to and maintain its dignity, and preserve the majesty of our laws.

The Government sent a note to Boyer, requiring him to set Mr. Horace at liberty. Mr. Horace has been released. Boyer, however, gives the following ground of grievance: 1st, That an annuity promised him in 1849, and fixed by law, has not been regularly paid him; 2d, That, after he had become reconciled to the port-of-entry law, the domestic trade was interdicted to him, simply because it was rumored by his native enemies that he was contemplating a descent upon the settlements in Grand Bassa County; 3d, That his confessions of repentance for the wrong he had done, by refusing, when commanded to do so, to surrender the goods of foreigners detained by him, were spurned by the Legislature; 4th, That his officers, while on a peaceful mission to the Government, were detained at Grand Bassa, and stripped of their insignia; 5th, That a present which he sent to the Government as an assurance of peace, was seized at Bassa; 6th, That the passage of the law interdicting the domestic trade seemed to be a last resort to crush him; 7th, That Senator Horace, by coming within the territory interdicted, violated the law which he himself assisted to make, and that he,

Boyer, under the circumstances, could not but act according to the natural impulse of a man. He has written to the Government, earnestly imploring a removal of the interdict.

On the other hand, it is clear that the tribes within our jurisdiction have no right to indulge in the spirit of reprisals which they manifest either towards ourselves or each other. When they have complaints against the laws or any proceedings of the Government, they should set forth their grievances in a proper manner. And no men know better the force and virtue of law than some of the powerful chiefs who preside over these tribes. Neither Boyer nor any other chief has any right to execute our laws, or to set up his authority against the majesty of the Republic.

But these chiefs and their subjects have, undoubtedly, certain rights, both natural and political, which should be highly respected by this Government and people. And when this is done, and the natives are not provoked by us to the commission of lawless deeds, or instigated by dishonorable foreigners to insubordination, there will subsist between us and them a permanent good understanding and the greatest cordiality of feeling.

MURDER AT SETTRA KROO. — Sometime in the month of October last, one James Douglas, of Greenville, Sinou, was wantonly murdered at Settra Kroo, by a native of that place. Immediately after intelligence of the tragical affair reached the Government, I sent down to Sinou a proclamation, interdicting all intercourse with Settra Kroo until such time as satisfaction should be given for the murder committed. By the vessel bringing the legislators to this city, I received a communication from the King and head men of Settra Kroo, assuring the Government that the murderer shall be delivered up to justice as soon as he can be placed in the hands of the Nanna Kroo natives.

SEIZURE FOR VIOLATING REVENUE LAW. — Presuming upon another illustration of the might of the British naval force on this coast over the just rights of the Republic, one J. M. Harris, a subject of Her Britannic Majesty's Government, who has for some time kept a trading establishment at Solyma contrary to the laws of the Republic, arrogantly sent, a few weeks ago, his vessel into the little Cape Mount River to prosecute a trade with the aborigines of that place, as if to see how far and with how much impunity he could contravene the laws of the Republic. It will be remembered that this vessel is one of the two that were brought into this port from Solyma by the gunboat "Quail," in 1860, to be tried for trading at that place contrary to our revenue laws, but were forcibly taken out of our harbor by Her Britannic Majesty's cruiser "Torch." The vessel, having been seized by order of the Government, has been brought to this port, and now lies in the river awaiting the investigation of her case by the proper authorities.

PROPOSAL FOR A BANK. — In connection with the subject of finance, I have further to inform you that the plan proposed by Messrs. McFarlan & Co., of London, for transacting financial business for this Government, and which was adopted by you at your last session, has not been acted upon by that firm; they preferring to operate on a totally different basis, merging their proposal into the plan of a bank, of which the details will be duly laid before you.

CODIFICATION OF THE LAWS. — The revision and compilation of our statute laws, which are at present in such inconvenient publications, require your authorization. I have to solicit an appropriation for this object.

EDUCATION. — During the year, Liberia College has continued in operation. The Preparatory Department, under the care of Mr. H. R. W. Johnson, has given the greatest satisfaction in the training of its scholars.

In connection with this I am happy to inform you, that we have intelligence from the United States of a growing and active spirit of emigration to Africa among the blacks. In a week or two, some five or six hundred will probably be landed on our shores. The Attorney General of this Republic, now on his way home, made an interesting tour, during the last summer, over a portion of the Western States; and he assures us, that, from what he has witnessed among the blacks with whom he came into contact, a steady stream of emigration has just begun. We are doubtless all glad to receive such intelligence. But the question that occurs to every thoughtful mind is, Can Liberia, with her feeble institutions, take up and absorb safely this influx of our down-trodden brethren, unaccustomed as they are to the duties and responsibilities of building up new States? I answer, without hesitation, that we can. But it becomes us, as legislators, and executors of law, to make provisions to guard and perpetuate more effectually the liberties of our country. And, among the provisions necessary, a most important, and, indeed, indispensable one, is the establishment of an efficient common-school system. We have in our statute books many laws referring to common schools, but they need revision and consolidation. Depend upon it, unless this matter is attended to, our free institutions will be in danger. Let knowledge be generally diffused, and we need not fear the debates and discussions which periodically take place among us as to our political affairs.

But the diffusion of education among us will, for some time, be dependent chiefly upon legislative action in the establishment and maintenance, throughout the country, of common schools. The Government must here, as in other countries, take this subject into its hands, — a subject which, to my mind, involves the whole matter of what is generally termed popular education, comprising not only schools established by the Government, but also mission schools in our townships or within our jurisdiction.

SYSTEM OF COMMON SCHOOLS. — By having the education of the people under some system — I mean something like the following — so as always to keep the subject of education prominently before the people: —

1. Let the different counties be divided into school districts, and let the people in those districts be taxed to provide school-houses and help to support the schools, the Government furnishing a certain amount.

2. Let a Secretary of Education be appointed, to regulate the educational interests of the country, in connection, if thought advisible, with a committee of Council. All appointments of instructors to common schools to be made by the Secretary, with the advice of the Council; and no teacher to be appointed without a certificate of capability from recognized examiners, *i.e.*, any of the professors in Liberia College, or any other well-known instructor.

3. School teachers to be examined twice a year by the Secretary of Education or his deputy.

4. Provision to be made for schools for girls, in which, besides mere book learning, they may be taught domestic economy and general habits of industry. This is a sore and pressing need of Liberia.

5. Children of the aborigines in our settlements and their neighborhood to have the same rights to education as emigrants; and the Government to have the right to establish schools in purely heathen districts.

Our brethren who flee from the United States to this country for freedom, find, on arriving here, a large and superabundant freedom; but they lose the advantages of enlarged education afforded them in their native country, — advantages which, since the war, have been increasing in various parts of the United States. It is therefore meet and proper that in a system of common schools, such as I have just referred to, efficiently established, they should find some compensation for the sacrifices they have voluntarily made.

PENSION RECOMMENDED. — Before closing this statement, I would request for Jonas Carey a stated pension during his lifetime. He is one of the only three male pioneers of Liberia surviving, and connecting the present with the past. He took part in the memorable battle of Dec. 1, 1822, on the issue of which depended the question whether Christian civilization should be established on this coast by black colonists from America, or not. He is now aged and feeble, and deserves whatever aid or patronage the government can render him.

CONCLUSION. — And now, in conclusion, I beg to assure you of the cordiality and cheerfulness with which I will co-operate with you in any measure for the promotion of the public weal. In all your deliberations, fail not to keep steadily before your mind the great object we should all have in view, viz — the vindication, up-building, and honor of the negro race, and the opening up of this great continent to civilization and religion. Keeping this elevated and glorious aim always before you, your labors will be considerably lightened, and harmony, peace, and fraternal feelings will mark your whole intercourse during the session.

D. B. WARNER.

MONROVIA, Dec. 6, 1866.

CHIEF MAGISTRATES OF LIBERIA.

This table is believed to include the names of all persons who were ever authorized to act as chief magistrates of Liberia. The original plan was, that an agent appointed by the Colonization Society should be the chief magistrate, and an agent appointed by the Government of the United States should have the care of the recaptured Africans: but the same person often held both offices; and there seems to have been an understanding, that, when either agent was absent, his duties should devolve on the other. After the adoption of the constitution proposed by Mr. Gurley, August, 1824, the duties of the Society's agent, in his absence, devolved on a vice-agent, elected by the people. After July, 1836, the Society's agent was styled governor, and the vice-agent, lieutenant governor. Since the Declaration of Independence, in 1847, presidents have been elected by the people. The names of all who are known to have acted as chief magistrates by authority from the Society or by popular election are placed in SMALL CAPITALS. The names of agents of the United States Government, who may have sometimes acted in that capacity, are placed in other type. The dates are given with as much completeness as has been practicable. Two agents of the Society and two of the Government died before the removal from Sierra Leone to Cape Mesurado; but their names none the less deserve to be retained. The names of physicians appointed by the Government or the Society, who may have acted as agents in case of necessity, are also given.

Dr. Samuel A. Crozer. — Instructions dated Dec. 10, 1819; sailed Feb. 6, 1820; died April 15, 1820.

Rev. Samuel Bacon. — Appointed Jan. 8, 1820; sailed Feb. 6, 1820; died May 21, 1820.

John P. Bankson. — Sailed Feb. 6, 1820; died May 13, 1820.

Rev. Daniel Coker, emigrant. — Appointed by Dr. Crozer, just before his death; he was the Society's agent at Campelar, and at Fourah Bay, Sierra Leone, where he remained when the other colonists removed to Cape Mesurado.

Rev. Ephraim Bacon. — Sailed Jan. 23, 1821; returned 1821.

Jonathan B. Winn. — Sailed Jan. 23, died Aug. 25, 1821.

Rev. Joseph Andrus. — Sailed Jan. 23, died July 28, 1821.

Christian Witlberger. — Sailed Jan. 23, 1821; returned June 4, 1822.

Dr. Eli Ayres. — Appointed July 25, 1821; acquired Cape Mesurado Dec. 15, 1821, and removed the colonists thither; appointed United-States Government agent, May 15, 1822; returned June 4, 1822; sailed again May 24; and returned December, 1823.

Elijah Johnson, emigrant. — Appointed by Dr. Ayres as Society's agent during his absence, from June 4, 1822.

Rev. Jehudi Ashmun. — Agent for the Society and the Government, sailed May 20, 1822; appointment confirmed, under the new constitution, August 1824; sailed, on his return, March 25, 1828; died Aug. 25, 1828.

Rev. R. R. Gurley. — Agent of the Society and Government, arrived Aug. 13, 1824; confirmed Ashmun's authority, under a new constitution, and returned Aug. 22, 1824.

Dr. John W. Peaco. — Arrived March 26, 1826; returned 1826.

Dr. George P. Todsen. — Appointed June, 1827; afterwards appointed Society's physician, Nov. 17, 1830, to 1834.

Rev. Lot Cary, emigrant. — Vice-agent, administered from Mr. Ashmun's departure, March 25, 1828; died Nov. 8, 1828.

Rev. Colston M. Waring, emigrant. — From Nov. 8 to Dec. 22, 1828.

CHIEF MAGISTRATES OF LIBERIA.

Dr. RICHARD RANDALL.—Appointed by the Society Sept. 8, and by the Government October, 1828; arrived Dec. 22, 1828; died April 19, 1829.

Dr. JOSEPH MECHLIN.—Appointed assistant agent and physician Oct. 17, 1828; succeeded Dr. Randall April 19, 1829; appointed agent Sept. 14, 1829; appointed Government agent to succeed Dr. Randall; returned May, 1830; sailed again October, 1830; returned July, 1832.

Dr. J. W. ANDERSON.—Appointed assistant agent and physician Jan. 1, 1830; arrived Feb. 27; died April 20, 1830.

ANTHONY D. WILLIAMS, emigrant.—Vice-agent, administered in Dr. Mechlin's absence in 1830, and after his departure in 1832.

Rev. JOHN B. PINNEY.—Appointed Oct. 24, 1833; from ill health, transferred his duties to Dr. Skinner in the summer of 1834.

Dr. EZEKIEL SKINNER.—Sailed as Society's physician June 21, 1834; appointed agent Jan. 26, 1835; returned late in 1836; again appointed physician Oct. 27, 1837.

ANTHONY D. WILLIAMS.—Formerly vice-agent, succeeded Dr. Skinner in 1836.

THOMAS BUCHANAN.—Appointed governor, Dec. 10, 1838, on the union of the settlement of the New-York and Pennsylvania Societies with the Commonwealth of Liberia. Also United-States Government agent. Arrived April 1, 1839; died Sept. 3, 1841. The last white chief magistrate.

Dr. J. W. Lugenbeel, Society's physician, and Government agent. Appointed by the Society July 27, 1843; sailed Sept. 16, 1843; returned May, 1849.

JOSEPH J. ROBERTS, emigrant.—Succeeded Gov. Buchanan, as lieut.-governor, Sept. 3. 1841; appointed governor Jan. 20, 1842; administered till the organization of the Republic, Jan. 3, 1848.

JOSEPH J. ROBERTS, emigrant, president, 1848 to 1856.
STEPHEN A. BENSON, emigrant, president, 1856 to 1864.
DANIEL B. WARNER, emigrant, president, 1864.

GOVERNORS OF MARYLAND IN LIBERIA.

Dr. JAMES HALL. — Founder and first governor. Appointed by the Maryland Colonization Society, October, 1833; sailed Nov. 23, 1833; purchased Cape Palmas, the site of the colony, by treaty, Feb. 13, 1834; resigned, and returned July, 1836. Dr. Hall had been assistant physician in Liberia from October, 1831, to June, 1833. As early as 1832, he urged the appointment of colored governors.

Dr. O. W. HOLMES, temporary agent, a few months from June, 1836.

JOHN B. RUSSWURM, emigrant. — Appointed 1836; died June 9, 1851.

Dr. SAMUEL F. MCGILL, emigrant. — Succeeded Gov. Russwurm in 1851; administered to June, 1854.

WILLIAM A. PROUT, emigrant. — Elected governor under the new Constitution of the colony as an independent state. Inaugurated, June 6, 1854; administered till April, 1856.

BOSTON J. DRAYTON, emigrant. — As lieutenant governor, he succeeded Gov. Prout in April, 1856, and administered till the annexation of the State to the Republic of Liberia, March 3, 1857.

GOVERNORS AT BASSA COVE.

Rev. Rufus Spalding. — The New-York Colonization Society, Dec. 13, 1833, while he was on his voyage to Liberia as a missionary, appointed him as their special agent to plant a new settlement under their auspices. He arrived at Monrovia Dec. 31, 1833; had the ordering of the erection of mission buildings at Bassa Cove, but was unable, from sickness, to visit that place. He returned in May, 1834.

Israel W. Searle. — Appointed by the same Society as sub-agent, Feb. 17, 1834. He was instructed to consult with Mr. Spalding as to a location for the proposed settlement, and to direct their attention to Cape Mount and Bassa Cove. He sailed June 23, 1834, and died in a few weeks after his arrival. That Society had already sent out a few emigrants.

EDWARD Y. HANKINSON. — Appointed by the Pennsylvania Colonization Society; sailed Oct. 24, 1834, with emigrants to found a colony at Bassa Cove. The two Societies were then negotiating on terms of co-operation.

THOMAS BUCHANAN. — Appointed by the united Societies; arrived at Monrovia Jan. 1, 1836.

Rev. JOHN J. MATTHIAS. — Appointed by the united Societies; arrived Aug. 4, 1837; returned, landing at New-York June 17, 1838.

Dr. WESLEY JOHNSON. — Succeeded Gov. Matthias as acting governor; administered till all the settlements were united under Gov. Buchanan in 1839.

MISSISSIPPI COLONY AT SINOU.

Rev. JOSIAH F. C. FINLEY. — Appointed by the Mississippi Colonization Society; sailed April, 1837; robbed and murdered by natives, while on a journey, September, 1838. The settlement was united with the Commonwealth of Liberia in 1839.

182 AMERICAN COLONIZATION SOCIETY.

TABLE OF EMIGRANTS SETTLED IN LIBERIA BY THE AMERICAN COLONIZATION SOCIETY.

Number	Names of Vessels	Date of Sailing	Massachusetts	Rhode Island	Connecticut	New York	New Jersey	Pennsylvania	Delaware	Maryland	Dist. Columbia	Virginia	North Carolina	South Carolina	Georgia	Alabama	Mississippi	Louisiana	Tennessee	Kentucky	Ohio	Indiana	Illinois	Missouri	Michigan	Iowa	Wisconsin	Texas	Ind. Territory	Barbadoes	Total	Total by Years
1	Elizabeth	Feb. 1820				40		33		2	2	9																			86	86
2	Nautilus	Feb., '21								8		25																			33	33
3	Strong	June, '22						12		25																					37	37
4	Oswego	Mar., '23						19		24		17																			60	
5	Fidelity	June, '23						1		4																					5	65
6	Cyrus	Jan., '24										103																			103	103
7	Hunter	Jan., '25									2	62	2																		66	66
8	Vine	Jan., '26	32																												32	
9	Indian Chief	Feb., '26								12		12	126																		150	182
10	Doris	Feb., '27				14				12		7	72																		92	
11	Doris	Nov., '27							2	65		22																			102	
12	Randolph	Dec., '27													27																27	222
13	Nautilus	Jan., '28								12		8	143																		163	163
14	Harriet	Jan., '29								17	2	125	1						2												147	

TABLE OF EMIGRANTS.

TABLE OF EMIGRANTS—Continued.

Number	Names of Vessels	Date of Sailing	Massachusetts	Rhode Island	Connecticut	New York	New Jersey	Pennsylvania	Delaware	Maryland	Dist. Columbia	Virginia	North Carolina	South Carolina	Georgia	Alabama	Mississippi	Louisiana	Tennessee	Kentucky	Ohio	Indiana	Illinois	Missouri	Michigan	Iowa	Wisconsin	Texas	Ind. Territory	Barbadoes	Total	Total by Years
15	Liberia	Dec., '29							2			42							13				1								58	205
16	Montgomery	April, '30								7	1	31	1		30																70	
17	Carolinian	Nov., '30			1					9		80	1		9		8														107	
18	Volador	Dec., '30										41	40			1															82	259
19	Reaper	Jan., '31								6																					6	
20	Criterion	July, '31								6		1	21					18													46	
21	Orion	Oct., '31								31																					31	
22	James Perkins	Dec., '31										291	47																		338	421
23	Crawford	Jan., '32													22																22	
24	Jupiter	May, '32				4						68	22	34	39		2														169	
25	America	July, '32									13	26	87																		126	
26	Jupiter	Nov., '32								1		37																			38	
27	Hercules	Dec., '32						1		1		1	20	146																	168	
28	Lafayette	Dec., '32						1		144		1																			146	
29	Roanoke	Dec., '32				6						98	20		2																127	796
30	American	Mar., '33																													6	
31	Ajax	May, '33			3							2	2		2			2	5	99	41		1								148	
32	Margaret Mercer	Oct., '33								1																					6	
33	Jupiter	Nov., '33										50						2													52	

TABLE OF EMIGRANTS—Continued.

Number	Names of Vessels	Date of Sailing	Mass.	R.I.	Conn.	N.Y.	N.J.	Penn.	Del.	Md.	D.C.	Va.	N.C.	S.C.	Ga.	Ala.	Miss.	La.	Tenn.	Ky.	Ohio	Ind.	Ill.	Mo.	Mich.	Iowa	Wisc.	Texas	Ind. Ter.	Barb.	Total	Total by Years
34	Argus	Dec., '33				2				12	37	7																				58	270
35	Ninus	Oct., '34								16		110																				127	127
36	Rover	Mar., '35								1		1				1	69															71	146
37	Louisiana	Mar., '35																9														9	
38	Indiana	June, '35				1									61																	62	
39	Independence	Dec., '35						4																								4	
40	Luna	Mar., '36										80	2																			82	234
41	Swift	April, '36															42															42	
42	Lona	July, '36										60			14																	74	
43	Roundout	Dec., '36									1	10	23																			34	
44	Oriental	May, '37						4											34													38	139
45	Emperor	Dec., '37										95												1							96	
46	Charl'e Harper	Dec., '37						4																								4	
47	Marine	Jan., '38											72																			72	109
48	Mail	May, '38															37															37	
49	Saluda	Feb., '39				2						13			2																	17	47
50	Saluda	Aug., '39										10	20																			30	

TABLE OF EMIGRANTS.

TABLE OF EMIGRANTS—Continued.

Number.	Names of Vessels.	Date of Sailing.	Massachusetts.	Rhode Island.	Connecticut.	New York.	New Jersey.	Pennsylvania.	Delaware.	Maryland.	Dist. Columbia.	Virginia.	North Carolina.	South Carolina.	Georgia.	Alabama.	Mississippi.	Louisiana.	Tennessee.	Kentucky.	Ohio.	Indiana.	Illinois.	Missouri.	Michigan.	Iowa.	Wisconsin.	Texas.	Ind. Territory.	Barbadoes.	Total.	Total by Years.
51	Saluda	Feb., '40										60	30			3				12		5									110	
52	Hobart	Sept., '40										1	4																		5	115
53	Rud'h Groming	Feb., '41										30							10	20											40	
54	Union	May, '41																	20	20											40	
55	Saluda	Oct., '41			1								4																		5	85
56	Mariposa	June, '42										16	10	14		5		81	84				14	2		3					229	
57	Globe	Dec., '42					1					18																			19	248
58	Renown	June, '43												3			77														80	
59	Latrobe	Nov., '43										5																			5	85
60	Lime Rock	Mar., '44															91														91	
61	Virginia	June, '44									7	33												18							58	
62	Chipola	Nov., '44																		21											21	170
63	Roanoke	Nov., '45				7						166	13	1																	187	187
64	Rothschild	Jan., '46																	25	34	2										61	
65	Chatham	May, '46				1															1										2	
66	Liberia Packet	Dec., '46						1				25																			26	89

186 AMERICAN COLONIZATION SOCIETY.

TABLE OF EMIGRANTS—Continued.

Number.	Names of Vessels.	Date of Sailing.	Massachusetts.	Rhode Island.	Connecticut.	New York.	New Jersey.	Pennsylvania.	Delaware.	Maryland.	Dist. Columbia.	Virginia.	North Carolina.	South Carolina.	Georgia.	Alabama.	Mississippi.	Louisiana.	Tennessee.	Kentucky.	Ohio.	Indiana.	Illinois.	Missouri.	Michigan.	Iowa.	Wisconsin.	Texas.	Ind. Territory.	Barbadoes.	Total.	Total by Years.
67	Mary Wilkes	Jan., '47				2					13	24	1			4		1		3				3								11	
68	Liberia Packet	Sept., '47																														40	51
69	Nehemiah Rich.	Jan., '48						8							6	23	35	37		28			6								129	
70	Amazon	Feb., '48				1						28	1																			44	
71	Liberia Packet	April, '48										134	4																			138	
72	Col. Howard	May, '48										8		45	54																	99	
73	Liberia Packet	Sept., '48				4		1			15			2																		31	441
74	Laura	Jan., '49															9	142														151	
75	Liberia Packet	Feb., '49				3		3			1	46	2																			55	
76	Clinto's Wright	April, '49																			19											21	
77	Huma	May, '49									1	2		50	131		2															181	
78	Liberia Packet	Aug., '49												11																		14	422
79	Liberia Packet	Jan., '50						1				69	65																			135	
80	Chieftain	Feb., '50												13	154																	167	
81	D. C. Foster	Mar., '50										37	1	14				7	35	19		17										78	
82	Liberia Packet	July, '50				2		1					12	9							19											56	
83	Edgar	Oct., '50				9		8			6	3							15													31	
84	Liberia Packet	Dec., '50			2	3																	1									38	505
85	Alida	Feb., '51														3		56	18	42		8	8	4							139	
86	Sea Mew	Mar., '51				15														15												15	

TABLE OF EMIGRANTS—Continued.

Number.	Names of Vessels.	Date of Sailing.	Massachusetts.	Rhode Island.	Connecticut.	New York.	New Jersey.	Pennsylvania.	Delaware.	Maryland.	Dist. Columbia.	Virginia.	North Carolina.	South Carolina.	Georgia.	Alabama.	Mississippi.	Louisiana.	Tennessee.	Kentucky.	Ohio.	Indiana.	Illinois.	Missouri.	Michigan.	Iowa.	Wisconsin.	Texas.	Ind. Territory.	Barbadoes.	Total.	Total by Years.
87	Baltimore	April, '51						3		44		6	3	28	98																126	
88	Liberia Packet	July, '51			20	4		2				136	13					1	25												56	
89	Zeno	Sept., '51	9									9	10																		36	
90	Morgan Dix	Nov., '51						14		30					67																149	676
91	Liberia Packet	Dec., '51																													155	
92	Julia Ford	Jan., '52					21	1	1		1	48	16			16	1	1	13	16	1										47	
93	Ralph Cross	May, '52						11	1		1		105	36	11		4														126	
94	Oriole	Oct., '52	2			3	16						39																		37	
95	Jos. Maxwell	Nov., '52									2	129			7			4						22							148	
96	Linda Stewart	Nov., '52						1														1									171	
97	Shirley	Nov., '52																									16			3	2	
98	Zebra	Dec., '52																													99	630
99	Banshee	April, '53	6			1		3				81	52		37	14	6	19	28	13	2	6							5		161	
100	Shirley	June, '53										6				1	5														11	
101	Adeline	June, '53										154	4						96	69	5	26									134	
102	Banshee	Nov., '53						32		8																					261	
103	Isla de Cuba	Nov., '53				4	16									15															53	
104	General Pierce	Dec., '53				1									56				85										5		163	783
105	Sophia Walker	May, '54	6									122	15	7	5			3	28	44				29							252	
106	Harp	June, '54				25	1								3				21												25	
107	Estelle	Oct., '54						1																							26	

TABLE OF EMIGRANTS—Continued.

Number	Names of Vessels	Date of Sailing	Massachusetts	Rhode Island	Connecticut	New York	New Jersey	Pennsylvania	Delaware	Maryland	Dist. Columbia	Virginia	North Carolina	South Carolina	Georgia	Alabama	Mississippi	Louisiana	Tennessee	Kentucky	Ohio	Indiana	Illinois	Missouri	Michigan	Iowa	Wisconsin	Texas	Ind. Territory	Barbadoes	Total	Total by Years
108	Euphrasia	Nov., '54						2				151										15									168	553
109	Gen. Pierce	Dec., '54				1									54				17	3	7										89	
110	Corn	May, '55								7		34							13	52											106	207
111	Corn	Nov., '55			7	13	11					21							31												53	
112	Lamartine	Dec., '55	4		1			7							1	4															48	
113	Elvira Owen	May, '56			2			1		4		57	41		85	2	14		42	67										1	321	538
114	M. C. Stevens	Dec., '56	6							1		103	13		56	3	1		13	19											217	
115	M. C. Stevens	May, '57		3		6						10	125			1			23					7							207	370
116	M. C. Stevens	Dec., '57								33		117								10											163	
117	G. T. Ackerly	Jan., '58				2						18	63																		2	167
118	M. C. Stevens	May, '58				1		1				4	8	3	7					14				4							108	
119	Morgan	Oct., '58				2		3		9		4						42		6											2	
120	M. C. Stevens	Nov., '58	20															5													53	
121	Homer	Dec., '58				2																									2	
122	Rebecca	April, '59						24		1		35		10	24																42	248
123	M. C. Stevens	May, '59				44				1																					99	
124	Mendi	May, '59				1												1	21												44	
125	M. C. Stevens	Nov., '59						11				19		5						1		3									63	

TABLE OF EMIGRANTS.

TABLE OF EMIGRANTS.—Continued.

Number	Names of Vessels.	Date of Sailing.	Massachusetts	Rhode Island	Connecticut	New York	New Jersey	Pennsylvania	Delaware	Maryland	Dist. Columbia	Virginia	North Carolina	South Carolina	Georgia	Alabama	Mississippi	Louisiana	Tennessee	Kentucky	Ohio	Indiana	Illinois	Missouri	Michigan	Iowa	Wisconsin	Texas	Ind. Territory	Barbadoes	Total	Total by Years
126	Mendi	April, '60				8																											8	
127	M. C. Stevens	May, '60	1		1			39		4	1	42		26	81		15		8	1			7			2					228	
128	M. C. Stevens	Nov., '60			5			32					17		5					2	1		11				7				80	316
129	Edward	April, '61				7																									7	
130	Teresa Bandell	July, '61												1																	1	
131	Justice Story	Aug., '61				1																									1	
132	John H. Jones	Nov., '61				6	6	13	4	12																					42	
133	Greyhound	Dec., '61				4																									4	55
134	Justina	Jan., '62					3	2												13		2									18	
135	M. C. Stevens	Nov., '62			2	2	11	5		10										1											47	65
136	M. C. Stevens	May, '63				4	18																4								26	26
137	Thomas Pope	Jan., '64	2			7		5																							18	
138	Thomas Pope	Sept., '64						5																							5	23
139	Greyhound	Jan., '65				1																									1	
140	M. A. Benson	Feb., '65	1																												1	
141	Cora	April, '65																												346	346	
142	Thomas Pope	June, '65				6		1																							7	
143	H. P. Russell	Nov., '65										172																			172	527

TABLE OF EMIGRANTS—Continued.

Number	Names of Vessels	Date of Sailing	Massachusetts	Rhode Island	Connecticut	New York	New Jersey	Pennsylvania	Delaware	Maryland	Dist. Columbia	Virginia	North Carolina	South Carolina	Georgia	Alabama	Mississippi	Louisiana	Tennessee	Kentucky	Ohio	Indiana	Illinois	Missouri	Michigan	Iowa	Wisconsin	Texas	Ind. Territory	Barbadoes	Total	Total by Years
144	Edith Rose	Mar., '66						4																							4	
145	Golconda	Nov., '66												262	194				144											600	600	
146	Edith Rose	Dec., '66						14																							14	
147	Forest Oak	Dec., '66	3																												3	621
	Totals		63	36	55	295	77	337	9	580	109	3,733	1,371	722	1,341	105	551	309	870	675	56	83	65	83	1	5	7	16	9	346	11,909	11,909

RECAPITULATION.

Massachusetts	63
Rhode Island	36
Connecticut	55
New York	295
New Jersey	77
Pennsylvania	337
Delaware	9
Maryland	580
District of Columbia	109
Virginia	3,733
North Carolina	1,371
South Carolina	722
Georgia	1,341
Alabama	105
Mississippi	551
Louisiana	309
Tennessee	870
Kentucky	675
Ohio	56
Indiana	83
Illinois	65
Missouri	83
Michigan	1
Iowa	5
Wisconsin	7
Texas	16
Indian Territory	9
Barbadoes	346
Total	11,909
Born free	4,541
Purchased their freedom	344
Emancipated to go to Liberia	5,957
"Freedmen"	753
From Barbadoes, W.I.	346
Unknown	68
Total	11,909

The Maryland State Colonization Society has settled at "Maryland in Liberia"......... 1,227

Total............ 13,136

Note.—The number of Recaptured Africans sent to Liberia by the Government of the United States, not embraced in the foregoing table, 5,722.

COST OF AFRICAN COLONIZATION.

The following Table will show the Annual Receipts of the American Colonization Society during the fifty years of its existence.

YEARS.	RECEIPTS.	YEARS.	RECEIPTS.
1817–9	$14,031 50	1853	$82,458 25
1820–2	5,627 66	1854	65,433 93
1823	4,758 22	1855	55,276 89
1824	4,379 89	1856	81,384 41
1825	10,125 85	1857	97,384 84
1826	14,779 24	1858	61,820 19
1827	13,294 94	1859	160,303 23
1828	13,458 17	1860	104,546 92
1829	20,295 61	1861	75,470 74
1830	26,683 41	1862	46,208 46
1831	32,101 58	1863	50,900 36
1832	43,065 08	1864	79,454 70
1833	37,242 46	1865	23,633 37
1834	22,984 30	1866	59,375 14
1835	36,661 49		$2,141,507 77
1836	33,096 88		
1837	25,558 14	The Maryland State Society, since its organization, received	$309,759 33
1838	10,947 41		
1839	51,498 36		
1840	56,985 62		
1841	42,443 68	The New-York State Society and Pennsylvania Society, during their independent condition, received	95,640 00
1842	32,898 88		
1843	36,093 94		
1844	33,640 39		
1845	56,458 60		
1846	39,900 03		
1847	29,472 84	The Mississippi Society, during its independent operations, received	12,000 00
1848	49,845 91		
1849	50,332 84		
1850	64,973 71		
1851	97,443 77	Making a total to January 1, 1867	$2,558,907 10
1852	86,775 74		

ORIGINAL MEMBERS OF THE SOCIETY.

H. Clay,
E. B. Caldwell,
Tho. Dougherty,
Stephen B. Balch,
Jno. Chalmers, Jun.,
Thos. Patterson,
John Randolph of Roanoke,
Robt. H. Goldsborough,
William Thornton,
George Clarke,
James Laurie,
J. I. Stull,
Dan'l Webster,
J. C. Herbert,
Wm. Simmons,
E. Forman,
Ferd'no. Fairfax,
V. Maxcy,
Jno. Loockerman,
Jno. Woodside,
William Dudley Digges,
Thomas Carberry,
Samuel J. Mills,
Geo. A. Carroll,
W. G. D. Worthington,

John Lee,
Richard Bland Lee,
D. Murray,
Robert Finley,
B. Allison,
B. L. Lear,
W. Jones,
J. Mason,
Mord. Booth,
J. S. Shaaf,
Geo. Peter,
John Tayloe,
Overton Carr,
P. H. Wendover,
F. S. Key,
Charles Marsh,
David M. Forest,
John Wiley,
Nathan Lufborough,
William Meade,
William H. Wilmer,
George Travers,
Edm. I. Lee,
John P. Todd,
Bushrod Washington.

SIXTY-NINTH

ANNUAL REPORT

OF THE

AMERICAN COLONIZATION SOCIETY:

WITH THE

MINUTES

OF THE

ANNUAL MEETING AND OF THE BOARD OF DIRECTORS,

JANUARY 17, 19 & 20, 1886.

WASHINGTON CITY:

COLONIZATION BUILDING, 450 PENNSYLVANIA AVENUE,

1886.

NORMAL SCHOOL STEAM PRESS
Hampton, Va.

American Colonization Society.

PRESIDENT,
1853. HON. JOHN H B. LATROBE.

VICE-PRESIDENTS:—

1838. Hon. Henry A. Foster, N. Y.
1841. Thomas R. Hazard, Esq., R. I.
1851. Rev. Robert Ryland, D. D., Ky.
1851. Hon. Frederick P. Stanton, D. C.
1853. Hon. Horatio Seymour, N. Y.
1859. Hon. Henry M. Schieffelin, N Y.
1861. Rev. J. Maclean, D. D., LL. D., N. J.
1866. Hon. James R. Doolittle, Wis.
1867. Samuel A. Crozer, Esq., Pa.
1870. Robert Arthington, Esq. England.
1872. Rev. Edward P. Humphrey, D. D., Ky.
1872. Harvey Lindsly, M. D., LL. D., D. C.
1874. Rev. Bishop R. S. Foster D. D., Mass.
1874. Rt. Rev. Wm. B. Stevens, D. D., Pa.
1884. Rt. Rev. Gregory T. Bedell, D. D , O.
1875. Rt. Rev. M. A. DeW. Howe, D. D., Pa·
1875. Samuel K. Wilson, Esq., N. J.

1876. Rev. Samuel E. Appleton, D. D., Pa.
1876. Rev. H. M. Turner, D. D., LL. D. Ga.
1877. Prest. E. G. Robinson, LL. D., R. I.
1877. Rev. William E. Schenck, D. D., Pa.
1878. Hon. Richard W. Thompson, Ind.
1878. Admiral Robert W. Shufeldt, U. S. N.
1880. Francis T. King, Esq., Maryland.
1880. Rev. Samuel D. Alexander, D.D., N.Y.
1881. Rev. Bishop H. W. Warren, D. D., Col.
1882. Henry G. Marquand, Esq., N. Y.
1884. Rev. George D. Boardman, D. D., Pa.
1884. Rev. Bishop E.G. Andrews, D.D., D.C.
1884. Rev. Edward W. Blyden,D.D.,Liberia.
1884. Rev. Otis H. Tiffany, D. D., N. Y.
1885. Rev. James Saul, D. D., Pa.
1886. Rt. Rev. Henry C. Potter, D.D.,N.Y.
1886. Hon. Alexander B. Hagner, D. C.

The figures before each name indicate the year of first election.

LIFE DIRECTORS.

1840.	Thomas R. Hazard, Esq.........*R. I.*	1869.	Charles H. Nichols, M. D...*N. Y.*
1851.	Rev. John Maclean, D.D., LL.D.*N.J.*	1870.	Daniel Price, Esq............*N. J.*
1852.	James Hall, M. D...............*Md.*	1871.	Rev. William H. Steele, D.D. *N.J.*
1853.	Alexander Duncan, Esq.......*R. I.*	1871.	R't Rev. H. C. Poiter, D. D., *N. Y.*
1864.	Alexander Guy, M. D..........*Ohio.*	1873.	Rev. George W. Samson, D. D. *N.Y.*
1868.	Edward Coles, Esq............*Pa.*	1878.	Rev. Edw. W. Appleton, D. D., *Pa.*
1869.	Rev. Joseph F. Tuttle, D. D...*Ind.*	1883.	Rev. James Saul, D. D.,......*Pa.*

1885. William Evans Guy, Esq........*Mo.*

DELEGATES FOR 1886.

PENNSYLVANIA COLONIZATION SOCIETY.—Rev. Samuel E. Appleton, D. D., Rev. Edward W. Appleton, D. D., Rev. Wilbur F. Paddock, D. D., Edward S. Morris, Esq., John Welsh Dulles, Esq., Arthur M. Burton, Esq.

Sixty-Ninth Annual Report.

In presenting the Sixty-Ninth Annual Report of the transactions and events in which THE AMERICAN COLONIZATION SOCIETY has been directly interested, that which touches it most deeply is the death of four Vice Presidents, whose character and influence lent an efficiency and importance to their support of the cause of African Colonization.

NECROLOGY.

HON. FREDERICK T. FRELINGHUYSEN, elected in 1869, was a member of the distinguished family whose virtues and services adorn not only the history of the State of New Jersey but of the Republic. He was a man of solid abilities and worth, of the highest honor and humblest faith, and of transparent sincerity, wise discrimination and refined sensibility. Like his illustrious uncle, Hon. Theodore Frelinghuysen, also a zealous Vice President, he contributed by his voice, his pen and his purse to the strength of the Society.

REV. S. IRENEUS PRIME, D. D., elected in 1869, rendered very valuable services to the Church and Nation as preacher and platform speaker, as author and editor, as a leader in religious and philanthropic enterprises, and as a staunch defender of everything right and good. He was from the beginning a steadfast friend of this Society, always ready with sagacious counsel and hearty co-operation, frequently attending its meetings and those of the Board of Directors. In the hearts of Christians of every denomination, in this and other lands, will his name be held in lasting and loving remembrance.

REV. JAMES C. FINLEY M. D., elected in 1854, will be gratefully remembered by his broad sympathies with every effort and institution that tended to the promotion of righteousness and peace in the earth. A grandson of Rev. James Caldwell, of revolutionary fame, and son of Rev. Robert Finley D. D., the founder of this Society, his faith, his hope and his love in the great cause always shone brightly, and his memory will not cease to inspire those who remain.

HON JAMES GARLAND, elected in 1838, was a ready sympathiser with the neglected, the afflicted and the needy, and a liberal contributor to their wants. He was kindly, courteous and unostentatious in his intercourse with his fellow men, and singularly loving and tender in the sacred privacy of private life. He was probably the oldest

Judge in the country, only retiring when in his ninety-second year and after he had become totally blind. The eyes, here closed to earth's fading beauties, have opened forever, it is believed, on the transparent glories of the brighter and better world.

Intelligence has also been received of the death of EX-PRESIDENT ANTHONY W. GARDNER, the last of the old statesmen of Liberia. He was born in Southampton County, Virginia, arrived at Monrovia with his parents in 1831, when eleven years of age, and was frequently called by his fellow-citizens to responsible positions— among them twice Vice President and three times President of the Republic. He had a liberal and accurate conception of the work to be done by Liberia, and labored to carry out that conception in the foreign and domestic affairs of the country. He was a member of the Convention in 1846 which drafted the Constitution of Liberia, and was the last surviving signer of the Declaration of Independence.

FINANCES.

The receipts during the year 1885 have been:—

Donations	$ 3,911 20
Legacies	533 78
Emigrants in aid of passage	547 50
For Education in Liberia	418 40
From other sources, including $500. from securities realized	2,019 25
Receipts	7,430 13
Balance 1 January, 1885	1,927 40
Making available	9,357 53
The disbursements have been	9,316 47
Balance 31 December, 1885	$ 41 06

The Society, with many of the religious and benevolent organizations, has suffered by the embarrassments resulting from fluctuations in the financial condition of the country. In the future as in the past, the Society's ability to carry on its work will be enlarged or restricted as its revenue is increased or diminished. Its methods are economical and its labors are necessary in a direction where other agencies cannot serve. Friends of the cause are invited to remember the Society in their Wills, and generous contributions are solicited from the living, of larger amounts than are made at the present time.

EMIGRATION.

Fifty-two emigrants were sent by the bark *Monrovia*, which sailed from New York on the 28th February. They arrived out on the 3d

April, and at once proceeded to Brewerville. Thirty-eight were from Calvert, Texas, and fourteen from Montgomery, Ala. Twenty-seven were twelve years of age and upwards, eighteen were between two and twelve years old, and seven were under two years of age. Eighteen were reported to be communicants in regular standing of evangelical churches. Of the adult males twelve were farmers and one an experienced house-carpenter.

The class of people selected and aided is shown by the following description of those above reported from Montgomery, Ala., of whom Rev. R. C. Bedford thus wrote to the *American Missionary*:— "The occurrence of most interest in our church of late is the departure of fourteen of our number for Liberia. They left yesterday. They comprise two of our best families. One family consists of ten— husband and wife, with seven children, from one year old to seventeen, and the husband's mother, about seventy : the other a family of four—husband and wife and two children, one year old and ten. These families are in very good circumstances, industrious and well-respected. Their going is the result of long meditation, beginning even in the days of slavery. Their object seems to be to make a permanent home for themselves and children, combined with much of a missionary spirit. A farewell meeting was held in our church last Sunday morning, which was largely attended, and much interest was manifested. A nice purse was made up to help them on their journey. I shall not be surprised if some of our best young people do not turn before long in the direction of Africa as a missionary field."

Reports represent that most of these immigrants have portions of their lands planted and that some are occupying and others are preparing to occupy their own houses.

Brewerville is stated to grow in importance. As an outlet and starting point to the rich and populous interior it has no rival. It is situated on and is extending along a highway which is said to have been travelled for centuries and which reaches to the Niger. The Poor river, which runs to the settlement from the interior, affords another means of communication with the wealthy districts.

Emigration to Liberia every year under the auspices of the American Colonization Society has been uninterrupted for the past sixty-five years. Those now reported make the number sent since the civil war to be 3,790, and a total from the beginning of 15,788, exclusive of 5,722 recaptured Africans which we induced and enabled the Government of the United States to settle in Liberia, making a grand total of 21,510 persons to whom the Society has given homes in Africa.

Every settlement in Liberia is calling for population from the United States. Hon. Z. B. Roberts, one of the Justices of the Supreme Court, writes under date of Greenville, July 24: "Sinoe County was planted by your philanthropy in common with the other portions of Liberia. It is heavily timbered, has a fertile soil, a bar for shipping at all seasons of the year, and a river abounding in fish, including superior oysters. Our evergreen palm trees lift up their towering heads—waving majestically their glossy limbs and broad leaves, their trunks filled with crimson fruit for home use and for exportation. There is room here for Africa's sons in America to enjoy with us this God given land. Emigrants are needed:—those that will resolve in coming to labor for the elevation of themselves, their children and their race. Men whose bosoms swell with a deep love of liberty—mechanics, farmers, miners and teachers are greatly desired. I emigrated here in 1849, and cease not to thank the American Colonization Society for aiding me to come, and my Heavenly Father for good health and prolonging my life."

APPLICATIONS.

The movement for removal to Liberia continues to increase. Hundreds of letters, whose writers earnestly request the aid of the Society to settle in that Republic, have been received during the year. These come from nearly all the States, but especially from North Carolina, Texas and Arkansas. Testimonials from leading white citizens commend the applicants as "the most enlightened and enterprising colored men of the district:" as "some of our best residents and we hate to have them leave us:" and as "worthy of all the Society can do for them." Others are described as "good people:" that they "own lots or houses, but cannot get any cash for them," and as "able to do much good in Liberia."

A cautious estimate would be that five hundred thousand of the people of color are considering the question of emigration to Liberia, finding but little scope in the land of their birth for their industrial energies and race aspirations.

LIBERIA.

The general aspects of Liberia are thus described by Hon. C. T. O. King, Mayor of Monrovia:—

"*Agriculture.* There is a steady growth in agriculture. The area of coffee culture has been increased 25 per cent. and renewed attention given to sugar-cane planting. The wilderness is disappearing before the energy and thrift of the settlers. Continue to send men like Hill, Moore, Newton, Batese, Miles, Knox, Burgess and North—hardy, experienced and self-reliant agriculturalists and mechanics. This is the class most needed here and the best suited to the country.

"*Commerce.* Nothwithstanding the depression in trade along the Coast, we have no cause to complain. Four of our citizen-merchants, one from this city, two from Grand Bassa, and one from Sinoe County, lately returned from England, where they went on their own business concerns. There is no part of Africa so well adapted to the capital and enterprise of Americans as this Republic and the wealthy interior to which it is an inlet.

"*Religion.* The several denominations are doing a valuable work in and adjoining Liberia. The Roman Catholics are specially active and are zealously collecting means for the erection of a church edifice in this city. The Church of England points with pride to Bishop Crowther as an outcome of its work at Sierra Leone. So may the Episcopal Church in the United States claim Bishop Ferguson as a legitimate result of its training here on missionary ground.

"*Temperance.* Efforts are making to bring about the repeal of the $2,000 revenue act, under which no spirituous liquors whatever have been brought into the Republic during the year. It is not probable that this restrictive legislation will be soon disturbed."

LIBERIA'S NORTHWEST BOUNDARY.

"The Havelock Draft Convention," fixing the North-West boundary of Liberia at the South-East bank of the Manna river, was signed at Sierra Leone, November 11, by Governor Sir Samuel Rowe, Comissioner on behalf of the British Government, and Hon. Messrs Henry W. Grimes and Benjamin Anderson, Commissioners on the part of Liberia. The final adjustment of this question is confidently expected to exert a favorable influence on the commercial and economic life of the two States whose territories are thus made conterminous. The most important English speaking communities on the Coast of Africa, of one race and identical in destiny, they easily enter into each other's feelings, and this formal connection of territory is calculated to bring about a more marked and practical recognition of their identity of interests, and to induce the Colony and the Republic to co-operate more closely for the spread of civilization and religion.

EDUCATION.

The American Colonization Society's schools are reported to have been regularly attended and with encouraging results: that at Arthington having 20 male and 26 female scholars, of whom 19 are Aborigines, and the school at Brewerville 34 Liberian and 4 native boys. The increasing number of children and the rapid extension of this settlement make additional educational facilities necessary. A high school, with an industrial department, is very desirable.

The Hall Free School, at Cape Palmas, under the auspices of the Maryland State Colonization Society, is stated to have 50 pupils of both sexes and nativities.

The Anna Morris School, at Arthington, is said to have 49 boys and 23 girls; of the former of whom 27 are natives. This interesting school was founded and is sustained by the disinterested efforts of Edward S. Morris Esq., of Philadelphia, Pa.

The Presbyterian Board of Foreign Missions report 4 schools and 101 pupils; also the Alexander High School, at Clay-Ashland, with 51 male and 27 female scholars: of the latter of whom 15 are native boys and 3 are native girls.

The Board of Missions of the P. Episcopal Church maintain, as reported by Bishop Ferguson, 4 boarding schools containing 251 scholars, and 9 other schools with 284 scholars. These are mostly native youths, and the Hoffman Institute, at Cavalla, is for the training of clergymen and catechists born in Africa.

All Saints Hall, at Beulah, Grand Bassa County, Miss Margaretta Scott, principal, is said to have 10 girls under instruction.

The Lutheran Mission schools, at Muhlenburg, are stated to have 127 scholars, of whom 73 boys and 15 girls are in the boarding department, and 23 boys and 16 girls are day pupils,—largely natives of the country.

The Woman's Baptist Foreign Missionary Society have two schools in Grand Bassa County, but no late statement as to the beneficiaries has been furnished.

Returns for the quarter ending March 31, show 40 primary and grammar schools with 1106 scholars supported by the Government of Liberia, as follows: —

Montserrado County, 24 schools and 476 pupils.
Grand Bassa County, 10 " " 329 "
Sinoe County 6 " " 301 "

No report appears from Maryland County, in many instances the number of scholars is not given, and there is nothing to indicate the sex or nativity of those reported.

The Liberia College was inaugurated Jan'y 23, 1862, and the first regular term began Feb'y 2, 1863. The schools which had chiefly prepared its first pupils were closed soon after it opened. The latest statement gives 14 pupils in the College, (of whom 6 are in the Freshman, 3 in the Sophomore and 5 in the Junior classes;) 35 in the Preparatory department and 21 in the female school.

Prof. Hugh M. Browne arrived in this country in July, and he and Prof. T. McCants Stewart have ceased to be connected with the College. Prof. Martin H. Freeman has been appointed President *pro tem*, and an iron roof and considerable repairs have been ordered to the College building. Several causes have led to the suspension, for the present, of the establishment of an Industrial department, and the removal of the College site to the interior.

The Liberia College is supported by the Trustees of Donations for Education in Liberia, at Boston, and the New York State Colonization Society. The Pennsylvania Colonization Society helps to meet the salary of the teacher of the female school.

The foregoing returns, incomplete and imperfect as they are, show an attendance for instruction of 303 males, 138 females, and 1792 whose sex is not stated, making a grand total of 2233.

The feeling is becoming general in Liberia that the time is not far distant when an earnest effort should be made for the support of its educational and religious institutions from the resources of the country. It is felt that provision should be made on the spot for the higher education of the people that it may not be exposed to the inconvenience which a state of absolute dependence upon friends at a distance must necessarily entail. Help in the first instance is indispensable to youthful communities, but help all the time becomes demoralizing and obstructive.

COLONIZATION.

Within the last twenty years England's engagements in other portions of the globe have prevented her from giving much attention to a former field of her operations. But quite recently, owing to the activity of the Germans in annexing territory in West Africa, and the military movements of the French in Senegambia, she has been aroused from apparent indifference to the possibilities of West Central Africa. Liberia, unfortunately, was the first to fall victim to her resuscitated energies. Forty miles of Liberian territory have been taken to extend the seaboard of the Colony of Sierra Leone, which before consisted of only mountains and swamps. Her appetite thus whetted for African territory, she has since proclaimed a Protectorate over the entire Niger delta, and over Bechuanaland, in South Africa. The whole of the Niger mouths are now under British protection, while France is striving to establish control over the upper portion of the river. The continued depression of trade and loss of revenue at Sierra Leone, notwithstanding the territorial accession from Liberia, has induced the Home Government to enlarge the powers of

Sir Samuel Rowe, the Governor-in-chief of the Colony, with a view to annexation on the north and east of the settlement.

Coincident with the granting of this power was the arrival, in August, of a conquering Mandingo military force on the North-Western frontiers of the Colony. This army, setting out from the country east of Liberia for the purpose of clearing the highways from Medina, Kankan and Sego for trade, has achieved marvellous conquests over powerful tribes which have for more than a century exercised capricious control over the trade from the gold regions of Boure and the rich districts of Sego.

The people who have achieved these conquests belong to the Koniah or Western Mandingoes, first made known to the world by Mr. Benjamin Anderson of Liberia—in his "Narrative of a Journey to Musardu" from Monrovia. Mr. Anderson was enabled to perform this journey through the liberality of a Vice President of this Society, Hon. H. M. Schieffelin, in 1868, who also bore the expense of the publication of his book.

The Government of Liberia, availing itself of the efforts of Mr. Anderson, entered into a treaty with the King of Musardu, an important city of Koniah, and subsequently opened communications with Ibrahima Sissi, King of Medina, the capital of Koniah. Since then, Samudu, the commander of the force which has appeared before Sierra Leone, raised an army, dethroned the King and united under his banner all the Mohammedan tribes for hundreds of miles and is now master of the country between the Niger and Sierra Leone.

The apparent neglect by England of her opportunities in West Africa has not arisen from a want of appreciation of its great commercial advantages, but she knows that for the effective management of those countries she will need more than money. Human agency in numerical strength will be required. It is a significant and suggestive fact that though West Africa is one of the fairest, most beautiful and most fruitful portions of the globe, (Bishop Taylor calls Liberia "the garden spot of West Africa") containing forests of the most valuable timber, enriched with districts impregnated with precious metals, yet comparatively little has been done to occupy the interior regions with the agencies of civilization or Christianity; and millions exist to-day in the heart of Africa who know nothing of the outside world.

The lesson taught by all experience is this:—that the interior of Africa can be reached and the Coast can be effectively occupied for commercial and colonization purposes but in one way, and that is through colonies of civilized Negroes : for *only they can colonize equa-*

torial Africa and live. But England, France and Germany have no means of securing such colonists. England cannot offer inducements to Negroes in the West Indies to go and build up the waste places of their fatherland. Such a proposition would in a few years depopulate her West Indies and reduce some of the wealthiest of those islands to poverty-stricken wildernesses. She cannot send recaptured Africans from her colonies at Sierra Leone, Gambia or Lagos. They have not enough civilization in its relations to the industrial arts or to commerce. France cannot depopulate Gaudaloupe or Martinique to transplant Negroes to the interior of Senegal or Goree. Germany has no colonies of civilized Negroes from which to get a supply for her African projects. The only man then available for the great work of opening Africa to commerce and civilization is the Negro of America. He can live there, for it is the *habitat* of his race, and being fully civilized and Christian too, he is the Agent, *and the only Agent that the world contains* adapted to this purpose. He has proved his adaptation and efficiency in the work thus far accomplished by the Republic of Liberia.

It is stated that "the British Government has expended immense sums to keep the peace and to promote trade along the route between Sego and Sierra Leone." But the principle of the Liberia establishment has done more and will do more to keep the peace and promote trade than all the wealth of England without colonists can do.

Now the American Colonization Society is the only organized agency for developing this important influence—for transferring to this vast and productive field the only agents that can profitably cultivate it. The amalgamation of civilized agencies with the indigenous elements is the only statesmanlike and effective mode of settling the difficulty of Africa's civilization: and the only agencies available for such amalgamation are in the United States.

TREASURER'S REPORT.

DR. *Receipts and Disbursements of the AMERICAN COLONIZATION SOCIETY in the year 1885.* CR.

Received Donations,	$3,911 20	Paid Passage and settlement of Emigrants, . . . $5,353 42
" Legacies, ...	533 78	" Education in Liberia, " 418 40
" Emigrants toward passage,	547 50	" Taxes, insurance and repairs of Colonization Building, 558 28
" Subscriptions to African Repository,	33 25	" Paper and printing the African Repository, . . . 362 06
" Rent of Colonization Building,	1,486 00	" Salary of Secretary and Treasurer, office expenses,
" For Education in Liberia, .	418 40	printing, postage, expenses of Annual Meeting, and
		costs of contested Wills, ... 2,624 49
Receipts,	$6,930 13	Payments, $9,316 47
Securities realized, . . $500 00		Balance December 31, 1885. . . . 41 06
Balance January 1, 1885. . 1,927 40	2,427 40	
Total, ...	$9,357 53	Total, ... $9,357 53

The Committee on Accounts have examined the Treasurer's account for the year 1885 and the vouchers for the expenditures, and find the same correct.

REGINALD FENDALL,
EDWARD S. MORRIS, } Committee.
ARTHUR M. BURTON.

Washington, D. C., *January 19, 1886.*

MINUTES OF THE SOCIETY.

WASHINGTON, D. C. *January* 17, 1886.

The Sixty-Ninth Anniversary of THE AMERICAN COLONIZATION SOCIETY was celebrated this evening at 7:30 o'clock, in Foundry Methodist E. Church, Vice President Dr. Harvey Lindsly LL. D., in the chair.

Rev. H. R. Naylor, D. D., pastor of the Church, conducted the devotional exercises, and Rev. George W. Samson, D. D., of New York, led in prayer.

The Chairman stated that a dispatch had been received from Hon. John H. B. Latrobe, President, announcing his inability to be present on the occasion, and the Chairman presented the Sixty-Ninth Annual Report of the Society, an abstract of which had been printed and distributed in the pews.

Rev. B. Sunderland, D. D., of Washington, D. C., delivered the Annual Discourse.

Rev. B. Sunderland pronounced the benediction,

COLONIZATION ROOMS, *January* 19, 1885.

The Annual Meeting of THE AMERICAN COLONIZATION SOCIETY was held to day at 3 o'clock P. M., agreeably to Article 4 of the Constitution and to notice published in THE AFRICAN REPOSITORY.

In the absence of the President, detained at his home by "chronic bronchial trouble," Rev. Samuel E. Appleton, D. D., Senior Vice President in attendance, took the chair and called the Society to order.

The Minutes of the Anniversary Meeting on the 17th inst, were read, and with the Minutes of the Annual Meeting of January 20, 1885. were approved.

Rev. Drs. Edward W. Appleton, James Saul and Wilbur F. Paddock were appointed a Committee to nominate the President and Vice Presidents for the ensuing year.

On motion of Rev. Dr. George W. Samson, it was

Resolved. That the thanks of this Society be presented to Rev. Dr. Sunderland for his practical presentation of the interests of this Society and Liberia, and that a copy be requested for publication.

Resolved. That the thanks of the Society are tendered to Rev. Dr. Naylor and the Trustees of Foundry Methodist E. Church for its use last Sunday evening for our 69th Anniversary.

Rev. Dr. Edward W. Appleton, Chairman of the Committee on Nominations, presented a report, recommending the election of the following:—

PRESIDENT,
1853. HON. JOHN H. B. LATROBE.

VICE-PRESIDENTS:—

1838. Hon. Henry A. Foster, N. Y.	1876. Rev. Samuel E. Appleton, D. D., Pa.
1841. Thomas R. Hazard, Esq., R. I.	1876. Rev. H. M. Turner, D. D. LL. D., Ga.
1851. Rev. Robert Ryland, D. D., Ky.	1877. Prest. E. G. Robinson, LL. D., R. I.
1851. Hon. Frederick P. Stanton, D. C.	1877. Rev. William E. Schenck, D. D., Pa.
1853. Hon. Horatio Seymour, N. Y.	1878. Hon. Richard W. Thompson, Ind.
1859. Hon. Henry M. Schieffelin, N. Y.	1878. Admiral Robert W. Shufeldt, U. S. N.
1861. Rev. J. Maclean, D. D. LL. D., N. J.	1880. Francis T. King, Esq., Maryland.
1866. Hon. James R. Doolittle, Wisconsin.	1880. Rev. Samuel D. Alexander, D. D., N.Y.
1867. Samuel A. Crozer, Esq., Pa.	1881. Rev. Bishop H. W. Warren, D. D. Col.
1870. Robert Arthington, Esq., England.	1882. Henry G. Marquand, Esq., N. Y.
1872. Rev. Edward P. Humphrey, D. D., Ky.	1884. Rev. George D. Boardman, D. D., Pa.
1872. Harvey Lindsly, M. D. LL. D., D. C.	1884. Rev. Bishop E. G. Andrews, D.D., D. C.
1874. Rev. Bishop R. S. Foster, D. D. Mass.	1884. Rev. Edward W. Blyden, D. D. Liberia.
1874. Rt. Rev. Wm. B. Stevens, D. D., Pa.	1884. Rev. Otis H. Tiffany, D. D., N. Y.
1874. Rt Rev. Gregory T. Bedell, D. D , O	1885. Rev. James Saul, D. D., Pa.
1875. Rt. Rev. M. A. DeW. Howe, D. D., Pa.	1885. Rt. Rev. Henry C Potter, D. D., N. Y.
1875. Samuel K. Wilson, Esq., N. J.	1886. Hon. Alexander B. Hagner, D. C.

The figures before each name indicate the year of first election.

Whereupon on motion, it was

Resolved, That the Report be accepted and approved, and that the Society elect the officers nominated by the Committee.

Resolved. That the Society hereby expresses its sincere gratification at the presence on this occasion of Mrs. Ex-President Roberts of Liberia.

On motion, Adjourned.

WM. COPPINGER, *Secretary*.

MINUTES OF THE BOARD OF DIRECTORS.

WASHINGTON, D. C., *January* 19, 1886.

THE BOARD OF DIRECTORS OF THE AMERICAN COLONIZATION SOCIETY met this day at 12 o'clock, M., in the Colonization Building, No. 450 Pennsylvania Avenue, N. W.

In the absence of the President of the Society, Rt. Rev. Henry C. Potter, D. D., was chosen to preside, and prayer was offered by Rev. Dr. Wilbur F. Paddock.

Mr. William Coppinger was appointed Secretary of the Board.

The unprinted parts of the Minutes of the last meeting were read, and the Minutes were approved.

Rev. Drs. Samson, E. W. Appleton and Saul were appointed a Committee on Credentials: who retired and subsequently reported, through their Chairman, the following named Delegates appointed for the year 1886, viz:

PENNSYLVANIA COLONIZATION SOCIETY. Rev. Samuel E. Appleton D. D., Rev. Edward W. Appleton D. D., Rev. Wilbur F. Paddock D. D., Edward S. Morris, Esq., John Welsh Dulles, Esq., Arthur M. Burton, Esq.

The following Directors were stated to be in attendance:—

DIRECTORS FOR LIFE. Rt Rev. Henry C. Potter, D. D., Rev. George W. Samson, D. D., Rev. Edward W. Appleton, D. D., Rev. James Saul, D. D.

EXECUTIVE COMMITTEE. Hon. Peter Parker, Hon. Charles C. Nott, Reginald Fendall, Esq., Rev Thomas G. Addison, D. D., Rev. Byron Sunderland, D. D., Justice William Strong.

Whereupon, on motion, it was

Resolved. That the report of the Committee on Credentials be accepted and approved, and the gentlemen named be received.

On motion, it was

Resolved. That Rev. John W. Chickering, D. D., and Admiral R. W. Shufeldt, U. S. N., be and they are hereby invited to share in the counsels of the Board.

The Secretary presented and read the Sixty-Ninth Annual Report of the American Colonization Society.

Whereupon, on motion, it was

Resolved. That the Annual Report be accepted and referred to the standing Committees according to its several topics.

The Secretary presented and read the Statement of the Executive Committee for the past year.

The Treasurer presented and read his Annual Report, with the certificate of audit, also a list of the property of the Society, and a statement of receipts by States in the year 1885.

Whereupon, on motion, it was

Resolved. That the Statement of the Executive Committee and the Treasurer's Report for the past year, with the accompanying annual papers, be accepted, and that so much of them as relate to Foreign Relations, Finance, Auxiliary Societies,

Agencies, Accounts, Emigration, and Education, be referred to the several standing Committees in charge of those subjects respectively.

The Chairman announced the STANDING COMMITTEES:—

COMMITTEE ON FOREIGN RELATIONS;—Rev. Dr. Edward W. Appleton, Justice William Strong, Rev. Dr. James Saul.

COMMITTEE ON FINANCE:—Reginald Fendall, Esq. Edward S. Morris, Esq, Arthur M. Burton, Esq.

COMMITTEE ON AUXILIARY SOCIETIES:—Rev. Dr. Samuel E. Appleton, Rev. Dr. Thomas G. Addison, John Welsh Dulles, Esq.

COMMITTEE ON AGENCIES:—Rev. Dr. Thomas G. Addison, Rev. Dr. Edward W. Appleton, D. D., Rev. Dr. Wilbur F. Paddock.

COMMITTEE ON ACCOUNTS:—Reginald Fendall, Esq., Edward S. Morris, Esq., Arthur M. Burton, Esq.

COMMITTEE ON EMIGRATION:—Rev. Dr. Byron Sunderland, Rev. Dr. James Saul, Hon. Charles C. Nott.

COMMITTEE ON EDUCATION:—Rev. Dr. George W. Samson, Rev. Dr. James Saul, Edward S. Morris, Esq.

On motion, it was

Resolved, That a Committee be appointed to nominate the Executive Committee and the Secretary and Treasurer for the ensuing year.

Rev. Drs. Paddock and Saul, and Mr. Morris were appointed the Committee.

Letters of regret were read from Hon John H. B. Latrobe, January 18, Rev. Dr. John Maclean, January 18, and Rev. Dr. William H. Steele, December 29.

Rev. Dr. Paddock, Chairman of the special Committee on Nominations, presented a report recommending the election of the following:

SECRETARY AND TREASURER:—William Coppinger, Esq.

EXECUTIVE COMMITTEE:—Hon. Peter Parker, Hon. Charles C. Nott, Reginald Fendall, Esq., Rev. Thomas G. Addison, D. D., Rev. Byron Sunderland, D. D., Justice William Strong, Dr. William W. Godding.

Whereupon, on motion, it was

Resolved, that the report be accepted and approved, and that the Board elect the gentlemen nominated by the Committee.

The following proposed amendment to the Constitution of the Society was considered, and, on motion, approved; and its further consideration was deferred until the next annual meeting of the Board of Directors, viz:

Resolved, That the word "five" in line 3 of Article 5 of the Constitution be changed to two.

On motion, it was

Resolved, That the Executive Committee nominate to the Board of Directors the appointment of Honorary Secretaries in the several States.

On motion, it was

Resolved, That the Board do now adjourn to meet in these rooms to-morrow morning at 11 o'clock.

Adjourned.

WASHINGTON, D. C., *January* 20, 1886.

THE BOARD OF DIRECTORS met this morning at the appointed hour in the rooms of the Society.

Rev. Dr. Samuel E. Appleton was chosen to preside, and at his request Rev. Dr. Sunderland offered prayer.

The Minutes of yesterday's meeting were read and approved.

A telegram of this date was read from Hon. John H. B. Latrobe, expressing deep regret at his inability to leave home and to preside at this session of the Board, and tendering his kind regards to the members in attendance.

Whereupon, on motion, it was

Resolved, That this Board has learned with sincere regret of the enforced absence of the Hon. John H. B. Latrobe, who has so ably filled the office of President of the American Colonization Society for many years.

Resolved, That this Board desires to express its deep sympathy with the President in his present illness, and heartily unites in the hope that his health may be so restored as to enable him to preside over the deliberations of this body.

Resolved, That a copy of these resolutions be transmitted to President Latrobe by the Secretary of this Society.

On motion, it was

Resolved, That Edward R. Wood Esq., of Philadelphia, Pa. be and he is hereby invited to a seat in the Board.

Rev. Dr. Edward W. Appleton, Chairman of the Standing Committee on Foreign Relations, verbally reported progress: and the report was, on motion, accepted and approved.

Mr. Fendall, Chairman of the standing Committee on Finance, presented and read the following report, which was, on motion, accepted and approved:

The Committee on Finance respectfully report that they have examined the securities of the Society and find them correct; and they cannot too earnestly recommend that greatly increased means be raised to prosecute the work of the Society.

Rev. Dr. Addison, from the standing Committee on Auxiliary Societies, presented and read the following resolution as their report; and it was, on motion, accepted and adopted:

Resolved, That it is important that the Parent Society should be aided and supported in its great work by Auxiliary Societies in the United States, and that the Executive Committee be directed to use its best efforts to increase the number of such Auxiliary Societies.

Rev. Dr. Addison, Chairman of the standing Committee on Agencies, presented and read the following resolution as their report; and it was, on motion, accepted and adopted:

Resolved, That the policy of employing agents for collecting funds and advocating the cause of Colonization in different parts of the country, be approved, and its continuance earnestly recommended to the Executive Committee.

The Board took a recess to call upon the President of the United States: and at 1:20 o'clock P. M. resumed its session.

Mr. Fendall, Chairman of the standing Committee on Accounts, presented and read the following report, which was, on motion, accepted and approved:

The Committee on Accounts have examined the Treasurer's Account for the year 1885 and the vouchers for the expenditures, and find the same correct.

Rev. Dr. Sunderland, Chairman of the standing Committee on Emigration, presented and read the following report, which was, on motion, accepted and approved:

The Committee on Emigration respectfully beg leave to report that:

Year by year your Committee on Emigration, stirred by the ever increasing needs of the hour, has sounded the tocsin of Liberian Colonization. Swift changes have been passing before our eyes in regard to Africa, within a brief period. "The Free State of the Congo" has occupied a distinguished conclave of explorers, ministers and diplomats in the capital of the German Empire. All Europe is rushing in upon Africa, from one motive or another. The solitude of the mountains and the shadows of the valleys are startled by the tramp of Caucasian enterprise, eager to establish control of some sort over the possibilities of the African future. Never was there such a scramble among the great Christian Powers to establish interests in Africa, since the day that the infant Saviour of mankind was sheltered in the heart of Egypt. Meanwhile the people of this country, who heard, on the 1st day of January, 1863, Lincoln's mighty word like a voice from the sky, amid the thunders and carnage of civil war, proclaiming freedom to every slave throughout the land, have had twenty-three years to consider the question of their duty and their destiny. They are now seven millions. Of these, half a million are, at this moment, anxiously looking across the sea, and longing for the land of their fathers, as did the captive Jews at Babylon.

When emancipation set those millions free, Mr. Lincoln foresaw the necessity of finding means for their departure out of the country, and on his recommendation Congress created a commission and set apart at different times, a large sum for their deportation, and though these projects came to no practical result in the confusion and exigency of the times, yet they ought to settle forever the principle upon which Congress would be justified in now devoting generous sums of money for emigration to the Negro Republic.

Liberia is waiting to receive them. All the facts before brought to our attention, in proof of this urgency to hasten them there, have, with the lapse of time, been only augmented and intensified. The cry is louder than ever. The *basis* of feeling is fast changing among the people of color. *Before*, it was suspicion and distrust of the motive and influence of Colonization. *Now*, they begin to act from higher incentives and grander considerations. The light of this venerable Society is beginning to be comprehended in quarters where it was so long excluded. Emigration by Africans, of Africans, and for Africans is coming to be the pibroch of thousands who would hail to-day the means of exodus from America. It is not simply the selfish gain of which they dream, but an inspiration of Heaven, which, like a mighty wind, is filling heart and mind and soul and sense, to render aid to the children of the mighty land of Ham.

Since this Committee was appointed yesterday a treatise by T. McCants Stewart, one of the young men sent out only two years since, to be a professor in the

College of Liberia, has been perused, and while he avows himself (p. 104) to be "not a colonizationist," the whole weight of his book is a powerful argument for emigration. The very matters which he exhibits to show the weakness of Liberia, are to us reasons trumpet-tongued, why we should at once pour in a tide of selected emigration upon her waste places—why we should lose no time in "strengthening the things that remain."

There is one paragraph wherein, while as a rule he seems to write with candor, he has made himself liable to misconstruction, and it is this (p. 74) where he says: "If I could influence the Colonization Society, I would earnestly plead with them to stop making emigration their objective point and use their funds mainly in internal improvements, opening roads, building bridges, fostering industries, and especially in establishing a system of agricultural and industrial education, beginning with the common schools." What! would he have emigration cease? Why, one half the human race has been in a state of emigration since Abraham left Ur of the Chaldees. Emigration to America began so soon as this continent was discovered and it has not ceased to this hour. The first necessity of a state is *men*. Napoleon when asked "What France most needed." replied *"mothers!"* The matters to which he would have this Society turn its attention and its funds, are grand and worthy objects, but they are objects, to promote which, the State and the Church exist. That such assistance should be rendered as may be practicable in the beginning is plain, but to do these things for a people once put upon their feet, is to keep them in a perpetual state of babyhood, and to deprive them of that brawn and muscle which the rigor of self discipline and the hardships of self reliance alone can furnish.

What Liberia most needs to-day, in our view, is, that one quarter of its territory, now unoccupied by a civilized and Christian population, should be filled with 10,000 of the choicest men, women and children that can be found in half a million, and that they should be sent there not by the tardy and inadequate aid of private beneficence, but by an appropriation of a million dollars, voted by Congress and sanctioned by the President under safeguards and guaranties, the wisest that human judgment can invent. At the annual meeting of this Society in 1852, the great Webster presided. He sat in the chair of Henry Clay, whose illness caused his absence. By his side sat President Fillmore. It was the last meeting of the Society which either of these great men attended. On that occasion Mr. Webster used these words: "It appears that this emigration is not impracticable. What is it to the great resources of this country to send out 100,000 persons a year to Africa? In my opinion * * it is within our Constitution, it is within the powers and provisions of the Constitution," and then he goes on to confirm his position by the example of Irish emigration to this country, a million and a half of Irish people having arrived in the short period of 4 or 5 years! Soon after, Webster died, and we are here to-day to make a beginning of emigration on a larger scale.

Let us hope we have struck the chord at last which Webster and those who were assembled with him felt trembling within them, and that before another year is spent we shall hear grand echoes from every quarter of the land;—and that for Africa—the signal of regeneration, reversing the circuit of the sun shall hail all nations.—"*Eastward* the Star of empire takes its way!"

Rev. Dr. Samson, Chairman of the standing Committee on Education, presented and read the following report, and it was, on motion, accepted, and the accompanying resolutions were adopted:—

The Committee on Liberian Education respectfully report: The Educational statistics gathered by the Secretary during the past year and presented in the Annual Report inaugurate the same era twenty years ago introduced by the U.S. Bureau of Education. These reports show the essential mutual dependence and co-ordination in Liberia as in the United States, of common schools for all children, of Church and other schools for higher and religious education, and of a College giving scientific and literary completeness of culture. They emphasize the reports of this Board in years past in every respect. As to common schools, they indicate the absolute necessity, not only of Liberian legislation, but of such aid from without as the Peabody fund has furnished to our Southern States. They put into just prominence the invaluable aid of Church, Mission and other high schools. They repeat the wisdom of men like Bloomfield and the counsels that have ruled at Hampton Institute: that manual labor prepares educated youth for the practical pursuits into which nearly all, though educated, must hereafter enter; while it may furnish in large part the means of their present support.

Your Committee recommend the adoption of the following resolutions:—

Resolved, That the statistics this year reported demonstrate the importance of bringing the facts as to Liberian educational provisions before the Liberian people and their American friends both as a guide and stimulus in the future.

Resolved, That the effort should be encouraged to increase in this country contributions for an Industrial Department in Liberia College, for Mission and other High Schools, and for the securing of a fund to aid and stimulate, as does the Peabody fund, common school education throughout the Liberian Republic.

On motion, it was

Resolved, That the Annual Report of the Society be referred to the Executive Committee for publication.

Rev. Dr. Chickering offered prayer, and the Board of Directors adjourned.

WM. COPPINGER, *Secretary*.

TABLE OF EMIGRANTS SETTLED IN LIBERIA BY THE AMERICAN COLONIZATION SOCIETY.

CONTINUED FROM THE SIXTY-FIRST ANNUAL REPORT.

Number	Name of Vessels.	Date of Sailing.	Mass.	New York.	Penn.	Dist. Col.	Virginia.	N. Carolina.	S. Carolina.	Georgia.	Florida.	Alabama.	Miss.	Tenn.	Illinois.	Missouri.	Texas.	Arkansas.	Kansas.	Nebraska.	Total.	Total by Years.
164	Liberia,	June, 1878						61			6						12				70	
165	Monrovia,	Dec., 1878	14					4									11				31	101
166	Monrovia,	June, 1879	3					13	1									42			44	
167	Monrovia,	Dec., 1879	2					45	5									76			47	91
168	Liberia,	May, 1880						7													6	
169	Monrovia,	May, 1880																			60	
170	Liberia,	Nov., 1880						5	5					1					3		76	
171	Tuck Sing,	Nov., 1880																			1	143
172	Liberia,	June, 1881						5			3	6									14	
173	Monrovia,	Dec., 1881						30				7									38	52
174	Monrovia,	Nov., 1882		1			1	19		1			2					4	1		22	27
175	Monrovia,	July, 1883						12							7				8	3	31	
176	Monrovia,	Dec., 1883	1					7					1						2	7	22	53
177	Monrovia,	April, 1884			4			21													34	
178	Monrovia,	Oct., 1884			3							14							20	7	47	83
179	Monrovia,	Feb., 1885														17	38				52	52
	Total.		20	2	7	3	4	229	6	1	12	27	3	1	7	17	61	145	38	17		600

TABLE OF EMIGRANTS.

EMIGRANTS SENT BY THE AMERICAN COLONIZATION SOCIETY.

Year.	No.	Year.	No.	Year.	No.	Year.	No.
1820	86	1837	138	1854	553	1871	247
1821	33	1838	109	1855	207	1872	150
1822	37	1839	47	1856	538	1873	73
1823	65	1840	115	1857	370	1874	27
1824	103	1841	85	1858	167	1875	23
1825	66	1842	248	1859	248	1876	21
1826	182	1843	85	1860	316	1877	53
1827	222	1844	170	1861	55	1878	101
1828	163	1845	187	1862	65	1879	91
1829	205	1846	89	1863	26	1880	143
1830	259	1847	51	1864	23	1881	52
1831	421	1848	441	1865	527	1882	27
1832	796	1849	422	1866	621	1883	53
1833	270	1850	505	1867	633	1884	81
1834	127	1851	676	1868	453	1885	52
1835	146	1852	630	1869	169		
1836	234	1853	783	1870	196		

Total 14,547
The Maryland State Colonization Society has settled in Maryland, Liberia, 1,227

Total 15,774

NOTE.—The number of Recaptured Africans sent to Liberia by the Government of the United States, not embraced in the foregoing table, is 5,722, making a grand total of 21,496 to whom the Colonization Society has given homes in Africa.

COST OF AFRICAN COLONIZATION.

The following table shows the Annual Receipts of the American Colonization Society:

Year.	Receipts.	Year.	Receipts.	Year.	Receipts.
1817-9	$14,031 50	1843	$36,093 94	1865	$23,633 37
1820-2	5,627 66	1844	33,640 39	1866	59,375 14
1823	4,758 22	1845	56,458 60	1867	53,190 48
1824	4,379 89	1846	39,900 03	1868	49,959 52
1825	10,125 85	1847	29,472 84	1869	62,269 78
1826	14,779 24	1848	49,845 91	1870	28,372 32
1827	13,294 94	1849	50,332 84	1871	29,348 80
1828	13,458 17	1850	64,973 71	1872	33,337 22
1829	20,295 61	1851	97,443 77	1873	33,335 71
1830	26,683 41	1852	86,775 74	1874	14,749 28
1831	32,101 58	1853	82,458 25	1875	12,125 79
1832	43,065 08	1854	65,433 93	1876	13,961 34
1833	37,242 46	1855	55,276 89	1877	11,812 72
1834	22,984 30	1856	81,384 41	1878	15,419 41
1835	36,661 42	1857	97,384 84	1879	18,302 37
1836	33,076 88	1858	61,820 19	1880	10,862 04
1837	25,558 44	1859	160,303 23	1881	8,523 66
1838	10,947 41	1860	104,546 92	1882	10,342 91
1839	51,498 36	1861	75,470 74	1883	14,091 87
1840	56,985 62	1862	46,208 46	1884	10,673 24
1841	42,443 68	1863	50,900 36	1885	6,930 13
1842	42,898 88	1864	79,454 70		

Total	$2,579,120 16
The Maryland State Colonization Society since its organization, received	309,759 33
The New York State Colonization, Society and the Pennsylvania Colonization Society, during their independent condition, received	95,640 00
The Mississippi Colonization Society, during its independent operations, received	12,000 00
Making a total to January 1, 1886	$2,996,519 49

SEVENTIETH ANNUAL REPORT

OF THE

American Colonization Society:

WITH THE

MINUTES

OF THE

ANNUAL MEETING and of the BOARD OF DIRECTORS,

JANUARY 16, 18 & 19, 1887.

WASHINGTON CITY:
COLONIZATION BUILDING, **450** *PENNSYLVANIA AVENUE,*
1887.

NORMAL SCHOOL STEAM PRESS,
HAMPTON, VA.

AMERICAN COLONIZATION SOCIETY.

PRESIDENT,
1853. HON. JOHN H. B. LATROBE.

VICE-PRESIDENTS,

1836. Hon. Henry A. Foster, N. Y.
1851. Rev. Robert Ryland, D. D., Ky.
1851. Hon. Frederick P. Stanton, Va.
1859. Hon. Henry M. Schieffelin, N. Y.
1866. Hon. James R. Doolittle, Wisconsin.
1867. Samuel A. Crozer, Esq., Pa.
1870. Robert Arthington, Esq., England.
1872. Rev. Edward P. Humphrey, D.D., Ky.
1872. Harvey Lindsly, M. D., LL. D., D. C.
1874. Rev. Bishop R. S. Foster, D. D., Mass.
1874. Rt. Rev. Wm. B. Stevens, D. D., Pa.
1874. Rt Rev. Gregory T. Bedell, D. D., O.
1875. Rt Rev. M. A. DeW. Howe, D.D., Pa.
1875. Samuel K. Wilson, Esq. N. J.
1876. Rev. Samuel E. Appleton, D. D., Pa.
1876. Rev. H. M. Turner, D. D., LL. D., Ga.

1877. Prest. E. G. Robinson, LL. D., R. I.
1877. Rev. William E. Schenck, D. D., Pa
1878. Hon. Richard W. Thompson, Ind.
1878. Admiral Robert W. Shufeldt, U. S. N.
1880. Francis T. King, Esq., Maryland.
188 . Rev. Samuel D. Alexander, D.D., N.Y
1881. Rev. Bishop H. W. Warren, D.D., Col.
1882. Henry G. Marquand, Esq., N. Y.
1884. Rev. George D. Boardman, D. D., Pa.
1884. Rev. Bishop E. G. Andrews, D. D., D.C.
1884. Rev. Edward W. Blyden, D.D., Liberia.
1884. Rev. Otis H. Tiffany, D. D., Pa.
1885. Rev. James Saul, D. D., Pa.
1886. Rt. Rev. Henry C. Potter, D. D., N. Y.
1886. Hon Alexander B. Hagner, D. C.
1887. Hon. Robert S. Green, N. J.

The figures before each name indicate the year of first election.

LIFE DIRECTORS.

1852. JAMES HALL, M. D..............*Md.*
1853. ALEXANDER DUNCAN, Esq........*R. I.*
1864. ALEXANDER GUY, M. D........*Ohio.*
1868. EDWARD COLES, Esq............*Pa.*
1869. REV. JOSEPH F. TUTTLE, D. D..*Ind.*
1869. CHARLES H. NICHOLS, M. D....*N. Y.*
1870. DANIEL PRICE, Esq.............*N. J.*
1871. Rev. WILLIAM H. STEELE, D. D. *N. J.*
1871. R't. Rev. H. C. POTTER, D. D...*N. Y.*
1873. Rev. GEORGE W. SAMSON, D. D. *N. Y.*
1878. Rev. EDW'D W. APPLETON, D. D., *Pa.*
1883. Rev. JAMES SAUL, D. D.,........*Pa.*
1885. WILLIAM EVANS GUY, Esq........*Mo.*

DELEGATES FOR 1887.

PENNSYLVANIA COLONIZATION SOCIETY.—Rev. Samuel E. Appleton, D. D., Edward S. Morris, Esq., Rev. Alfred Elwyn.

SEVENTIETH ANNUAL REPORT.

The Seventieth year of THE AMERICAN COLONIZATION SOCIETY has not been exempt from the afflictions common to humanity. Death has removed three of its Vice-Presidents—two of whom were also Directors—who had long evinced the deep interest felt by them in our beneficent enterprise.

NECROLOGY.

1. HON HORATIO SEYMOUR, elected in 1863, was twice chosen Governor of the State of New York, but his influence upon the public mind extended over his whole active career, and was wide as the nation. He was an orator and statesman of the old school—firm in his convictions, earnest in their advocacy, dignified, high-minded and incorruptible. In him the Republic has lost one of its most useful and illustrious citizens.

2. THOMAS R. HAZARD, ESQ., elected in 1841, was the soul of human kindness, noted for his utter freedom from affectation and his Christian charity. He was one of our earliest and most faithful friends, and an eloquent advocate and generous supporter, contributing, in 1840, one thousand dollars to constitute himself a Director. His life will be held in grateful remembrance for what he did through this Society, as through others, to promote the well-being of the oppressed and the poor, of the ignorant and the degraded.

3. REV. JOHN MACLEAN, D. D., LL. D., elected in 1861, was long the President of the New Jersey State Auxiliary, and for the last thirty-five years a Director of this Society, giving his time and thought, his labor and his means to the promotion of the cause. He was just in judgment, wise in counsel, and practical in methods. The power of his intellect, the vastness of his knowledge, the mingled strength and beauty of his character, and that harmony of all his life which the spirit of Christian faith and holiness gave—mark this venerable man, even within the lofty circle of those eminent men among whom his name must stand, as one worthy of his fellows.

FINANCES.

The receipts during the year year 1886 have been:

Donations	$2,046 00
Legacies	40,485 33
Emigrants toward cost of passage	65 00
For education in Liberia	418 40
Interest	93 33
From other sources	1,814 40
Receipts	$44,922 46
Balance 1 January, 1886	41 06
Making available	$44,963 52
The disbursements have been	39,130 85
Balance 31 December, 1886	$5,832 67

Early in the year the funds of the Society were largely augmented by a generous legacy, and it is to this that its present efficiency is mostly due. An appeal is made to the friends of the Society, not only for liberal gifts during their life time, but for provision from their estates after they are departed.

EMIGRATION.

One hundred and two emigrants were given passage in the bark Liberia (3) April 12, and the bark Monrovia (107) October 30. The first of these vessels completed her voyage at Monrovia, May 27, and the latter arrived at Cape Palmas, December 24. Most of these people are agriculturists, and were commended for their sobriety, industry and integrity. Two were from Rockingham, N. C., ninety-six from Lancaster County, S. C., four from Darlington, S. C., seven from Gainesville, Florida, and one from Topeka, Kansas. Sixty-one are between the ages of 12 and 60, forty-one between 12 and 2 years, and eight are less than 2 years. Forty-six were reported as Church communicants. Of the adult males twenty-two are farmers, and one blacksmith, one carpenter and one school teacher. The baggage of the people and the stores for their support during the first six months after arrival, accompanied them.

It is represented from Liberia that "the late immigrants are generally prospering, and they are perfectly satisfied with their new homes and prospects. They are taking upon themselves the duties and resposibilities of really free citizens, while they feel that they have reached a higher plane of manhood."

Emigration to Liberia every year under the auspices of The American Colonization Society has been uninterrupted for the past sixty-six years. Those now reported make the number sent since the civil war to be 3,900, and a total from the beginning of 15,898, exclusive of 5,722 recaptured Africans which we induced and enabled the Government of the United States to settle in Liberia, making a grand total of 21,620 persons to whom the Society has given homes in Africa.

APPLICATIONS.

The appeal of very many thousands of the people of color for homes in the land of their ancestors continues to come unsought to the Society. The applications this year have been marked by some striking features—mostly, the applicants have been more numerous and of higher grade than ever before, and there is a greatly increased looking to Congress for assistance to remove to Liberia.

Among the petitions which have reached Congress from colored men in various parts of the States of North Carolina, South Carolina, Georgia, Florida, Alabama, Mississippi, Louisiana, Texas, Arkansas, Tennessee, Indiana, Missouri and Kansas, and the Indian Territory, was the following:

"To the Senate and House of Representatives, in Congress assembled:

"The memorial of the undersigned, citizens of Groveton, Trinity County, Texas, respectfully represents:

" 1. That we are descendants of people torn from Africa and brought to this country, where, for two hundred years, their children have contributed by their labor to increase the wealth of every portion of the United States. We greatly desire now to go to the land of our forefathers and make it our home; but have not the means of paying our passage, or providing for our immediate wants on landing in Liberia.

" 2. Low wages and high rents, and a despair of doing better in the future, compel us to emigrate. The main reason urged why we should remain here is, that our labor and our votes are needed in this country: a suggestion, the force of which we fail to perceive, believing the country can very well dispense even with our presence.

" 3. The attractions of Liberia are rich virgin lands, freedom from competition with any but our own race, and assurance of superior position. The entire continent of Africa is open to the intelligent and industrial class, and the road to useful employment, as well as to Christian enterprise and an honorable nationality, is wide and inviting.

" Your petitioners therefore respectfully and earnestly ask Congress to pass a bill appropriating not exceeding $100 per capita, to be expended, under the direction of the American Colonization Society, in paying the expenses of emigrants to Liberia, and the providing there of six months' shelter and support of ourselves and children."

In the Senate of the United States, April 6, as officially published in the *Congressional Record* of April 7, Senator Plumb of Kansas is reported to have said :

"I present a petition by a large number of colored citizens of the State of Kansas, praying for assistance to enable them to go to Africa. I will venture to ask that the petition itself, with the names of the officers who subscribed it, not the individual subscribers, be read, as it is somewhat remarkable. The petition, I think, perhaps should be referred to the Committee on Foreign Relations. I am not particular about the reference which is had, but it comes to me accompanied by letters from prominent citizens of Topeka, where these people live, speaking of their character most favorably, and also of the very thorough determination that they have in this matter; and by reason of that sincerity and earnestness which they have manifested I hope that the petition, wherever it goes, will meet with consideration."

The petition was referred as suggested, after being read by the Chief Clerk, as follows :

" To the Members of the Senate and House of Representatives of Congress :

"*Whereas*, we, the Negroes of the United States, were brought from Africa and sold as slaves in this country, and served as such from 1620 to 1865 : and *Whereas*, we were set free without a penny and left at the mercy of our late masters and their brothers, who owned all this country from the Atlantic to the Pacific, and for over two hundred years had regarded us as inferiors and slaves : and *Whereas*, there are sixteen thousand of us who have already returned to Africa ; and *Whereas*, there are thousands of us in humble circumstances who yet wish to return to Africa, and there try to build up a United States in Africa, modeled after this Government, and under the protecting care of the same, for the elevation of the African and for the pepetuity of our race, which is here losing its identity by intermixture with the white races, and other troubles, etc.: *Therefore,*

" We, the members of the African Emigration Association, and such citizens as are willing to aid and encourage us, ask you for an appropriation to be disbursed through such a channel as in your judgment you may direct. It is the purpose of this petition to help only those who wish to go to Africa, in whatever part of the United

States they may be found. The head of the Association is for the present to be found at Topeka, Kans. It was established September 17, 1881. Approved by the Association March 27, 1886. Officials: George Charles, president; Antony Griffin, vice-president; John Smith, chaplain; W. Johnson, chaplain; Lewis Lee, treasurer; Charles Charles, secretary."

To the foregoing specimens of the movement, individual and organized, for Government aid, and the reasons assigned for it and for emigration, it seems proper to add a letter addressed to the Society by the Governor of a leading State:

"Executive Office,
———— ———, August 26, 1886.

DEAR SIR:
The Rev. Wm. Slatter, colored, who is a native of this State, and who emigrated to Liberia in 1869, and remained there nearly fifteen years, has called on me with some friends of his to ask my intervention, as Governor of their State, in securing to him and some 300 other persons of his color, transportation from this country to Liberia. Their hope is to have the Government send them over. If this can be done, how can it be effected? If it cannot be done—then can the Colonization Society do anything for them in that way? Hoping to hear from you soon in regard to this. I am,

Respectfully yours,
———— ————.

African Colonization has been approved by formal resolutions, after full discussion, by Congress repeatedly, and by the Legislatures of Massachusetts, Connecticut, New York, New Jersey, Pennsylvania, Delaware, Maryland, Virginia, Louisiana, Tennessee, Kentucky, Ohio and Indiana. Several of these States have acted upon it repeatedly, and appropriated money—Maryland granting $10,000 annually for twenty-five years, for its support. It is a cause which is identified with the dearest and most valuable interests of the country as well as with the objects of humanity, and the benevolent designs of Christian effort. It is an undertaking sufficiently great for the care and treasury of the nation.

LIBERIA.

The following statement of affairs in Liberia has been kindly furnished by Hon. C. T. O. King, Mayor of Monrovia:

"AGRICULTURE—Our agricultural progress, especially as to the porduction of sugar and coffee, is encouraging. The forests are giving way before the energy and march of civilization, and with marked effect upon the climate. Our rainy seasons are not so long nor the waterfall so heavy as formerly, and the general health is much improved.

"COMMERCE.—The depression in trade throughout the world has unfavorably affected this Republic, and caused a considerable falling off in the national revenue. Our merchants have endeavored to contract rather than expand their business, and are anxiously waiting for a revival of trade in Europe and America, so that they may participate. Leading minds are desirous of extending trade in the interior, but the low price of African products abroad does not justify the venture.

"EDUCATION—The schools of low grades are doing very well, and those of the American Colonization Society at Brewerville and Arthington are in a highly prosperous condition and yielding satisfaction. The educational work carried on by the Episcopal Mission at Cape Mount promises largely for the future of Liberia. Bishop William Taylor has commendable schemes for reaching and instructing the natives. The colored Baptists of the United States have begun an important educational work on the beautiful lake east of Cape Mount.

"THE COLLEGE.—Extensive repairs are being prosecuted on the College building; meanwhile, Prof. Freeman, the acting President, will visit America to recruit his health."

A revival of religious interest is reported in the Methodist and Baptist churches of the Republic. Rev. P. Moort wrote from Monrovia, Sept. 7: "The Episcopal Church of this Diocese held in May last, in this city, a convocation of its clergy, presided over by Bishop Ferguson. Comprising a portion of this body's work was the ordaining of three Priests and one Deacon. The convocation awakened great interest. Never was there in the Capital, at any one time, such a number of Episcopal ministers; meetings were held almost every evening; and to bring matters to a close a grand missionary meeting was held. On that occasion the church (Trinity) was filled with an attentive audience. I had the pleasure of visiting Beulah, twenty miles up the St. John's river, a little before I started for Monrovia. This station is doing a glorious work. Both sides of the St. John's river are a natural paradise. No one who has not seen them can imagine the beauty and grandeur of these interior sceneries."

Judson A. Lewis, Esq., United States Consul at Sierra Leone, in an official report dated November 6, says:

"Liberia is an interesting instance of American benevolence and foresight. Founded by a philanthropic Society, having its headquarters at Washington, it has, with its slender resources, accomplished a great work for this part of Africa, and seems to present an inviting field for enterprising black men from America.

"Many of the people have emigrated from the United States, and are more favorable to the extension of American influence in the country than of any other. The Constitution is modeled after our own. The President and Vice-President are elected for two years. The Legislature consists of a Senate and House of Representatives, and all other branches of the civil service are the same as those of the United States. The right of suffrage is based upon a slight property (real estate) qualification.

"From all accounts which I have been able to gather, Liberia is rich in natural resources. In mineral and agricultural capacity it is thought to be without a rival in this part of Africa. The country seems particularly adapted to the successful raising of coffee, and this Liberia coffee, has within the last few years acquired, I believe, a reputation very high. The immigrants from the United States, especially in recent years, have been devoting more attention to its cultivation. They are pushing their settlements towards the interior and enlarging their farms.

"Some of the Liberian farmers and merchants have made money and live in comfortable and even elegant style. In the month of July last, four Liberian merchants from different parts of the Republic, passed here on board the English mail steamer on their way to Europe for business or pleasure. They were all colored men, born in the United States and emigrated to Liberia when children.

"The great needs of Liberia are civilized population and capital, both of which can be readily furnished from the colored population of the United States. Fifty thousand Negroes, located about fifty miles from the Coast, would fill the lower Niger Valley with a wholesome industrial influence.

"I shall be glad if anything I have written may quicken American enterprise in this direction, either of a commercial or agricultural nature. Such undertakings, properly and intelligently conducted, would, I think, not fail to be remunerative and confer great blessings upon this continent."

Bishop William Taylor is the most recent disinterested testimony in favor of Liberia. He truly calls it "the garden spot of West Africa" and he adds: "There is a grand future for Liberia if they will learn by what they have seen and suffered in the past fifty years."

INTERIOR SETTLEMENTS.

The Republic of Liberia, occupying some five hundred miles of territory on the West African Coast, with an indefinite interior, was founded by a Society of American citizens.

The Republic has been acknowledged as a Sovereign and Independent State by all the leading Powers of Europe and America. It is the only Independent Christian nation on the Continent of Africa. It has recently been cited by international lawyers to prove that communities formed by private persons for industrial and commercial purposes may, in the course of time, assume sovereign rights. Senator Morgan, of the United States Senate Committee on Foreign Relations, in his report in 1881 on the International Congo Association, said:

"The people of the United States, with but little assistance from the Government, have established a free Republic in Liberia, with a Constitution modeled after our own, and under the control of the Negro race: its commerce is valuable: its government is successful, and its people are prosperous

"The success of the Liberian Colony has demonstrated the usefulness of that system of dealing with a social question which is, to the people of the United States, of the highest importance. It has also established a recognized precedent in favor of the right of untitled individuals to found States in the interests of civilization in barbarous countries, through the consent of the local authorities, and it has given confidence to those who look *to the justice of the nations for the restoration of the emancipated Africans to their own country, if they choose to return to it.*"

"This great duty has, so far, been left entirely to the efforts of citizens of the United States, and it has been supported almost exclusively by their personal contributions. The Governments of the world have been slow even to recognize the State just founded by the courage and means of private citizens, but it is now firmly established in the family of nations, and is everywhere recognised as a free and independent nation.

"This pleasing history of progress, attended with peace and prosperity in Liberia, has given rise to a feeling of earnest interest among the people of the United States in the questions which arise from the recent discovery by their countryman, H. M. Stanley, of the great river which drains Equatorial Africa."

From the commencement of the career of this Americo-African State—or even before its commencement, when the idea of its establishment was first mooted - it was regarded with jealousy by European Governments having possessions on the Coast. Attempts were from time to time made by foreign adventurers to hamper its growth and circumscribe the area of its jurisdiction. But through the prompt interference of American benevolence these efforts were thwarted. The territory adjacent to the settlements were purchased and a continuous seaboard was secured, from the river Shebar to the river San Pedro, bought, as the late venerable Dr. Archibald Alexander has said, "and paid for with money, and doubly paid for by the blood of the emigrants shed in its defence."

Notwithstanding numerous drawbacks, Liberia has prospered, and owing to its endeavor to establish itself firmly on the Coast, there has been hitherto no opportunity for extending inland. The policy of the American Colonization Society has always contemplated interior settlements. In the 24th Annual Report, as far back as 1841, it is said:

"The Executive Committee have been for some time anxious to open a road from the Coast to the mountain country, with a view of making a settlement, believing it will prove much more healthy than those on the seaboard and thus render the acclimating fever harmless. When the Colony was commenced there were many reasons for settling on the Coast—limited means, the want of all facilities for transportation, and the hostile character of the native Kings, all rendered it impossible to establish a Colony in the interior."

This interesting enterprize could not be carried out to any extent, owing to exigencies on the Coast. It was of vital interest to the settlements, which were scattered along three hundred miles of Coast, with intervals between of from one hundred to two hundred miles, that the interjacent territory should be kept free from the plots of foreigners, which, if successful with the Aborigines would, it was felt, lead to a dismemberment of the Colony. But, unfortunately, without the arms of Briaereus and the eyes of Argus (qualities possessed by a powerful neighbor north of the young State) the Republic being unable to keep watch over every inch of territory, the Aboriginal inhabitants in the exposed positions on the North-West came under the influence of foreign traders, and international complications brought on through their intrigues opened the way for the British Government to seize, at one stroke, forty miles of Liberian territory in that direction, and annex it to Sierra Leone, thus making the terrritories of the two countries conterminous.

There is now an opening and a warm welcome awaiting American Negro settlers in the healthy and wealthy country interior of Liberia: and there are thousands of strong men, mechanics, farmers, school-teachers and ministers, in the United States, ready to go and occupy. These are making constant applications to the Society for help to reach that land of promise for themselves and their children.

It is believed that the time is at hand for the friends of Africa to establish on the highlands interior of Liberia a settlement to be occupied by a selected company of emigrants. It is becoming every day more and more evident that the agency of the Republic as a support to missionary work is indispensible. On this subject a recent West African paper, the *Methodist Herald*, published at Sierra Leone, says;

"We are persuaded that the most effectual method of establishing and spreading Christianity and civilization in Africa is the planting of colonies of Christian and civilized blacks. The Aboriginal wars, which now distract the neighborhood of the settlement, would be permanently put down by the founding of agricultural and trading colonies in the harried districts.

"Experience has proved that the isolated successes achieved by missionaries, white or black, are not permanent in their results, and that if it is desired to produce any widespread and lasting effect upon the social, moral and natural condition of Africa, the agency of the colony is indispensable. When the native sees men of his own race combining under social, municipal and national laws and regulations, developing into successful husbandmen, mechanics, traders, etc., and secure in the enjoyment of the fruits of their own labor, he will be incited to imitate the example and share in the advantages of those around him."

Bishop Ferguson, in his Annual Report, observes:

"The Government of Liberia exercises an influence and authority over the different tribes as never before: the favorable result of which is a cessation of tribal wars and free intercourse. At the close of every year delegates from all the tribes who have entered into solemn compact with the Government—now numbering twenty-four in Maryland County—meet at Harper to discuss matters appertaining to the interests of all, and to receive an annual stipend—which is given on condition that the articles of the compact have been faithfully kept during the year. Among other things stipulated in the compact is a promise on their part to keep the roads and river open for free passage, and to maintain peace with all. For the tribes living on the Cavalla river and in the far interior this is an important desideratum. Heretofore, upon the slightest pretext, some petty tribe, living on the river or other highway into the interior, would endeavor to prevent all passage by them. Our missionaries have often been hindered, and in some instances roughly handled, in their visits to the interior, through this evil. It will be readily seen, therefore, that this success on the part of the Liberia Government greatly facilitates the work of advancing the Gospel into the regions beyond."

The American Colonization Society needs the means for the passage to Africa and the establishment in Liberia of a goodly num-her of choice families from this country about fifty miles in a direct line from the Coast, and for the opening of a good road to the settlement. It presents the subject to the serious consideration of the friends of humanity and progress, with the earnest request that they will send donations to aid in this important enterprize—that an interior settlement, with all its grand facilities for religion and science, or agriculture and commerce may, within the year at least be commenced, as one of a series which, it is hoped, will, in the course of time, extend to the Niger.

TREASURER'S REPORT.

Receipts and Disbursements of the AMERICAN COLONIZATION SOCIETY in the year 1886.

DR.		CR.
Received Donations,	$2,046 00	Paid Passage and settlement of Emigrants, $10,481 14
" Legacies,	40,485 33	" Education in Liberia, 418 40
" Emigrants toward passage,	65 00	" Taxes, insurance and repairs of Colonization Build'g, 455 55
" Subscriptions to African Repository,	37 40	" Paper and printing the African Repository, 387 75
" Rent of Colonization Building,	1,777 00	" Salary of Secretary and Treasurer, office expenses, printing, postage, expense of meetings, and costs of contested Wills, 2,799 01
" For Education in Liberia,	418 40	
" Interest on temporary Investments,	93 33	" Temporary Investments, 24,589 00
Receipts,	$44,922 46	Disbursements, $39,130 85
Balance January 1, 1886,	41 06	Balance December 31, 1886, 5,832 67
Total,	$44,963 52	Total, $44,963 52

The Committee on Accounts have examined the Treasurer's Account for the year 1886, and the vouchers for the expenditures, and find the same correct.

REGINALD FENDALL, } Committee.
EDWARD S. MORRIS,

Washington, D. C., *January* 18, 1887.

MINUTES OF THE SOCIETY.

WASHINGTON, D. C., *January* 16, 1887.

THE AMERICAN COLONIZATION SOCIETY celebrated its Seventieth Anniversary in the P. Episcopal church of the Epiphany, G street, above 13th, N. W., Washington, D. C., on Sunday evening, January 16, 1887.

Hon. John H. B. Latrobe, of Baltimore, Md., President of the Society, occupied the chair, and the services were conducted by Rev. S. H. Giesy, D. D., assisted by Rev. Alexander Crummell, D. D., of Washington, D. C.

The Seventieth Annual Report of the Society was presented by President Latrobe, with the statement that an abstract of it had been printed and placed in the pews.

The Annual Discourse was delivered by Rev. Charles H. Hall, D. D., of Brooklyn, N. Y.: Text, Philippians, 2d chap. and 3d verse.

The exercises were closed with the benediction by Rev. S. H. Giesy, D. D., rector of the church.

COLONIZATION ROOMS, *January* 18, 1887.

The Annual Meeting of THE AMERICAN COLONIZATION SOCIETY was held to-day at 3 o'clock, P. M., agreeably to Article 4 of the Constitution and to notice in THE AFRICAN REPOSITORY.

The President, Hon. John H. B. Latrobe, in the chair.

The Minutes of the Anniversary on the 16th inst., were read, and with the Minutes of the Annual Meeting of January 19, 1886, were approved.

Rev. Alfred Elwyn and Hon. Charles C. Nott were appointed a Committee to nominate the President and Vice Presidents of the Society for the ensuing year.

On motion of Rev. Samuel E. Appleton, D. D., it was

Resolved, That the thanks of the Society are tendered to the Rev. Charles H. Hall. D. D., for his able presentation of the interests of this Society and of Liberia, and that a copy of the same is requested for publication.

Resolved, That the thanks of the Society are tendered to the Rev. Dr. S. H. Giesy and the Vestry of the church of the Epiphany for the use of the church last Sunday evening for our Seventieth Anniversary.

Rev. Alfred Elwyn, Chairman of the Committee on Nominations, presented and read a report recommending the re-election of the present President and Vice Presidents, and the election of Hon. Robert S. Green, of New Jersey, as an additional Vice President, as follows :—

PRESIDENT,

1853.   HON. JOHN H. B. LATROBE.

VICE-PRESIDENTS,

1838. Hon. Henry A. Foster, N. Y.	1877. Prest. E. G. Robinson, LL. D., R. I.,
1851. Rev. Robert Ryland, D. D., Ky.	1877. Rev. William E. Schenck, D. D., Pa.
1851. Hon. Frederick P. Stanton, Va.	1878. Hon. Richard W. Thompson, Ind.
1859. Hon. Henry M. Schieffelin, N. Y.	1878. Admiral Robert W. Shufeldt, U. S. N.
1866. Hon. James R. Doolittle, Wisconsin.	1880. Francis T. King, Esq., Maryland.
1867. Samuel A. Crozer, Esq., Pa.	1880. Rev. Samuel D. Alexander, D.D., N.Y.
1870. Robert Arthington, Esq., England.	1881. Rev. Bishop H. W. Warren, D.D., Col.
1872. Rev. Edward P. Humphrey, D.D., Ky.	1882. Henry G. Marquand, Esq., N. Y.
1872. Harvey Lindsly, M. D., LL. D., D. C.	1884. Rev. George D. Boardman, D. D., Pa.
1874. Rev. Bishop R. S. Foster, D. D., Mass.	1884. Rev. Bishop E.G. Andrews, D.D., D.C.
1874. Rt. Rev. Wm. B. Stevens, D. D., Pa.	1884. Rev. Edward W. Blyden, D.D., Liberia.
1874. Rt Rev. Gregory T. Bedell, D. D., O.	1884. Rev. Otis H. Tiffany, D. D., Pa.
1875. Rt. Rev. M.A. DeW. Howe, D.D., Pa.	1885. Rev. James Saul, D. D., Pa.
1875. Samuel K. Wilson, Esq. N. J.	1886. Rt. Rev. Henry C. Potter, D. D., N. Y.
1876. Rev. Samuel E. Appleton, D. D., Pa.	1886. Hon Alexander B. Hagner, D. C.
1876. Rev. H. M. Turner, D. D., LL. D., Ga.	1887. Hon. Robert S. Green, N. J.

The figures before each name indicate the year of first election.

Whereupon, on motion, it was

Resolved, That the Report be accepted and approved, and that the Society elect the officers nominated by the Committee.

On motion, Adjourned.

WM. COPPINGER, *Secretary*.

MINUTES OF THE BOARD OF DIRECTORS.

WASHINGTON, D. C., *January* 18, 1887.

THE BOARD OF DIRECTORS OF THE AMERICAN COLONIZATION SOCIETY met this day at 12 o'clock, M., in the rooms of the Society, No. 450 Pennsylvania Avenue, N W., Washington, D. C.

The President, Hon. John H. B. Latrobe, took the chair, and prayer was offered by Rev. Samuel E. Appleton, D. D.

Mr. William Coppinger was appointed Secretary of the Board.

The unprinted portions of the Minutes of the last meeting, January 19 and 20, 1886, were read, and the Minutes were approved.

Reginald Fendall, Esq., and Rev. Samuel E. Appleton, D. D., were appointed a Committee on Credentials; who retired and subsequently reported, through their Chairman, the following named Delegates appointed for the year 1887 :

PENNSYLVANIA COLONIZATION SOCIETY: Rev. Samuel E. Appleton, D. D., Edward S. Morris, Esq., Rev. Alfred Elwyn.

EXECUTIVE COMMITTEE: Hon. Peter Parker, Hon. Charles C. Nott, Reginald Fendall, Esq., Rev. Thomas G. Addison, D. D., Rev. Byron Sunderland, D. D., Dr. William W. Godding.

Whereupon, on motion, it was

Resolved, That the Report of the Committee on Credentials be accepted and approved, and the gentlemen named be received as members of the Board.

On motion, it was

Resolved, That Mrs. Jane R. Roberts, widow of President Roberts, of Liberia, and Rev. John W. Chickering, D. D., of Massachusetts, be and they are hereby invited to share in the counsels of the Board.

The Secretary presented and read the Seventieth Annual Report of the American Colonization Society.

Whereupon, on motion, it was

Resolved, That the Annual Report be accepted and referred to the standing Committees according to its several topics.

The Secretary presented and read the Statement of the Executive Committee for the past year. Also a list of property of the Society, and a Statement of receipts by States in the year 1886.

The Treasurer presented and read his Annual Report of receipts and disbursements, with the certificate of audit.

Whereupon, on motion, it was

Resolved, That the Statement of the Executive Committee and the Treasurer's Report for the past year, with the accompanying Annual papers, be accepted, and that so much of them as relate to Foreign Relations, Finance, Auxiliary Societies, Agencies, Accounts, Emigration, and Education, be referred to the several standing Committees in charge of those subjects respectively.

The President appointed the STANDING COMMITTEES, as follows:

COMMITTEE ON FOREIGN RELATIONS:- Hon. Peter Parker, Rev. Alfred Elwyn.

COMMITTEE ON FINANCE:—Reginald Fendall, Esq., Edward S. Morris, Esq.

COMMITTEE ON AUXILIARY SOCIETIES:— Rev. Samuel E. Appleton, D. D., Rev. Thomas G. Addison, D. D.

COMMITTEE ON AGENCIES:—Rev. Thomas G. Addison, D. D., Dr. William W. Godding.

COMMITTEE ON ACCOUNTS:—Reginald Fendall, Esq., Edward S. Morris, Esq.

COMMITTEE ON EMIGRATION:—Rev. Byron Sunderland, D. D., Dr. William W. Godding.

COMMITTEE ON EDUCATION:—Rev. Samuel E. Appleton, D. D., Hon. Charles C. Nott.

Mrs. Roberts presented to the Board the enterprise of establishing a Hospital at Monrovia, for the care and relief of sick and destitute seamen, and of Liberian and native sufferers by disease and disability of mind and body.

Whereupon, on motion, it was

Resolved, That the subject be referred to the Executive Committee, with power.

The Board proceeded to the consideration of the proposed amendment to Article Fifth of the Constitution of the Society, approved at the last annual meeting of the Board, and that Article was unanimously amended to read as follows:

Article 5. There shall be a Board of Directors composed of the Directors for Life and of Delegates from the several Auxiliary Societies. Each of such Societies shall be entitled to one Delegate and an addititional Delegate for every two hundred dollars paid into the treasury of this Society within the year ending on the 31st of December. Provided, That no Auxiliary shall be entitled to more than four Delegates in any one year.

Letters excusing their absence from this meeting were presented and read from the following named Life Directors, viz.: Dr. James Hall, Claremont, Md., December 8; Rev. Edward W. Appleton, D. D., Ashbourne, Pa., January 5; Rev. William H. Steele, D. D., Newark, N. J., January 7; Edward Coles, Esq., Philadelphia, Pa., January 12; Dr. Charles H. Nichols, New York, January 14; Rev. George W. Samson, D. D., New York, January 17; and Rev. James Saul, D. D., Philadelphia, Pa., January 17.

On motion, it was

Resolved, That a Committee be appointed to nominate the Executive Committee and the Secretary and Treasurer for the ensuing year.

Edward S. Morris, Esq., and Rev. Samuel E. Appleton, D. D., were appointed the Committee.

Edward S. Morris, Esq., Chairman of the Special Committee on Nominations, presented and read a report recommending the re-election of the following:

SECRETARY AND TREASURER—William Coppinger, Esq.

EXECUTIVE COMMITTEE—Hon. Peter Parker, Hon. Charles C. Nott, Reginald Fendall, Esq., Rev. Thomas G. Addison, D. D., Rev. Byron Sunderland, D. D., Justice William Strong, and Dr. William W. Godding.

Whereupon, on motion, it was

Resolved, That the report be accepted and approved, and that the Board elect the officers nominated by the Committee.

On motion, it was

Resolved, That the Board do now adjourn to meet in these rooms to-morrow at 12 o'clock. M.

Adjourned.

WASHINGTON, D. C., *January* 19, 1887.

THE BOARD OF DIRECTORS met to-day at 12 o'clock, M., in the rooms of the Society, President Latrobe in the chair.

Prayer was offered by Rev. Byron Sunderland, D. D.

The Minutes of yesterday's meeting were read and approved.

Hon. Peter Parker, Chairman of the standing Committee on Foreign Relations, reported that, in their opinion, no business justifying a written report had been referred to them. Whereupon, on motion, the report was accepted and approved.

Reginald Fendall, Esq., Chairman of the standing Committee on Finance, presented and read the following report, which was, on motion, accepted and approved:

The Standing Committee on Finance respectfully report, that they have examined the Securities of the Society and find them correctly stated, and in the possession of the Treasurer.

Rev. Thomas G. Addison, D. D., from the standing Committee on Auxiliary Societies, presented and read the following resolution as their report, and it was, on motion, accepted and adopted:

Resolved, That it is important that the Parent Society should be aided and supported in its great work by Auxiliary Societies in the several States, and that the Executive Committee be directed to use its best efforts to increase the number of such Auxiliary Societies, and to secure a more general appointment of Delegates to the Annual Meeting of this Board of Directors.

Mr. Fendall, Chairman of the standing Committee on Accounts, presented and read the following report, which was, on motion, accepted and approved:

The Committee on Accounts have examined the Treasurer's Account for the year 1836, and the vouchers for the expenditures, and find the same correct.

Rev. Byron Sunderland, D. D., Chairman of the Standing Committee on Emigration, presented and read the following report, which was, on motion, accepted and approved, and the accompanying resolution was adopted:

For several years this Society has been specially calling public attention to the subject of the emigration of colored people to Liberia, and endeavoring to bring all the facts bearing on the subject to the notice of the people and the Government, with a view of crystallizing and concentrating public sentiment upon the one great work which we believe this Government should undertake—that of aiding such of the Negroes as desire it to return to the land of their fathers more rapidly and under more favorable conditions than can be done by any private beneficence or by the organized efforts of our own Society; and there is very decided indication of the fact that what has been done by us has not been altogether fruitless. It has been indeed questioned and criticised in no very amiable spirit in several quarters, and as yet the apathy and indifference of Congress have scarcely been disturbed: but a new interest has been awakened in the country, especially among the colored people themselves; and one of the most kindly suggestions in regard to Liberia appears in the late message of President Cleveland to the present Congress. Petitions are beginning to pour into Congress from various combinations and organizations of the Negroes for aid in this noble undertaking. The idea of African colonization is taking a deeper hold of the public mind, and broader views of the whole question are being entertained. As evidence of this we may cite the fact that appeals more emphatic have been made to his Society by the colored people themselves than in any single year before. These appeals come from a class evidently of higher intelligence and character, and they indicate a more serious purpose from a more decided conviction taught by the experience of a quarter of a century that Africa is the proper field for the development of the colored race, and needs this immigration from America more for the sake of the future of that Continent than for the private welfare of individuals.

Petitions to Congress have been sent during the past winter from no less than thirteen States and from the Indian Territory, praying for aid to colonization. These have come from the colored people in almost every quarter of the country where the Negro population is most dense.

A recent memorial addressed to President Cleveland, under date of December 30th, 1886, has been received by our Secretary from colored people in the State of Mississippi, setting forth in the most pathetic terms the miserable condition of the Negroes, and the utter hopelessness of improvement which has taken possession of them, and breathing the most earnest prayers that something may be suggested or undertaken by the Government for their relief. And they feel to-day that the most effectual relief will be to send them back to the land of their fathers. A communication of the same purport came to our Secretary under late of January 12th, 1887, in behalf of a large number of colored people in South Carolina;

Hundreds of these people could be collected at different points in the South in a very short time ready to go to Africa. Indeed so great a desire do they manifest for emigration to their fatherland that swindling knaves of their own race have already been trading on their credulity, and selling them bogus tickets of transportation. These tickets they have purchased at the cost of all the money they had in the world, and now having been duped and robbed they are left in the most pitiful condition.

"A special from Charleston, S. C., says: 'On Monday some curiosity was occasioned by thirty Negroes leaving Rock Hill on the afternoon train. They bought tickets to Fort Mill, when they met about three hundred more Negroes who were there awaiting the arrival of a special train that they said had been chartered to take them to New York, whence they were to sail for Liberia. The train has not yet arrived, and the railroad officials say that no arrangements have been made for any train. The Negroes are waiting at Fort Mill, where they are exposed to the cold without sufficient clothing. They are confident that their train will come. It seems that some one has been inciting the colored people to leave their homes, sell their property, and go to Liberia; as an inducement giving them a red badge or ticket, for a consideration, which would convey them to New York. The party who sold the tickets has never turned up. The condition of these duped Negroes is pitiful. The majority of them have sold everything they have in the world in order to pay for their fraudulent tickets. The agent has cleared several thousand dollars by his heartless trick."

An African Emigration Association was established September 17, 1881, at Topeka, Kansas, for the purpose of promoting the same objects which we have in view; and during the last year, they also petitioned Congress for aid in this great work.

The United Trans-Atlantic Society, founded June 16th, 1885, and whose objects are the same as ours, have put forth a ringing circular, calling upon the people of their own race and all the friends of African colonization to come forward and aid them to "bridge the ocean that the sons and daughters of Ham may return to their God-given inheritance, and Ethiopia regain her ancient renown and be enhanced with modern splendor."

At a meeting of colored people in Columbia, South Carolina, in honor of Emancipation Day, the colored orator from Salisbury, North Carolina, Rev. J. C. Price, in eloquent and impressive terms advocated the very doctrine of which the American Colonization Society has been so long in this country almost the sole exponent and defender.

"COLUMBIA, S. C., January 3.—The colored people of this city and the surrounding country to-day had a grand celebration of Emancipation Day. The orator of the day was Prof. J. C. Price, of North Carolina, colored. He took for his subject, 'The American Negro, His Future and His Peculiar Work.' His advice to his race was to pay less attention to the past and look to the glorious future. He said the Negroes had the mind and ability; all they needed was confidence. The Negro could do what any other man could. He was opposed to amalgamation, and he did not believe in it. The peculiar work of the American Negro was the redemption of their race in Africa, which was their own country. If the white man could find gold, diamonds, and other riches in Africa, why not the Negro? It was the duty of the American Negro to go to Africa and reclaim their country, civilize the Negroes there, give them manual and intellectual education, and show them the way to build up the country. The speaker was a well-educated man."

And upon this question of emigration to Liberia, there begins to be a new stir in certain quarters. The men who have jeered at our venerable Society as an "old corpse" begin to find that it is a lively "old corpse," which yet has life enough in it to stir up editors of newspapers and magazines, authors of books, narrow-eyed Puritans, crazy orators at Negro conventions, and sinister critics who have little knowledge of, and less sympathy with, the grand objects which for seventy years our Society through all weathers has kept steadily before it.

We appreciate most highly the fidelity, the devotion and loyalty of the Pennsylvania Auxiliary, and we hope to comply with their timely suggestion "to give in future reports the figures showing as nearly as possible the number of applicants for emigration." A recent statement of a newspaper in Philadelphia, called "*The Record*," that "the great difficulty which the Society has had to contend against has been the reluctance of colored people to emigrate from this country to Liberia," &c., is wholly misleading and directly in the teeth of manifold and constantly accumulating facts. And to the sapient writer in the "*The Evening Telegram*," who charitably reminds us that "figures will go a great deal further towards demonstrating that the Society is earning its expenses than any amount of word-spinning," we have to say that before another year has passed over his head he will be gratified with figures enough to overwhelm him with the conviction that "the Society is earning enough to pay expenses," and that all murmurers like himself must clear the way for free, open, rapidly-increasing emigration to Liberia.

"*Resolved*, That in view of the demand for the data in reference to the number of applicants for emigration to Africa, the Secretary of this Society, with Dr. Sunderland as a committee, be requested to prepare a circular giving these data for a term of fifteen years past, that it may be broadcast with the view of informing the public of the actual truth of the case."

Rev. Thomas G. Addison, D. D., Chairman of the standing Committee on Agencies, presented and read the following resolution as their report, and it was, on motion, accepted and approved:

Resolved, That the policy of employing Agents for collecting funds and advocating the cause of Colonization in different parts of the country be approved, and its continuance earnestly recommended to the Executive Committee.

On motion, it was

Resolved, That the Annual Report of the Society be referred to the Executive Committee for publication.

The Minutes of to-day to this point were read and, on motion, approved. President Latrobe made an address, expressing a high sense of personal regard and esteem for the members of the Board, Rev. Thomas G. Addison, D. D., offered prayer, and the Board, on motion, adjourned.

WM. COPPINGER, *Secretary*.

ADDENDA TO REPORT ON EMIGRATION.

The following brief statement is appended in compliance with the resolution reported by the Committee on Emigration, page 24.

The original statement, made in the Annual Report of the Society for 1885, was as follows:

"A cautious estimate would be that five hundred thousand of the people of color are considering the question of emigration to Liberia, finding but little scope in the land of their birth for their industrial energies and race aspirations."

Following this appeared, in various forms, at different times, a similar representation as to the number of Negroes who were seeking information on the subject of emigration to Africa as their fatherland. In Dr. Sunderland's address before he Society, a year ago, he made the following statement:

"Yet to-day half a million of Father Snowden's people are seeking light from the 'ten-horned monster,' and turning a wistful gaze on the far-off fatherland."

These representations have been called in question, in various quarters, through the public press; and the suggestion of the Pennsylvania Auxiliary that hereafter, to meet the issue so raised as to the number of the colored people who are month by month seeking information from the American Colonization Society, the future reports should contain the statistics on the subject so far as the correspondence can show them.

The subjoined table of the number of actual applications for emigration, from year to year, for the last fifteen years, and also other statistics from the correspondence of colored people throughout the country in support of the estimate first announced, as cited above, is presented:—

Year	Number	Year	Number
1872	17	1881	48
1873	8	1882	51
1874	23	1883	95
1875	17	1884	133
1876	21	1885	180
1877	90	1886	169
1878	98		
1879	53		1037
1880	34		

' It would swell the proportion of the present document beyond any reasonable necessity to insert the whole of the correspondence for the period of the last fifteen years, but a fair specimen of this correspondence for a period of five months *only* ending December 31, 1886, is here given, as follows, the statements being in the exact language of the correspondents, as also the names of the places from which they write:

Green Hill, Miss.....................500 persons.
Cureton's, S. C......................140 families.
Sunflower, Miss ....A large body.
Prospect, S. C........................500 of us.

Rome, Ga	500 families.
Forestville, N. C	A number of choice families.
Nashville, Tenn	Some 200 have signed.
Denison, Texas	Several valuable men.
Tradesville, S. C.	Great many wanting to go.
Quincy, Florida	500 or 600 families
Edenton, N. C	A club.
Fort Mill, S. C	400 head.
Waxhaw, S. C	Want vessel to carry 1000 persons.
Wichita, Kansas	Colony.
Glendale, Miss	A number of us.
Belair, S. C	300 persons.
Denver, Col	A Society.
Harrison, N. C	Hundreds are willing.
Richburgh, S. C	Many ready to go.
Mars Hill, Ark	A large number.
Concord, Florida	Thousands.

It is proper to add, as Dr. Sunderland expressed in his address above cited, that "the Society has done nothing to bring about this state of things. The only activity in this direction has been information imparted at the request of the Negroes."

It appears to be a spontaneous movement on the part of the Negroes themselves who are awaking to broader views, both of their own mission and destiny and of the great work of the American Colonization Society.

SEVENTY-FIRST ANNUAL REPORT

OF THE

American Colonization Society:

WITH THE

MINUTES

OF THE

ANNUAL MEETING and of the BOARD OF DIRECTORS,

JANUARY 15, 17, & 18 1888.

WASHINGTON CITY:
COLONIZATION BUILDING, 450 PENNSYLVANIA AVENUE.
1888.

NORMAL SCHOOL STEAM PRESS,
HAMPTON, VA.

AMERICAN COLONIZATION SOCIETY.

PRESIDENT,
1853. HON. JOHN H. B. LATROBE.

VICE-PRESIDENTS.

1838. Hon. Henry A. Foster, N. Y.
1851. Rev. Robert Ryland, D. D., Ky.
1851. Hon. Frederick P. Stanton, Va.
1859. Hon. Henry M. Schieffelin, N. Y.
1866. Hon. James R. Doolittle, Wisconsin.
1867. Samuel A. Crozer, Esq., Pa.
1870. Robert Arthington, Esq., England.
1872. Harvey Lindsly, M. D., LL. D., D.C.
1874. Rev. Bishop R.S. Foster, D.D., Mass.
1874. Rt. Rev. Gregory T. Bedell, D. D., O.
1875. Rt. Rev. M.A.De W.Howe, D.D., Pa.
1875. Samuel K. Wilson, Esq., N. J.
1876. Rev. Samuel E. Appleton, D. D., Pa.
1876. Rev. H.M. Turner, D.D., LL. D., Ga.
1877. Prest. E. G. Robinson, LL. D., R. I.
1877. Rev. William E. Schenck, D. D., Pa.

1878. Hon. Richard W. Thompson, Ind.
1878. Admiral Robert W. Shufeldt, U. S. N.
1880. Francis T. King, Esq., Maryland.
1880. Rev. Samuel D. Alexander, D.D., N.Y.
1881. Rev. Bishop H.W.Warren, D.D., Col.
1882. Henry G. Marquand, Esq., N. Y.
1884. Rev. George D. Boardman, D.D., Pr.
1884. Rev. Bishop E.G. Andrews, D.D, D.C.
1884. Rev. Edw'd W. Blyden, D.D., Liberia.
1884. Rev. Otis H. Tiffany, D. D., Pa.
1884. Rt. Rev. Henry C. Potter, D.D., N.Y.
1886. Hon. Alexander B. Hagner, D. C.
1887. Hon. Robert S. Green, N. J.
1888. Hon. William Strong, D. C.
1888. Rev. J. Aspinwall Hodge, D. D., Ct.
1888. Arthur M. Burton, Esq., Pa.

The figures before each name indicate the year of first election.

LIFE DIRECTORS.

1852. James Hall, M. D........*Md.*	1870. Daniel Price, Esq.........*N. J.*
1853. Alexander Duncan, Esq.....*R. I.*	1871. Rev. William H. Steele, D.D. *N. J.*
1864. Alexander Guy, M. D......*Ohio.*	1871. R't. Rev. H. C. Potter, D. D..*N. Y.*
1858. Edward Coles, Esq..........*Pa.*	1873. Rev. George W. Samson, D D. *N. Y.*
1869. Rev. Joseph F. Tuttle, D. D..*Ind.*	1878. Rev. Edw'd W. Appleton, D. D., *Pa.*
1869. Charles H. Nichols, M. D....*N. Y.*	1885. William Evans Guy, Esq......*Mo.*

DELEGATES FOR 1888.

Pennsylvania Colonization Society.—Robert B. Davidson, Esq., Rev. William E. Schenck, D. D., Arthur M. Burton, Esq., Gilbert Emley, Esq.

SEVENTY-FIRST ANNUAL REPORT.

The record of the Seventy-First year of THE AMERICAN COLONIZATION SOCIETY is marked by the death of three Vice Presidents.

NECROLOGY.

1. RT. REV. WILLIAM BACON STEVENS, D. D., LL. D., elected in 1874, was of simple manners, sound judgment and so drew to himself the confidence of men by the faithful discharge of duty that leadership was accorded him by those who saw his fine qualities. He was for many years active in the Pennsylvania Auxiliary as a Manager, and at the time of his death its esteemed President. The Society will retain the benefit of his great influence and wise work, while it lifts eyes full of tears for his loss to the home of his glory.

2. REV. JAMES SAUL, D. D., elected in 1885, was conservative in his principles and of strong convictions of duty. He was one of the founders of the Louisiana Colonization Society, and more recently a zealous Vice President of the Pennsylvania Auxiliary. Dr. Saul was especially concerned in religious work among the colored people of the United States, and several institutions for their improvement have enjoyed his benefactions in liberal gifts. He demonstrated the blessedness of living with noble aims and dying in the accomplishment of holy purposes.

3. REV. EDWARD P. HUMPHREY, D, D., LL. D., elected in 1872, was a man of superior endowments and elevation of character, full of sympathy for the helpless and distressed. His devotion to African Colonization gave the Society a claim upon him which he always fully recognized, and his position enabled him to make his friendship for it of practical value. Always ready in suggestion and execution, he was among those upon whom it surely relied, and his place will not be readily filled.

Full of generous sympathies and earnest in his efforts to promote the best welfare of his fellow-beings, BENJAMIN COATES, ESQ., who died at his residence in Philadelphia, Pa., March 7, will long be pleasantly remembered in the wide circles where he had become known. His far-seeing interest in the Republic of Liberia, and his contributions for the promotion of her national life, entitle him to the gratitude not only of Liberians but all friends of Africa.

FINANCES.

The receipts during the year 1887 have been:—

Donations	$1,726 00
Legacies	14,031 00
Emigrants toward cost of passage	433 45
For common schools in Liberia	1,418 40
Interest	1,584 44
Other sources	1,723 14
Receipts	20,916 43
Balance 1st January, 1887	5,832 67
Making available	26,749 10
The disbursements have been	18,499 19
Balance 31st December, 1887	$8,249 91

EMIGRATION.

One hundred and twenty-four persons have been given passage by the bark "Monrovia," from New York, viz.: March 5, (51), for Cape Palmas; July 20, (2), for Brewerville, and December 3, (71), for Cape Mount. Nearly all of these were in families of character, intelligent and industrious, who were influenced to remove to Liberia by information from relatives and friends who had preceded them. One was from New York City; two from Norfolk, Va.; one from New Berne, N. C.; three from Raleigh, N. C.; thirty-seven from Charlotte, N. C.; fifteen from Fort Mill, S. C.; ten from Gainesville, Florida; eight from Helena, Ark.; and forty-seven from Muscogee, Indian Territory. Seventy-one are twelve years old and over; forty-four are between two and twelve, and nine are less than two years of age. Fifty-two were reported as communicants in Evangelical Churches. Of the adult males twenty-five are farmers, two are teachers, and one each a carpenter, painter, blacksmith and shoemaker, and one a licensed minister of the gospel.

A number of Liberians joyfully returned to their homes on each voyage of the "Monrovia;"—prominent among whom may be named, the widow and five children of Ex-President Payne, Prof. Martin H. Freeman, and the wife, daughter and grandchild of the Rev. Dr. Blyden.

Letters from Liberia state "The new arrivals are doing well;" "Those who came by the 'Azor,' and located at Royesville and Burnsville, are succeding admirably;" ",The recent additions to Cape Palmas are mostly contented and happy in their own homes and on their own lands, and are rejoicing in their improved condition and surroundings;" "They are a good class of people and promise to prove adequate to the task of helping to build up the Republic."

An intelligent emigrant writes :---"I thank God we were enabled to reach Cape Palmas December 24th, and were taken ashore the following day. All my company of ninety-seven persons landed in very good health. We are well pleased with our new homes, and if I keep the mind I now have I will never return to America to live. I find everything here just as represented—jacks, hogs, ox carts, &c. We like our ration arrangements also. The lands are rich indeed. Please do all you can to send out emigrants next winter."

Attention is invited to the fact that the last company of emigrants was dispatched to Cape Mount, the northwestern portion of the Republic, a region of which it is said that "there is nothing wanted but men, means, and enterprise, to make it one of the most flourishing commercial ports in Western Africa." The great highway from that part of the coast to the Valley of the Niger, passing through a rich and salubrious country, has its outlet at Cape Mount. It is expected that this company will occupy the fertile lands on the river or on the magnificent lake not far from the settlement.

Constant applications are received from other parts of the Republic for immigrants. It is probable that the Spring expedition will be sent to Sinoe, and that in the Fall to Bassa.

Emigration to Liberia every year under the auspices of the American Colonization Society has been uninterrupted for the past sixty-seven years. Those now reported make the number sent since the civil war to be 4024, and a total from the beginning of 16,022, exclusive of 5722 recaptured Africans which it induced and enabled the Government of the United States to settle in Liberia, making a grand total of 21,744 persons to whom the Society has given homes in Africa.

APPLICATIONS.

The people of color are loud in their appeals for help to reach the land of their fathers. The Society received during the year one hundred and eighteen new applications for passage to Liberia, and a much larger number of appeals from former applicants for aid. All these are purely voluntary and spontaneous.

In many instances the names and ages of applicants for emigra—

tion are furnished, but in the majority of cases a very general statement of numbers is alone given. The following quotations from the letters of recent correspondents, with the names of the places from which they wrote, show that it is not possible to give in figures the number of those seeking the Society's assistance:

Sandifer, N. C., the better class of people; *Wolfsville, N. C.*, a great many; *Valdosta, Geo.*, a colony; *Orlando, Fla.*, thirty-five or forty families; *Gainesville, Fla.*, a company; *Sturgis, Miss.*, many people; *Newton, Miss.*, more than five thousand citizens; *Houston, Texas*, some parties; *Galveston, Texas*, a crowd; *Trinity, Texas*, two or three thousand persons; *Conway, Ark.*, a large number of people; *Van Buren, Ark*, a society; *Memphis, Tenn.*, quite a number; *Chattanooga, Tenn.*, several families; *Makanda, Ill.*, a great many; *Carthage, Mo.*, several colored persons; *Kingman, Kan.*, lots of people; *Niota, Kan.*, twelve men of us and our families; *Muscogee, Indian Territory*, a large number of families.

The desire of the Negroes for emigration to the fatherland is sometimes said to be exaggerated by Colonizationists; but the *South-Western Christian Advocate*, edited by the Rev. Marshall W. Taylor, D. D., lately contained the following: "Shall we go to Africa or not? This is the question as it is not infrequently put to the editor of this paper by men who are ready to go to their fatherland. They want intelligent direction and quiet counsel, such as in most cases colored men are unable to obtain, since among us the most of our public-spirited like to be seen and heard in all they do. But Africa; shall Negroes of this country go there? Let the inferior masses remain here, wards of America, and if they wish to do so, let them drink up the blood of the various nationalities as a solution of the Negro problem. But our professional men, women, and families of characacter and money; let those who can do anything to produce something for his neighbors to consume, apply and carry along every art with the religion of civilization to that country. What, then, shall we go to Africa? Yes, if we are so situated that by going we can do something better for Africa than add to her pauper population."

Among the petitions submitted to Congress during the past session praying for an appropriation of one hundred dollars apiece to enable them to go to Liberia was one, as stated by the Senator who presented it, "from a committee of colored men who say they represent five thousand people."

And there recently appeared in *The Church at Home and Abroad* the following from Rev. H. N. Payne, Field Secretary of the Presbyterian Board for Freedmen: "Much as the colored people are attached to the places where they grow up, thousands of them would gladly go to Arkansas, to Texas, or *to any other place* where they would better their condition; but they cannot raise the money to emigrate, and must stay and suffer where they are."

This is disinterested testimony, put not half as strongly as the facts warrant. The "any other place" is Africa; and if these hapless creatures do not name Africa in the utterance of their tearful longings, it is because thousands do not dream that there is any possibility of ever getting to that Continent.

LIBERIA.

The prospects of Liberia are brightening. Hon. C. T. O. King Mayor of Monrovia, writes as follows:

"*Religious.*—The several denominations are moving on the even tenor of their way. The Liberia Conference of the Methodist Episcopol Church held its annual session in Clay-Ashland, February 3-7, Bishop William Taylor presiding. The statistics are: 21 traveling preachers, 56 local preachers, 2,628 full members, 361 probationers, 23 churches valued at $25,755; 37 Sunday-schools, with 371 officers and teachers, and 2,371 scholars. The collections during the last year were $400 for missions and $1,524 for ministerial support. Bishop Taylor, after inaugurating his great work on the Congo, is now turning his attention to Liberia, with the aim and desire of operating from that Republic as a base to the heart of Nigritia.

"The Baptist Convention reports 31 churches, 23 licensed ministers, and some 2,000 communicants. It has established a mission at Zodakie, eight miles from the nearest American settlement, where it owns five hundred acres of land and two buildings. Here is located the Rick's Institute for the education of native youth, named in honor of Mr. Moses U. Ricks, a well-to-do coffee planter at Clay-Ashland, and a contributor of $500 cash to the school.

"The Episcopalians are in good condition at Cape Palmas, but elsewhere they are not making much progress, owing to the scarcity of clergymen. The value of their efforts among the Greboes has just been demonstrated by the Christian converts during the rebellion at Cavalla, some seventy of whom, with their native rector, Rev. M. P. Valentine, preferred to leave their kindred, homes and property at that place, and start life anew among the American settlers at Cape Palmas, rather than unite with their heathen brethren in resistance to the Government of Liberia.

"THE SCHOOLS of the American Colonization Society at Arthington and Brewerville continue to be patronized by those for whom they are intended, and they are proving a valuable help to the rising generation of those growing settlements. I recommend that the Society establish a primary school at Cape Mount.

"AGRICULTURE, especially in this (Montserrado) county, is in a flourishing state. The coffee crop is large this season —our planters being stimulated to renewed energy by the advance last year in the selling price of the berry abroad. It would astonish and gratify any one to visit the St. Paul's river and see how the heavy forests have been made to give way to substantial buildings and coffee plantations, with rice, vegetables and fruits in their season. Through the thoughtful generosity of Hon. Henry M. Schieffelin in supplying neat wire for fencing, a number of our farmers are increasing their stock of cattle. I saw a few days ago at Brewerville, Mr. Howell Tyler utilizing African oxen in ploughing his land."

JUBILEE.

Eighteen Hundred and Eighty-Seven was a year of Centenaries and Jubilees. The centennial of the signing of the Constitution of the United States was observed, and Queen Victoria celebrated the fiftieth year of her reign. Sierra Leone rejoiced over the centennary of her existence, and the African Methodist Episcopal Church the centennary of its foundation: while President Cleveland of the United States and President Johnson of Liberia celebrated the Jubilee of their birth. It seemed to have been a year providentially appointed for retrospect. To millions it suggested a review of the past. The American and British nations have looked back upon their history, and, in doing so, the history of the whole world passed before them.

The Jubilee of the Secretary of the American Colonization Society suggests a review of the events which have transpired bearing upon the work of African Colonization and Liberia.

When the Secretary, October 17, 1837, became connected with Colonization, the Society was twenty years old. Nearly all the original founders of the Society and of Liberia were living and active. In Africa the colonists had obtained a permanent foothold, having been fifteen years in occupation.

The question of the outlet of the Niger had just been settled by the Landers: but the grand results of modern exploration in Africa had not yet been achieved: therefore, as an officer of a Society whose operations were in A'rica, the Secretary has had the opportunity of watching closely and following with practical interest, the whole series of brilliant explorations witnessed by the present generation. He has seen the large blank spaces which confronted him on the map of Africa in the office in Philadelphia, in 1837, gradually filled up, until now the Continent seems alive with a busy, stirring population, with rivers and lakes, with cities and manufactories, with agriculture and commerce.

In 1837, the Colony of Liberia existed in separate settlements under different administrations, independent of and unconnected with each other, responsible to different organizations in this country: viz: Monrovia and its adjacent settlements were under the American or Parent Society: Bassa Cove and Edina under the Pennsylvania and New York Societies; Cape Palmas under the Maryland State Society, and Sinoe, just established, under the Mississippi Society.

This condition of things threatened to be fruitful of serious evils to the young colonies: and warnings from Africa made a deep impression upon the friends of Colonization generally and especially those responsible for the management of the several Societies. They felt the importance of uniting the settlements under one central Government. Much diversity of opinion prevailed as to the best means of accomplishing the object. Those who preferred united-action in Liberia, finding their views sustained by many of the most talented and experienced of the settlers, and others who had been Agents and Governors of the colonists, proposed a Convention of Delegates from the American Colonization Society, the New York and Pennsylvania Colonization Societies and the Maryland State Colonization Society; which was held in Philadelphia, September, 25, 1838. At the Convention a general form of union was discussed and a Committee was appointed to prepare a plan, to be submitted to the several Societies for their consideration. At the Annual Meeting of the Board of Directors of the American Colonization Society, held in Washington City, January 5, 1839, a Constitution for the United Colonies, under the name and style of the COMMONWEALTH OF LIBERIA was adopted: and Thomas Buchanan Esq , of Philadelphia, Pa., was appointed Governor. Mr. Buchanan had resided about a year in Liberia as Governor of Bassa Cove, where he was beloved by the colonists and respected by the native Kings. It was believed that a more competent man could not be found to preside over the interests of Liberia and carry into operation the provisions of the new Constitution.

Governor Buchanan was the first and last white Governor of the Commonwealth, and the last white man who presided over the affairs of Liberia. He died, after nearly three years of hard labor, September 3, 1841, and was succeeded in the office of Governor by Mr. Joseph Jenkins Roberts, an emigrant from Virginia of twelve years residence in the country. After six years of successful administration of their own affairs, the people, in Convention assembled, July 26, 1847, constituted and declared themselves a "free, sovereign and independent State, by the name and title of the REPUBLIC OF LIBERIA."

Cape Palmas or "Maryland in Liberia"—the colony of the Maryland State Colonization Society—continued its separate existence under the faithful auspices of that Society until 1854, when it became a free and independent nation by the name of the State of Maryland in Liberia. In 1857, the State entered the Republic proper as the County of Maryland in Liberia.

The next events of importance affecting Colonization and Liberia were the emancipation of the slaves in the United States, and the recognition of the Independence of Liberia by the Government of the United States.

January 21, 1864, the Secretary was unanimously elected by the Board of Directors at Washington City to take the place of the Rev. R. R. Gurley as Corresponding Secretary of the American Colonization Society. Mr. Gurley had been relieved from the cares and duties of that office and assigned an honorary relation in connection with the Society. President Warner, Liberia's third President, had just been inaugurated for his first term.

In 1865, a new departure was taken by the Society in sending emigrants to Liberia from beyond the limits of the United States. Three hundred and forty-six persons were sent by the Society from Barbadoes, W. I., to Monrovia:—a step whose wisdom has been abundantly vindicated by the valuable agricultural and other improvements introduced by them into the Republic.

In 1867, the Society celebrated its Semi-Centennial Anniversary. In 1873, by the death of the Rev. William McLain D. D., the offices of Financial Secretary and Treasurer devolved upon the Secretary. In 1874, he was appointed Consul General of the Republic of Liberia for the United States.

The removal of the Secretary from Philadelphia to Washington was coincident with a very important era in the Society's work. The abolition of slavery had produced new conditions in the whole field of its operations in America, and it appeared before the world under a new aspect. It could no longer be charged with the guilt of rendering slavery more secure by deporting the restless and discontented among the slaves. The *raison d' etre* of the Anti-Slavery Society, which had been its professional antagonist and accuser, having ceased, that organization passed away. But when its work was done, the work of the American Colonization Society assumed larger and more serious proportions. As might have been expected, and as was foreseen by the founders of the Society, the coming of liberty to the millions in the South brought the general desire for exodus from the house of bondage. Applications to the Society for passage to Liberia multiplied and continue to multiply. The great mass of the Negro population of America, whatever may be said to the contrary, cling with a restless and irrepressible longing to the land of their fathers. While the learned Negroes hesitate and the colored gentlemen argue, the mass of Africa's descendants are calling for the means of egress from the country of their exile.

But the ability of the Society to answer the earnest calls of the weary exiles diminished, on the arrival of emancipation, in proportion to their number, and the conditions of the Society's work were modified and new methods had to be adopted. The pressure still continues,

In looking back upon the fifty years' work of the Society, the Secretary cannot have one moments' misgivings as to the methods and line of policy pursued. He believes, and has through all his active life believed, in the grandeur and practicability of the Colonization scheme. If he has any—the slightest—cause for regret it will be that, hampered in its financial resources, the Society has not been able to carry out in its operations every detail of its policy—to adhere more closely to the letter and spirit of its fundamental principles.

The Secretary feels that though devoting his energies to the building up of a Christian Nation of Negroes in West Africa, he has been lending a hand, through the only available agency to help forward the regeneration of a Continent and the intellectual and moral progress of a race: and that for Africa, not all the discoveries of the last century have been so important as the founding of THE AMERICAN COLONIZATION SOCIETY.

HON. PETER PARKER, M. D.

Since the foregoing was prepared, the Society has been called to sorrow over the departure from earth of the senior member of the Executive Committee. That body, at a special meeting held January 12, 1888, adopted the following minute:—

"*Resolved*, That the Executive Committee hereby record their deep sense of the loss they have sustained in the death of their late beloved associate, HON. PETER PARKER, M. D. They recall with gratitude and admiration his twenty-eight years faithful service in the cause of African Colonization, his unwearied diligence, his unvarying courtesy, his wise counsels, and the gentle suavity of tone and manner which so truly indicated the Christian kindness and sympathy of his heart.

Resolved, That in heartfelt sympthy the foregoing be communicated to the bereaved widow and son of our venerated friend."

TREASURER'S REPORT.

Dr. *Receipts and Disbursements of the* AMERICAN COLONIZATION SOCIETY *in the year 1887.* Cr.

Received Donations,	$1,726 00	
" Legacies,	14,031 00	
" Emigrants toward passage,	433 45	
" Subscriptions to African Repository,	24 25	
" Rent of Colonization Building,	1,697 00	
" For Education in Liberia,	1,418 40	
" Interest on temporary investments,	1,584 44	
" Investment realized	1 89	
Receipts,	$20,916 43	
Balance January 1, 1887	5,832 67	
Total,	$26,749 10	

Paid Passage and settlement of Emigrants		$12,543 15
" Education in Liberia,		668 40
" Taxes, insurance and repairs of Colonization Building,		558 57
" Paper and printing the African Repository,		359 46
" Salary of Secretary and Treasurer, office expenses, printing, postage, expense of meetings, and cost of contested Wills,		2,969 61
" Temporary Investments		1,400 00
Disbursements,		$18,479 19
Balance December 31, 1887.		8,249 91
Total,		$26,749 10

The Committee on Accounts have examined the Treasurer's Account for the year 1887, and the vouchers for the expenditures, and find the same correct.

REGINALD FENDALL,
ROBERT B. DAVIDSON, } *Committee.*
WILLIAM E. SCHENCK.

Washington, D. C., *January 17, 1888.*

MINUTES OF THE SOCIETY.

WASHINGTON, D. C., *January* 15, 1888.

THE AMERICAN COLONIZATION SOCIETY celebrated its Seventy-First Anniversary in the New York Avenue Presbyterian Church, Washington, D. C., on Sunday evening, January 15, 1888.

The services were conducted by Rev. W. A. Bartlett, D. D., pastor of the church, who also presented the Seventy-First Annual Report of the Society, stating that a printed abstract of the Report had been distributed in the pews.

The Annual Discourse was delivered by Rev. J. Aspinwall Hodge, D. D., of Hartford, Conn., on the text, Psalm 67, 4 : " Oh, let the nations be glad and sing for joy, for Thou shall judge the people righteously and govern the nations upon earth."

The benediction was pronounced by Rev. Dr. Hodge.

COLONIZATION ROOMS, *January* 17, 1888.

The Annual Meeting of THE AMERICAN COLONIZATION SOCIETY was held to-day at 3 o'clock P.M., in the rooms of the Society.

In the absence of the President, Rev. William. E. Scheck, D. D., senior Vice-President in attendance, presided.

The Minutes of the Anniversary meeting on the 15th inst. were read, and with the Minutes of the Annual Meeting of January 18, 1887, were approved.

Rev. Dr. Thomas G. Addison and Dr. William W. Godding were appointed a Committee to nominate the President and Vice-Presidents for the ensuing year.

On motion of Hon. Charles C. Nott, it was

Resolved, That the Society gratefully acknowledges the able, eloquent and fearless presentation of the cause of African Colonization by the Rev. J. Aspinwall Hodge, D. D., in his address before the Society in the city of Washington on its Seventy-First Anniversary; and that a copy of the Address be requested for publication.

Resolved, That the thanks of the Society be tendered to the Pastor, Trustees, and Congregation of the New York Avenue Presbyterian Church in the city of Washington, for the use of that church on the occasion of the Seventy-First Anniversary of the Society.

Rev. Dr. Addison, Chairman of the Committee on Nominations read a report, recommending the re-election of the present President and Vice-Presidents, and the election of Hon. William, Strong of the District of Columbia, Rev. J. Aspinwall Hodge, D. D., of Connecticut, and Arthur M. Burton, Esq., of Pennsylvania, as additional Vice-Presidents, as follows:

PRESIDENT,

1853. HON. JOHN H. B. LATROBE.

VICE-PRESIDENTS.

1838. Hon. Henry A. Foster, N. Y.
1851. Rev. Robert Ryland, D. D., Ky.
1851. Hon. Frederick P Stanton, Va.
1859. Hon. Henry M. Schieffelin, N. Y.
1866. Hon. James R. Doolittle, Wisconsin.
1867. Samuel A. Crozer, Esq., Pa.
1870. Robert Arthington, Esq., England.
1872. Harvey Lindsly, M. D., LL. D., D.C.
1874. Rev. Bishop R.S. Foster, D.D., Mass.
1874. Rt. Rev. Gregory T. Bedell, D. D., O.
1875. Rt. Rev. M. A. De W. Howe, D.D., Pa.
1875. Samuel K. Wilson, Esq., N. J.
1876. Rev. Samuel E. Appleton, D. D., Pa.
1876. Rev. H. M. Turner, D.D., LL. D., Ga.
1877. Prest. E. G. Robinson, LL. D., R. I
1877. Rev. William E. Schenck, D. D., Pa.

1878. Hon. Richard W. Thompson, Ind.
1878. Admiral Robert W. Shufeldt, U. S. N.
1880. Francis T. King, Esq., Maryland.
1880. Rev. Samuel D. Alexander, D.D., N.Y.
1881. Rev. Bishop H. W. Warren, D.D., Col.
1882. Henry G. Marquand, Esq., N. Y.
1884. Rev. George D. Boardman, D.D., Pa.
1884. Rev. Bishop E. G. Andrews, D.D., D.C.
1884. Rev. Edw'd W. Blyden, D.D., Liberia.
1884. Rev. Otis H. Tiffany, D. D., Pa.
1884. Rt. Rev. Henry C. Potter, D.D., N.Y.
1886. Hon. Alexander B. Hagner, D. C.
1887. Hon. Robert S. Green, N. J.
1888. Hon. William Strong, D. C.
1888. Rev. J. Aspinwall Hodge, D. D., Ct.
1888. Arthur M. Burton, Esq., Pa.

The figure before each name indicate the year of first election.

Whereupon, on motion, it was

Resolved, That the Report be accepted and approved, and that the Society elect the officers nominated by the Committee.

On motion, Adjourned.

WM. COPPINGER, *Secretary*.

MINUTES OF THE BOARD OF DIRECTORS.

WASHINGTON, D. C., *January* 17, 1888.

THE BOARD OF DIRECTORS OF THE AMERICAN COLONIZATION SOCIETY met this day at 12 o'clock M. in the rooms of the Society, No. 450 Pennsylvania Avenue, N. W., Washington, D. C.

In the absence of Hon. John H. B. Latrobe, President of the Society, Dr. Charles H. Nichols was chosen to preside.

Prayer was offered by Rev. Thomas G. Addison, D. D.

Mr. William Coppinger was appointed Secretary of the Board.

The unprinted portions of the minutes of the last meeting, January 18 and 19, 1887, were read, and the minutes were approved.

Rev. Dr. Schenck and Messrs. Davidson and Emley were appointed a Committee on Credentials; and they retired and subsequently reported through their Chairman, the following named Delegates appointed for the year 1888:

PENNSYLVANIA COLONIZATION SOCIETY.—Robert B. Davidson, Esq., Rev. William E. Schenck, D. D., Arthur M. Burton, Esq., Gilbert Emley, Esq.

The following DIRECTORS were stated to be in attendance:

DIRECTORS FOR LIFE.—Dr. Charles H. Nichols, Right Rev. Henry C. Potter, D. D.

EXECUTIVE COMMITTEE.—Hon. Charles C. Nott, Reginald Fendall, Esq., Rev. Thomas G. Addison, D. D., Rev. Byron Sunderland, D. D., Dr. William W. Godding.

Whereupon, on motion, it was

Resolved, That the Report of the Committee on Credentials be accepted and approved, and the gentlemen named be received as members of the Board.

The Secretary presented and read the Seventy-First Annual Report of the American Colonization Society.

Whereupon, on motion, it was

Resolved, That the Annual Report be approved, and referred to the Standing Committees according to its several topics.

The Secretary presented and read the Statement of the Executive Committee for the past year and accompanying papers. Also a list of property of the Society, and a Statement of receipts by States in the year 1887.

The Treasurer presented and read his Annual Report of receipts and disbursements, with the certificate of audit.

Whereupon, on motion, it was

Resolved, That the Statement of the Executive Committee and the Treasurer's Report for the year 1887, with the accompanying Annual and other papers, be accepted, and that so much of them as relate to Foreign Relations, Finance, Auxiliary Societies, Agencies, Accounts, Emigration, and Education, be referred to the several Standing Committees in charge of those subjects respectively.

The Chairman appointed the STANDING COMMITTEES, as follows:

COMMITTEE ON FOREIGN RELATIONS AND ON EDUCATION.—Hon. Charles C. Nott, Right Rev. Henry C. Potter, D. D., Robert B Davidson, Esq.

COMMITTEE ON FINANCE AND ON ACCOUNTS.—Reginald Fendall, Esq , Robert B. Davidson, Esq , Rev. William E. Schenck, D. D.

COMMITTEE ON AUXILIARY SOCIETIES AND ON AGENCIES.—Rev. Thomas G. Addison, D. D., Rev. Byron Sunderland, D. D., Gilbert Emley, Esq.

COMMITTEE ON EMIGRATION.—Arthur M. Burton, Esq.; Rev. William E. Schenck, D. D., Dr. William W. Godding.

On motion of Mr. Emley, it was

Resolved, That a Committee be appointed to nominate the Executive Committee and the Secretary and Treasurer for the ensuing year.

Mr. Emley, Judge Nott, and Rev. Dr. Schenck, were appointed the Committee.

Letters were read from the following named Directors presenting excuse for absence: Rev. G. W. Samson, D. D., January 10; Rev. Edward W. Appleton, D. D., January 11; Rev. William H. Steele, D. D., January 13; and Dr. James Hall, January 14; and from Hon. John H. B. Latrobe, President, January 20.

On motion it was

Resolved, That the Board do now adjourn to meet in these rooms at 10 o'clock to-morrow morning.

Adjourned.

WASHINGTON, D. C., *January* 18, 1888.

THE BOARD OF DIRECTORS met this morning at 10 o'clock in the rooms of the Society, Dr. Nichols in the chair.

Prayer was offered by Rev. Dr. Schenck.

The minutes of yesterday's meeting were read and approved.

Judge Nott, Chairman of the Standing Committee on Foreign Relations and on Education, reported that no business had been referred to them calling for a report.

Whereupon, on motion, it was

Resolved, that the report be accepted and approved.

Mr. Davidson, from the Standing Committee on Finance and on Accounts, presented the following reports; which were read, and on motion they were accepted and approved:

The Standing Committee on Finance respectfully report, that they have examined the Securities of the Society and find them correctly stated, and in the possession of the Treasurer.

The Standing Committee on Accounts have examined the Treasurer's Account for the year 1887, and the vouchers for the expenditures, and find the same correct.

Rev. Dr. Addison, Chairman of the Standing Committee on Auxiliary Societies and on Agencies, read the following as their report; and it was, on motion, accepted and the resolution was adopted:

WHEREAS, The Board of Directors have again and again passed resolutions favorable to the establishment of Auxiliary Societies in the different States, and to the employment of Agents to make known the objects of the Society and collect funds for its work. Be it

Resolved, That the Executive Committee be urgently requested to carry out, wherever expedient or practicable, the policy so often and emphatically endorsed by this Body:

Dr. Godding, from the Standing Committee on Emigration, read the following report; and it was, on motion, accepted and approved:

The awakened interest throughout Christendom in the development of the Continent of Africa, the large number of applicants for aid to emigrate thither, and the present financial resources of the Society would seem to justify the expectation that the present year would witness the embarkation of a goodly number of colonists under the auspices of the American Colonization Society, to aid in the great work of Christianizing and civilizing Africa.

This is pre-eminently the work for which the Society was organized, and believing that it is also the Master's work, and that under Providence emigration has in all ages been a highly important means whereby the civilization of the world has been developed and extended, your Committee offer the following suggestions as pertinent to the subject.

Since these emigrants go to make themselves a country and a home on the virgin soil of a new world, to aid in creating communities in what relatively speaking is still the wilderness, to bring schools to barbarism, to plant the cross among the idols of paganism and the tents of Islam, to help maintain the institutions of a free government among a people apparently needing to be taught the first principles of finance and political economy; and since the number of persons who can receive aid to emigrate at the hands of this Society is necessarily limited, we respectfully submit for the consideration of the Executive Committee, whether in selecting persons who are to be aided in emigrating by the funds of the Society, preference should not be given to Christian young men and women of African blood who are in the full vigor of life, and who by their education and talents would be capable of organizing here in America a community of their own with the churches, schools and industries necessary to its successful maintenance and growth.

That they further consider whether it would not be well in each company sent out, that some organization should be attempted so that each band should go equipped as a distinct colony with its artizans, its agriculturists, its teachers and its ministers of Christ, electing its officers and making to itself a community of interests, with the laws and regulations governing that community. Might not such a company, properly officered with men of the right stamp, landing on a new shore, be capable, like the Mayflower of old, of founding there an empire for itself?

Mr. Emley, Chairman of the Special Committee on Nominations read a report, recommending the election of the following officers:

SECRETARY AND TREASURER.—William Coppinger, Esq.

EXECUTVE COMMITTEE.—Hon. Charles C. Nott, Reginald Fendall, Esq., Rev. Thomas G. Addison, D. D., Rev. Byron Sunderland, D. D., Justice William Strong, Dr. William W. Godding, and Rev. Adoniram J. Huntington, D. D.

Whereupon, on motion, it was

Resolved, That the report be accepted and approved, and that the Board elect the officers nominated by the Committee.

On motion, it was

Resolved, That the Annual Report of the Society be referred to the Executive Committee for publication.

On motion it was

Resolved, That the Board greatly miss the presence and counsels of its honored President on this occasion, and tender to him our hearty good wishes for continued health and usefulness.

Rev. Dr. Addison offered prayer, and the Board, on motion, adjourned.

WM. COPPINGER, *Secretary.*

SEVENTY-SECOND

ANNUAL REPORT

OF THE

AMERICAN COLONIZATION SOCIETY,

WITH THE

MINUTES

OF THE

ANNUAL MEETING and of the BOARD OF DIRECTORS,

JANUARY 13, 15 & 16, 1889.

———:o:———

WASHINGTON CITY:
COLONIZATION BUILDING, 450 PENNSYLVANIA AVENUE,
1889.

AMERICAN COLONIZATION SOCIETY.

PRESIDENT.
1853. HON. JOHN H. B. LATROBE.

VICE-PRESIDENTS.

1838. Hon. Henry A. Foster, N. Y.	1878. Hon. Richard W. Thompson, Ind.
1851. Rev. Robert Ryland, D. D., Ky.	1878. Admiral Robert W. Shufeldt, U. S. N.
1851. Hon. Frederick P. Stanton, Va.	1880. Francis T. King, Esq , Maryland.
1859. Hon. Henry M. Schieffelin, N. Y.	1880. Rev. Samuel D. Alexander, D.D., N.Y.
1866. Hon. James R. Doolittle, Wis.	1881. Rev. Bishop H. W. Warren, D.D., Col.
1867. Samuel A. Crozer, Esq., Pa.	1882. Henry G. Marquand, Esq., N. Y.
1870. Robert Arthington, Esq., England.	1884. Rev. George D. Boardman, D.D., Pa.
1872. Harvey Lindsly, M. D., LL. D., D.C.	1884. Rev. Bishop E.G. Andrews, D.D., N.Y.
1874. Rev. Bishop R.S. Foster, D.D., Mass.	1884. Rev. Edw'd W. Blyden, D.D., Liberia.
1874. Rt. Rev. Gregory T. Bedell, D.D., O.	1884. Rev. Otis H. Tiffany, D. D., Pa.
1875. Rt. Rev. M.A. DeW. Howe, D.D., Pa.	1884. Rt. Rev. Henry C. Potter, D.D., N.Y.
1875. Samuel K. Wilson, Esq., N. J.	1886. Hon. Alexander B. Hagner, D. C.
1876 Rev. Samuel E. Appleton, D.D., Pa.	1887. Hon. Robert S. Green, N. J.
1876. Rev. H.M. Turner, D.D., LL. D., Ga.	1868. Hon. William Strong, D. C.
1877. Prest. E. G. Robinson, LL. D., R. I.	1888. Rev. J. Aspinwall Hodge, D. D., Ct.
1877. Rev. William E. Schenck, D. D., Pa.	1888. Arthur M. Burton, Esq., Pa.

The figures before each name indicate the year of first election.

LIFE DIRECTORS.

1852. JAMES HALL, M. D.............Md.	1870. DANIEL PRICE, Esq..............N. J.
1853. ALEXANDER DUNCAN, Esq........R. I.	1871. Rev. WILLIAM H. STEELE, D. D. N. J.
1864. ALEXANDER GUY, M. D.........Ohio.	1871. R'T. Rev. H. C. POTTER, D. D....N. Y.
1868. EDWARD COLES, Esq..........Pa.	1873. Rev. GEORGE W. SAMSON, D. D. N. Y.
1869. REV. JOSEPH F. TUTTLE, D. D...Ind.	1878. Rev. EDWARD W. APPLETON, D. D., Pa.
1869. CHARLES H. NICHOLS, M. D....N. Y.	1785. WILLIAM EVANS GUY, Esq.,..... Mo.

DELEGATES FOR 1889.

PENNSYLVANIA COLONIZATION SOCIETY.--Arthur M. Burton, Esq., Robert B. Davidson, Esq., Rev. Alfred S. Elwyn, John Welsh Dulles, Esq.

SEVENTY-SECOND ANNUAL REPORT.

In opening the Seventy-Second Annual Report of THE AMERICAN COLONIZATION SOCIETY, it is pleasant to record that no vacancy occurred by death among the Vice-Presidents, Directors and other officers during the past year.

RECEIPTS AND DISBURSEMENTS.

There has been received during the past year $6,176.05. Of this amount $929.00 came from donations; $1,304.34 from legacies; $239.75 from applicants toward cost of passage; $418.40 for the support of common schools in Liberia; $1,599.56 from interest, and $1,685.00 from other sources. These amounts, with the balance in the treasury at the beginning of the year, $10,749.91, have placed at the disposal of the Society $16,925.96. The expenditures of the year have amounted to $13,007.60, leaving a balance in the treasury of $3,918.36.

There has also been received during the year a bequest by Mr. John West Mason, late of Newark, Illinois, of $1,000, "to be invested with or without additions until the income thence arising shall be suffient to meet the expenses of a pious young man of color, while being educated to preach the Gospel among the heathen of Africa; said income to bear the name of Theodore Lewis Mason, M. D." The principal has been accordingly invested and additions are invited.

EMIGRATION.

During the past year thirty-nine emigrants were sent by the bark "Monrovia," sailed from New York, June 2, for Sinoe, and fifteen by the same vessel, sailed from New York, November 3, for Monrovia. Of these six were from Boston, Mass.; one from Washington, D. C.; one from Afton, Va.; nineteen from Gainesville, Florida; eight from Rochelle, Florida; one from Ocala, Florida; nine from Sturgis, Miss.: one from Chicago, Ill.; and eight from Wyandotte, Kansas. Thirty are twelve years of age and over, seventeen are between twelve and two, and seven are less than two years old. Twelve were reported as communicants in the Baptist Church, six in the Methodist Church, and one in the Episcopal Church. Of the adults one is an ordained minister of the Gospel, one each a teacher, physician, and machinist, two are carpenters and eight are farmers.

They are an industrious and self-reliant class of people, mostly, influenced to remove by information received direct from acquaintances in Liberia. A liberal supply of stores and tools, and books and stationery accompanied them to aid their settlement and for the support of the schools of the Society in that Republic.

Several causes prevented the embarkation of more of the accepted applicants by the spring expedition; and the visitation of yellow fever and the danger of its introduction on the ship or in Liberia seemed to make it wise not to send people from the South during its prevalence. This malignant scourge having psssed away the Society is arranging and expects to dispatch larger parties of people during the coming spring and autumn.

Emigration to Liberia every year under the auspices of the American Colonization Society has been uninterrupted for the past sixty-eight years. Those now reported make the number sent since the civil war to be 4,078, and a total from the beginning of 16,076, exclusive of 5,722 recaptured Africans which it induced and enabled the Government of the United States to settle in Liberia, making a grand total of 21,798 persons to whom the Society has given homes in Africa.

Some of the emigrants lately sent to Cape Palmas have removed to and settled at Arthington and elsewhere on the St. Paul's river; most of those landed January 23d, at Cape Mount, have taken possession of their own houses and are reaping crops raised on their own lands, and commendable progress has been made by the company that reached Sinoe, July 19.

An intelligent Liberian wrote, September 11 : " I was glad to find that the stoppage of immigrants to Brewerville has had no other effect than to stimulate the settlers. They are now farming in earnest. Their coffee plantations are making large and permanent inroads into the forest. Bissell, Banks, William Hayes, Batese, Lucas, are among the enterprising ones who are pushing forward the interests of the settlement, with an unwavering belief that the country is theirs, and that they belong to the country."

APPLICATIONS.

The cry of thousands anxious to find a home in the ancestral land not only continues but to grow in volume and earnestness. During the past year the Society received a greatly increased number of applications for aid, and also several hundred renewed appeals for passage and settlement in Liberia.

As to numbers and the reasons assigned for emigration, the following extracts from late communications will speak:

Society Hill, S. C. " Is there any provision made for assisting the colored people of the United States in returning to their old home—Africa? I am a minister of the Gospel, a man of family, and I intend to leave America. A thousand or more persons wish to start with me if they can get passage. My people are convinced that this is a white man's country, and they want to go home. Will you help us?"

Palm Beach, Florida. " I desire to know what are the sawable timbers of Liberia as I desire to take with me a mill and fixtures for sawing timber. One hundred and thirty six good families want to go with me. They comprise men of all trades, including experienced farmers. Our object is to form a settlement of our own, and thus lead to success in Liberia."

Greenville, Miss. " A society of thirty members wanting to go to a country of our own."

New Orleans, La. " Six hundred very anxious to go to Liberia."

Foster, Texas. " Two thousand families preparing for Africa."

Magnolia, Ark. " Three thousand persons want passage."

Great Bend, Kansas. " Two hundred families getting ready, a few of whom are able to pay part of their expenses on the ship."

Goldsboro, N. C. " I am greatly interested in the redemption of Africa, because, first, it is my fatherland, and second, the labors of the American Negro are greatly needed there. I pray God that He may continue to bless abundantly the work of the American Colonization Society."

LIBERIA.

Sir Samuel Rowe, K. C. C. G., Governor of Sierra Leone and British Consul for Liberia, arrived at Monrovia, April 26, and on the following day, at the Executive Mansion, an exchange took place of the ratification of the Convention entered into at Sierra Leone, Nov. 5, 1885, for the settlement of the Liberian North-West boundary. Thus a question which had long stood in abeyance was practically and pleasantly brought to an end. It is stated that "Governor Rowe expressed himself as most agreeably surprised at what he saw at Monrovia, and in one of his speeches he declared that Liberia was a fixed fact, and he based that assertion, he said, on the evidences of progress and civilization he beheld on every hand. He made a visit to the Kroo village, now occupied by about two thousand Kroomen, and in a short address to them, congratulated them on their loyalty to the Liberian Government, and assured them of the friendly relations subsisting between her Majesty's Government and the Republic."

Bishop William Taylor thus represented the state of his work in Liberia and the condition of that Republic, in his Quadrennial report to the late General Conference of the Methodist Episcopal Church, viz.: "The Liberian Conference received me with great cordiality, and the members have ever since, without exception, manifested a loving, filial spirit of co-operation in the work of God. I have presided at each of the four sessions of the quadrennium, and have visited a majority of circuits and stations. The productive interests of Liberia are fairly prosperous. Within ten miles of Monrovia, up the St. Paul's river, there are ten steam sugar-cane crushing mills, and during the past year more than six hundred thousand pounds of coffee have been exported from Monrovia; but the great depreciation of African product values in European markets for several years past, caused hard times on all the West and South-West coast of that Continent. The Liberians live pretty comfortably and dress well on Sunday, but as a rule have no spare change for church and school purposes."

The Liberian correspondent of the *Weekly News* of Sierra Leone says: "The twenty-sixth of July, the anniversary of Liberia's independence, was celebrated at Monrovia in usual style. The oration was delivered by Arthur Barclay, Esq. It advocated the speedy incorporation of the Aborigines into the body, social and political, and was well received. Kroomen from the Kroo coast are settling in large numbers at Monrovia and near the neighboring rivers, engaging in trade and agriculture. Some of them at Monrovia show considerable enterprise. They are building substantial houses, importing goods from Europe and pushing trade with the interior. Under the guidance and stimulus of the colonists from America they are taking their place among the civilized agencies and giving a permanence and force to the work of civilization. The idea of a railway to the interior from the coast is much favored here, and it is hoped that the enterprise at Sierra Leone will be so completely successful as to encourage a similar effort from this point."

From an account in the *News* of Sierra Leone of a trip up the St. Paul's river, the following two paragraphs are taken: "The morning of the 18th of June the weather was excedingly inclement, and it continued to pour until 1 P. M. At 3 the party resumed their journey up the river. Passing by several coffee and sugar farms, among which were those of Hon. R. H. Jackson, Messrs. Cooper & Son, and Mr. Jesse Sharp, they reached the plantation of Mr. M. T. De Coursey about

4, where they were received with courtesy and cordiality by the intelligent and enterprising host and amiable hostess. After a few minutes' rest the company, led by the energetic proprietor, went out to inspect the agricultural operations. The sugar mill was visited, where, although they were not at work that day, Mr. De Coursey showed the engine and explained the various processes by which sugar is made. A walk through the farm revealed extensive areas covered with sugar-cane, coffee and cocoa. Mr. De Coursey has erected a substantial brick chapel for the religious instruction of his hands, who are all aborigines. The building is constructed entirely of native material. The brick was made on the bank of the river and the timber taken from the neighboring forest. The benches are solid and neat. The building is thoroughly furnished and plastered, and the wooden portions painted. Every other Sunday a clergyman of the P. Episcopal Church visits the farm to hold regular service. On alternate Sundays, Sunday-school is held.*

"Arthington is about thirty miles from the sea. The money, £1,000 sterling, for founding it was given to the American Colonization Society by Mr. Robert Arthington, of Leeds, England. The first emigrants from America arrived there in December, 1869, and begun their labors in a dense forest. They now have a large town of substantial frame houses, extensive coffee farms, fine roads and bridges, and are extending their settlement toward the interior. In the family of every settler are several aborigines, who work in the farms and workshops together. In this way the natives learn the language and industries of the settlers. I noticed in all these places that no broken English is spoken. As the natives come from the interior they learn the language at once and speak it like the settlers. The visitor to these settlements and farms must be impressed with the fact that this is the most effective way of civilizing and Christianizing Africa: teaching the people to work and to supply their necessities and improve their country according to civilized methods. Liberia is making a greater impression upon Africa than at first might be supposed."

EDUCATION

The Society's schools, including the Benjamin Coates School opened in January at Cape Mount, are reported to be growing in numbers and the pupils to be making commendable progress in scholarship.

---

* Mr. De Coursey went from Baltimore to Liberia under the auspices of the American Colonization Society, by the bark Liberia Packet, sailed July 20, 1851.

At a late meeting at Boston of the Trustees of Donations for Education in Liberia, the election of Prof. Martin H. Freeman as President of Liberia College was confirmed. The new President spent twelve years as a teacher in Avery Institute, Allegheny, Penna., immediately preceding his removal to Liberia in 1864, since which he has been connected with the College at Monrovia. At the last report there were eight students in the College and twenty-six in the Preparatory Department.

THE OUTLOOK.

The great Powers of Europe are vieing with each other and bringing into use diplomacy, money, agencies, and even armies and navies for commercial enterprise and colonial establishments in Africa. The United States has permanently founded, after some seventy years of philanthropic endeavor, the Republic of Liberia, possessing the attributes of a free and independent nation. But it should be distinctly noted that while European emigrants cannot live and flourish in the African torrid zone, the United States holds a commanding position in having several millions of Negroes adapted to those regions, of whom half a million are now seemingly desirous to remove to the congenial soil, climate and race of their ancestors.

Liberia has been appropriately termed the "open door" through which to commercialize, civilize, colonize and Christianize the equatorial portions of the "Dark Continent." Soudan, to the east, is represented to possess a population of fifty millions, having cities of from 10,000 to 100,000 inhabitants, living after a peaceful and somewhat industrial style, the soil productive and rich in natural values, and the climate stimulative to luxuriant growths. To open up this region, there is needed direct communication by steamships from this country for the carriage of Negro emigrants, and a railroad from Liberia to the Niger and Congo valleys, the latter to ultimately cross the Continent to the Nile and the Red Sea. It is suggested that nowhere could capital be better employed to secure an abundant market for the constantly increasing products and manufactures of America, than in penetrating this rich portion of Africa.

The American Colonization Society places the Negro in his own country to carve out his own way for himself, for his descendants and for his race. Liberia has thus far proved herself able to open the way not only for individuals, but for communities of Africans along five hundred miles of coast. In this she stands in interesting contrast to every other agency for Africa's upbuilding. She is furnishing the natural elements—an industrial civilization with its farms and workshops and schools and churches—its bustle and activity and affluence;

and has, to-day, under its transforming influence, hundreds and thousands of native Africans, who are becoming unconsciously, with no sudden shock to their prejudices or preconceived notions, the objects and promoters of Western ideas—of a social and political condition, which is sending out on the right and the left, the leaders of regeneration and reconstruction.

The American Colonization Society appeals for support in its work to Americans. The relations of this country to Africa stand upon a somewhat different basis from its relations to India, China, or Japan. Americans are debtors to the African Continent in a more practical sense than to the Asiatic, and God has given them abundant means for discharging the debt.

TREASURER'S REPORT.

DR. *Receipts and Disbursements of the* AMERICAN COLONIZATION SOCIETY *in the year* 1888. **CR.**

Received Donations,	$929 00	Paid Passage and settlement of Emigrants	$8,201 21
" Legacies,	1,304 34	" Education in Liberia,	1,068 40
" Emigrants toward passage,	239 75	" Taxes and repairs of Colonization Building,	518 60
" Subscriptions to African Repository	24 00	" Paper and printing the African Repository,	377 44
" Rent of Colonization Building,	1,661 00	" Salary of Secretary and Treasurer, office expenses, printing, postage, expense of meetings, and cost of contested Will,	2,441 95
" For Education in Liberia,	418 40	" Temporary Investment	400 00
" Interest on temporary investments,	1,599 56		
Receipts,	$6,176 05	Disbursements,	$13,007 60
Balance January 1, 1888	10,749 91	Balance December 31, 1888,	3,918 36
Total,	$16,925 96	Total,	$16,925 96

The Committee on Accounts have examined the Treasurer's Account for the year 1888 and the vouchers for the expenditures, and find the same correct.

JOHN WELSH DULLES,
ROBERT B. DAVIDSON, } *Committee.*
REGINALD FENDALL,

Washington, D. C., *January* 16, 1889.

MINUTES OF THE AMERICAN COLONIZATION SOCIETY.

Washington, D. C, January 13, 1889.

The American Colonization Society held its Seventy-Second Anniversary this evening in the First Baptist Church, 13th Street near G.

Services were conducted by Rev. Charles A. Stakely, pastor of the Church, who also presented the Seventy-Second Annual Report of the Society, stating that an abstract of the same had been printed and placed in the pews,

The Annual Discourse was delivered by Rev. R. M. Luther, D.D., of Philadelphia, Pa., text: Isaiah 24: 12; "Lord, Thou wilt ordain peace for us, for Thou hast wrought all our work in us."

The benediction was pronounced by Rev. Dr. Luther.

Colonization Rooms, January 15, 1889.

The Annual Meeting of The American Colonization Society was held to-day at 3 o'clock p, m., in the rooms of the Society.

In the absence of the President, Arthur M. Burton, Esq., of Philadelphia, Pa., a Vice President, presided.

The Minutes of the anniversary meeting on the 13th inst, were read, and with the Minutes of the annual meeting, January 17, 1888, were approved.

John Welsh Dulles, Esq., and Rev. Alfred L. Elwyn, were appointed a committee to nominate officers for the ensuing year: and they reported, recommending the re-election of the present President and Vice Presidents, as follows:—

PRESIDENT.
1853. HON. JOHN H. B. LATROBE

VICE-PRESIDENTS.

1838. Hon. Henry A. Foster, N. Y.	1878. Hon. Richard W. Thompson, Ind.
1851. Rev. Robert Ryland, D. D., Ky.	1878. Admiral Robert W. Shufeldt, U. S. N.
1851. Hon. Frederick P. Stanton, Va.	1880. Francis T. King, Esq , Maryland.
1859. Hon. Henry M. Schieffelin, N. Y.	1880. Rev. Samuel D. Alexander,D.D.,N.Y.
1866. Hon. James R. Doolittle, Wis.	1881. Rev. Bishop H.W.Warren, D.D., Col.
1867. Samuel A. Crozer, Esq., Pa.	1882. Henry G. Marquand, Esq., N. Y.
1870. Robert Arthington, Esq., England.	1884. Rev. George D. Boardman, D.D., Pa.
1872. Harvey Lindsly, M. D., LL. D., D.C.	1884. Rev. Bishop E.G.Andrews,D.D.,N.Y.
1874. Rev. Bishop R.S. Foster, D.D., Mass.	1884. Rev. Edw'd W.Blyden,D.D., Liberia.
1874. Rt. Rev. Gregory T. Bedell, D.D.,O.	1884. Rev. Otis H. Tiffany, D. D., Pa.
1875. Rt. Rev. M.A. DeW. Howe,D.D., Pa.	1884. Rt. Rev.Henry C.Potter, D.D.,N.Y.
1875. Samuel K. Wilson, Esq., N. J.	1886. Hon. Alexander B. Hagner, D. C.
1876. Rev. Samuel E. Appleton, D.D., Pa.	1887. Hon. Robert S. Green, N. J.
1876. Rev. H.M. Turner, D.D., LL. D.,Ga.	1888. Hon. William Strong, D. C.
1877. Prest. E. G. Robinson, LL. D., R. I.	1888. Rev. J. Aspinwall Hodge, D. D., Ct.
1877. Rev. William E. Schenck, D. D., Pa.	1888. Arthur M. Burton, Esq., Pa.

The figures before each name indicate the year of first election

Whereupon it was

Resolved, That the Report be accepted and approved, and that the Society elect the officers nominated by the Committee.

On motion,

Resolved, That the Society tenders its warmest thanks to Rev. Robert M. Luther, D. D., for his able, opportune and excellent Discourse before the Society on its Seventy-Second Anniversary, and that a copy of the same is hereby requested for publication.

Resolved, That the thanks of the Society is tendered to the Pastor, Deacons and Trustees of the First Baptist Church in the city of Washington, for opening their Church on the occasion of our Seventy-Second Anniversary.

On motion, adjourned.

WM. COPPINGER,
Secretary.

MINUTES OF THE BOARD OF DIRECTORS.

WASHINGTON, D. C., *January* 15, 1889.

THE BOARD OF DIRECTORS OF THE AMERICAN COLONIZATION SOCIETY met this day at 12 o'clock M. in the rooms of the Society, No. 450 Pennsylvania Avenue, N. W.

In the absence of Hon. John H. B. Latrobe, President of the Society, Dr. Charles H. Nichols was, on motion, invited to preside.

Prayer was offered by Rev. R. M. Luther, D. D.

Mr. William Coppinger was, on motion, appointed Secretary of the Board.

The unprinted portions of the Minutes of the last meeting, January 17 and 18, 1888, were read, and the Minutes were approved.

On motion,

Resolved, That Rev. John Miller, of Princeton, N. J., and Rev. R. M. Luther, D. D., of Philadelphia, Pa., are hereby invited to seats in the Board and to participate in its deliberations.

Dr. Godding, Mr. Fendall, and Judge Nott were appointed a Committee on Credentials; and they retired and subsequently reported, through their chairman, the following named Delegates appointed for the year 1889, viz.:

PENNSYLVANIA COLONIZATION SOCIETY—Arthur M. Burton, Esq., Robert B. Davidson, Esq., Rev. Alfred L. Elwyn, and John Welsh Dulles, Esq.

The following DIRECTORS were stated to be also in attendance:

LIFE DIRECTOR—Dr. Charles H. Nichols.

EXECUTIVE COMMITTEE—Hon. Charles C. Nott, Reginald Fendall, Esq., Rev. Thomas G. Addison, D. D., Rev. Byron Sunderland, D. D., Dr. William W. Godding, Rev. A. J. Huntington, D. D., and Hon. J. C. Bancroft Davis.

Whereupon it was

Resolved, That the Report of the Committee on Credentials be accepted and approved, and the gentlemen named be received as members of the Board.

The Secretary presented and read the Seventy-Second Annual Report of the American Colonization Society.

Whereupon it was

Resolved, That the Annual Report be approved, and referred to the Standing Committee according to its several topics.

The Secretary presented and read the Statement of the Executive Committee for the past year with accompanying papers, viz.:

Statement of property of the Society, and a Table of receipts by States in the year 1888.

The Treasurer presented and read his Report of receipts and disbursements in the year 1888, with the certificate of audit.

Whereupon it was

Resolved, That the Statement of the Executive Committee and the Treasrer's Report just read, with the accompanying financial and annual papers, be accepted, and that so much of them as relate to Foreign Relations, Finance, Auxiliary Societies, Agencies, Accounts, Emigration, and Education, be referred to the several Standing Committees in charge of those subjects respectively.

The Chairman appointed the STANDING COMMITTEES, as follows:

COMMITTEE ON FOREIGN RELATIONS AND ON EDUCATION.—Robert B. Davidson, Esq., Rev. Byron Sunderland, D. D. and Hon. Charles C. Nott.

COMMITTEE ON FINANCE AND ON ACCOUNTS.—John Welsh Dulles, Esq., Reginald Fendall, Esq., and Robert B. Davidson, Esq.

COMMITTEE ON AUXILIARY SOCIETIES AND ON AGENCIES.—Rev. Thomas G. Addison, D. D., Rev. Byron Sunderland, D. D., and Rev. Alfred L. Elwyn.

COMMITTEE ON EMIGRATION.—Arthur M. Burton, Esq., Dr. William W. Godding, and Prof. A. J. Huntington, D. D.

On motion,

Resolved, That a Committee be appointed to nominate the Executive Committee and the Secretary and Treasurer for the ensuing year.

Messrs. Burton, Davidson, and Dulles were appointed the Committee.

Letters were read from the following named Directors presenting an excuse for absence, vix.: Rt. Rev. H. C. Potter, D. D., December 8; Dr. James Hall, December 10; William E. Guy, Esq., December 13; Rev. G. W. Samson, D. D., January 5, and Rev. E. W. Appleton, D. D., January 12; and from Hon. John H. B. Latrobe, President, December 10.

On motion,

Resolved, That the Board do now adjourn to meet in these rooms at 11 o'clock to-morrow morning.

Adjourned.

WASHINGTON, D. C., *January* 16, 1889.

THE BOARD OF DIRECTORS met this morning at 11 o'clock, in the rooms of the Society.

In the absence of Life Director Dr. Charles H. Nichols, occasioned by sickness, Delegate Arthur M. Burton, Esq., was, on motion, invited to preside.

Prayer was offered by Rev. Alfred L. Elwyn.

The Minutes of yesterday's meeting were read and approved.

Mr. Davidson, Chairman of the Standing Committee on Foreign Relations and on Education in Liberia, presented and read a Report; and it was accepted and approved.

Mr. Dulles, Chairman of the Standing Committee on Finance and on Accounts, presented and read the following Reports; and they were accepted and approved:

The Standing Committee on Finance have examined the Securities belonging to the Society and find that they agree with the Statement of the Treasurer.

The Standing Committee on Accounts have examined the Treasurer's Account for the year 1888 and the vouchers for the expenditures, and find the same correct.

Rev. Dr. Addison, Chairman of the Standing Committee on Auxiliary Societies and on Agencies, read the following as their Report; and it was accepted and the resolution was adopted:

WHEREAS, The Board of Directors have again and again passed resolutions favorable to the establishment of Auxiliary Societies in the different States, and to the employment of Agents to make known the objects of the Society and to collect funds for its work; Be it

Resolved, That the Executive Committtee be urgently requested to carry out, wherever convenient or practicable, the policy so often and emphatically endorsed by this Body.

Dr. Godding, from the Standing Committee on Emigration, read the following report; and it was accepted and approved:

Your Committee, while commending the care that has been exercised in the past in the selection of emigrants would urge upon the Executive Committee the necessity of continued vigilance in this direction, that quality rather than quantity is what Africa needs in the way of emigrants; that the ability to pay their own passage money should be accepted as the best evidence of that energy on the part of the emigrant which will help to found States, and that beyond this the use of the funds of the Society in the way of aiding emigration should be limited, as far as practiecable, to defraying the expenses of God-fearing men and women of African blood capable of making their way in the communities where they now reside, who would be an element of strength and not of weakness in civilizing and Christianizing the new world to which they go.

Your Committee would especially commend the effort that is being made to place the emigrants in new communities, developing the fertile lands of the interior of Liberia, and would recommend that that policy be continued.

Mr. Dulles, from the Special Committee on Nominations, reported, recommending the election of the following:

SECRETARY AND TREASURER—William Coppinger.

EXECUTIVE COMMITTEE—Hon. Charles C. Nott, Reginald Fendall, Esq., Rev. Thomas G. Addison, D. D., Rev. Byron Sunderland,

D. D., Dr. William W. Godding, Rev. Aioniram J. Huntington, D. D., Hon. J. C. Bancroft Davis.

Whereupon it was

Resolved, That the report be accepted and approved, and that the Board elect the officers nominated by the Committee.

On motion,

Resolved, That the Annual Report of the Society be referred to the Executive Committee for publication.

Rev. Mr. Elwyn offered prayer and the Board adjourned.

WM. COPPINGER, *Secretary*.

SEVENTY-THIRD

ANNUAL REPORT

OF THE

AMERICAN COLONIZATION SOCIETY,

WITH THE

MINUTES

OF THE

ANNUAL MEETING and of the BOARD OF DIRECTORS,

JANUARY 19, 21 & 22, 1890.

WASHINGTON CITY:
COLONIZATION BUILDING, 450 PENNSYLVANIA AVENUE,
1890.

AMERICAN COLONIZATION SOCIETY.

President.

1853. HON. JOHN H. B. LATROBE.

Vice-Presidents.

1851. Rev. Robert Ryland, D. D., Ky.	1878. Admiral Robert W. Shufeldt, U. S. N.
1851. Hon. Frederick P., Stanton, Va.	1880. Francis T. King, Esq., Maryland.
1859. Hon. Henry M. Schieffelin, N. Y.	1880. Rev. Samuel D. Alexander, D.D., N.Y.
1866. Hon. James R. Doolittle, Wis.	1881. Rev. Bishop H. W. Warren, D.D., Col.
1867. Samuel A. Crozer, Esq., Pa.	1882. Henry G. Marquand, Esq., N. Y.
1870. Robert Arthington, Esq., England.	1884. Rev. George D. Boardman, D.D., Pa.
1874. Rev. Bishop R.S. Foster, D.D., Mass.	1884. Rev. Bishop E.G.Andrews, D.D., N.Y.
1874. Rt. Rev. Gregory T. Bedell, D.D., O.	1884. Prof. Edw'd W. Blyden, LL.D., Liberia.
1875. Rt. Rev. M.A. DeW. Howe, D.D., Pa.	1884. Rev. Otis H. Tiffany, D. D., Minn.
1875. Samuel K. Wilson, Esq., N. J.	1884. Rt. Rev. Henry C. Potter, D.D., N.Y.
1876. Rev. Samuel E. Appleton, D. D., Pa.	1886. Hon. Alexander B. Hagner, D. C.
1876. Rev. H. M. Turner, D.D., LL.D., Ga.	1887. Hon. Robert S. Green, N. J.
1877. Rev. E. G. Robinson, D.D., R. I.	1888. Hon. William Strong, D. C.
1877. Rev. William E. Schenck, D. D., Pa.	1888. Rev. J. Aspinwall Hodge, D. D., Ct.
1878. Hon. Richard W. Thompson, Ind.	1888. Arthur M. Burton, Esq., Pa.

The figures before each name indicate the year of first election.

LIFE DIRECTORS.

1853. ALEXANDER DUNCAN, Esq........R. I.	1871. Rev. WILLIAM H. STEELE, D. D., N. J.
1864. ALEXANDER GUY, M. D........Ohio.	1871. R't. Rev. H. C. POTTER, D. D, N. Y.
1868. EDWARD COLES, Esq........Pa.	1873. Rev. GEORGE W. SAMSON, D. D., N. Y.
1869. REV. JOSEPH F. TUTTLE, D. D...Ind.	1878. Rev. EDWARD W. APPLETON, D. D., Pa.
1870. DANIEL PRICE, Esq............N. J.	1885. WILLIAM EVANS GUY, Esq......Mo.

DELEGATES FOR 1890.

NEW JERSEY COLONIZATION SOCIETY—Gen Clinton B. Fisk, Samuel K. Wilson, Esq., Rev. John Mille.

PENNSYLVANIA COLONIZATION SOCIETY.—Rev. Samuel E. Appleton, D. D., Rev. William E. Schenck, D. D., Arthur M. Burton, Esq., Rev. A. L. Elwyn.

SEVENTY-THIRD ANNUAL REPORT.

NECROLOGY.

Two Vice Presidents and two Directors of The American Colonization Society, during the past year, have been removed by death.

HON. HENRY A. FOSTER, of New York, elected in 1838, was a man of rare culture and refinement, and of Christian patience, strong faith and bright hope. It has been fitly said of him that "he was faithful to all obligations, and his hands were full of good works."

DR. HENRY LINDSLY, of Washington, D. C., elected in 1872, and also a Member of the Executive Committee from 1840 and its Chairman from 1858 to 1886, when impaired health caused his resignation. Those who had the pleasure of frequent and intimate relations with Dr. Lindsly have no words to express their high appreciation of his character and his deeds. Few have won for themselves the exalted place which he long held in the hearts of men as a Christian philanthropist of rare wisdom, of tender sympathy and of unassuming generosity.

DR. JAMES HALL, of Maryland, who constituted himself a Director in 1852. This gentleman, being in feeble health, went to Liberia, in 1831, in the hope, which was partly realized, that the sea-voyage and a change of climate would improve it. He served as the Physician of this Society in its then feeble colony for some eighteen months, and returning to Baltimore was appointed Agent of the Maryland State Colonization Society. November 27, 1833. Dr. Hall embarked on the brig Ann with 18 emigrants, and stopping at Monrovia and Bassa, where he secured some thirty colonists, mostly able bodied adults, he arrived at Cape Palmas, January 25, 1834. The next day, negotiations were entered upon with the Native Chiefs for lands on which to settle the emigrants; and the deed selling Cape Palmas to the Maryland State Colonization Society was signed February 14, 1834. This brought into Liberia one of the most important sections of West Africa. Dr. Hall governed the Colony with uncommon skill, bravery, sagacity and perseverance for about three years, when he again returned to Baltimore to serve the Maryland Society and to promote the general cause in this country, notably as

Editor of the *Maryland Colonization Journal* and Manager of the emigrant ships Liberia Packet, the Mary Caroline Stevens and the Golconda. The mere statement of Dr. Hall's lengthened services in Africa and in the United States is in itself impressive. But those who had the privilege of working with him learned to highly appreciate his manly principles and unprejudiced judgment, and to regard him with no small measure of affection and respect. His tender consideration, combined with a firm, rigid sense of duty, his large experience and clear judgment, united to make his guiding and elevating influence a power among those with whom he was associated.

Dr. Charles H. Nichols, of New York, constituted a Director in 1869, and also a Member of the Executive Committee from 1872 to 1877, when he removed from Washington City. His interest in the work of the Society was profound and constant, and his services were faithful and valuable. He has left his impress upon his chosen profession and for many years the influence of his wise management of affairs will be felt and honored. He bequeathed an unstained name and the record of a useful and beneficial life.

RECEIPTS AND DISBURSEMENTS.

There has been received during the past year $17,144.15. Of this amount $1,395.00 came from donations; $11,331.98 from legacies; $387.60 from applicants toward cost of passage; $453.52 for education in Liberia; $1,683.86 from interest on temporary loans, and $1,892.19 from other sources. These amounts, with the balance in the treasury at the beginning of the year, $3,918.36, have placed at the disposal of the Society $21,062.51. The expenditures of the year have amounted to $17,426.25, leaving a balance in the treasury of $3,636.26.

EMIGRATION.

Sixty emigrants were sent during the year, viz; fifty by the bark "Monrovia," sailed April 6, from New York for Bassa, and ten by the bark "Liberia," sailed October 1, from New York for Brewerville. Of these, eight were from Oakland, Florida; eight from Conway, Ark.; three from Evansville, Ind.; sixteen from St. Louis, Mo.; eight from Great Bend, Kansas; one from Denver, Colorado, and sixteen from Muscogee, Indian Territory. Thirty-five were twelve years of age and upwards; twenty-one were between twelve and two, and four were less than two years. Fourteen were reported as communicants in Baptist churches and seven in Methodist churches. Of the adult males, fifteen are farmers and one is a blacksmith. A gentleman well competent to judge, voluntarily pronounced these companies to be composed of the most promising material that ever embarked at New York for Africa. They took with them an unusually large quantity of baggage and agricultural and mechanical tools, and they gave the Society some $250 toward the cost of passage, in addition to defraying their railroad fare from their homes to the port of embarkation.

Intelligence has been received of the arrival in Liberia of these people and that the majority of them have entered upon their lands with hopefulness.

Emigration to Liberia every year under the auspices of the American Colonization Society has been uninterupted for the past sixty-nine years. Those now reported make the number sent since the civil war to be 4,136 and a total from the beginning of 16,136, exclusive of 4,722 recaptured Africans which it induced and enabled the Government of the United States to settle in Liberia, making a grand total of 21,858 persons to whom the Society has given homes in Africa.

APPLICATIONS.

That there exists a wide and deep interest in Africa in the minds and hearts of the Negroes in the United States is again proven by the almost daily receipt, during the past year, of applications for passage and settlement in Liberia. Thousands upon thousands of these people are thus represented. The applicants include laborers, farmers, mechanics, lawyers, teachers, physicians and preachers, competent to broaden the foundation and strengthen the superstructure of civilized and Christian government in Africa.

These applications come not only from all the Southern States, but from the West and Northwest, from Nebraska, Colorado, California, Arkansas, and the Indian Territory—showing that there is no section of the United States where there is not only unrest among the Negro population, but a desire to remove to the land of their fathers. From information and appeals constantly received at this office, it is estimated that there are more than half a million of people at this time ready to go if the way were open. Let these appeals be heeded by those able to assist, and a blessing will come upon this country and upon vast regions of the " Dark Continent."

Much of the desire to remove to Liberia is produced by intelligence received direct from relatives and acquaintances in that Republic. The following extract from a letter written by Rev. Ezekiel Ezra Smith, Minister Resident and Consul General of the United States to Liberia, penned after a residence there of over a year breathes the wishes of old settlers and points out some of the material advantages awaiting new comers :—

"I am thoroughly aroused to the importance of awakening the Negro of the United States to realize and appreciate the blessings there are in store for him here in Africa. I want to see 5,000 or 10,000 of my brethren from the United States come over, bringing money, coupled with intelligence and experience, so that there may be a beginning to utilize the wonderful resources of this country, which are so abundant in almost every section of the Republic. I am quite sure that I have seen lying around here iron ore containing from 85 per cent. to 90 per cent. of iron. I have several times had pointed out to me beds of anthracite coal. I want to see men of push and ability come here and, in addition to cultivating this very fertile soil, develope and utilize these resources. These, to say nothing of the other and more valued or precious minerals, which are well known to lie embosomed here, are quite sufficient to induce the industrious and enterprising Negro of the States to come over."

EDUCATION.

The schools of this Society in Liberia are reported to be increasing in pupils and to be making satisfactory progress in their studies. The parents and others are also stated to manifest an appreciable interest for what is thus being done for the rising generation.

GOVERNMENTAL ACTION.

The time seems to have come when the Government of the United States should evince an active interest and give substantial aid in the emigration of its colored population. Many thousands of them have appealed to Congress for pecuniary assistance, and other thousands are anxiously expecting that body to appropriate the necessary means to enable them to pass over and erect for themselves a nation in their ancestral land.

During the first week of the present Congress two distinct resolutions and a bill were introduced in the Senate and appropriately referred:—as thus reported by a leading newspaper:—

"Senator Morgan introduced a resolution instructing the Senate Committee on Foreign Relations to inquire into the relations of the United States with the Congo State, and their political rights and powers in that country. The purpose of this resolution is to open the way for negotiations which will establish the right of colored emigrants from the United States to settle in the Congo State and will determine their status in that country.

"Senator Gibson introduced a resolution instructing the same Committee to inquire into the expediency and practicability of acquiring or setting apart a territory for the occupation of the colored citizens of the United States, and how far and in what manner the Government can and ought equitably to aid them.

"Senator Butler introduced a Bill to provide for the emigration of persons of color and to appropriate money to pay the expenses of their transportation when necessary.

"Only a voluntary emigration is contemplated, of course. The territory to be occupied by the emigrants is to be set apart exclusively for their possession and benefit. Those who desire to go but are unable to pay their way, will be furnished free transportation. The political and commercial rights and relations of the colonists, in whatever territory they shall occupy, are to be carefully determined and assured to them, by treaty and otherwise. And the Government of the United States is to give such equitable aid to the emigrants as may be necessary to their continued welfare and improvement in the colonies, including the establishment of a system of common school education for their children."

The Republic already founded by American benevolence in West Africa, with its vast area of fertile land and in possession of the religious, civil and social institutions of the United States, presents, for the time being at least, the most desirable field for the emigration of the Negroes of this country, and to that Republic they chiefly desire to go. They want a country and a nation of their own, where their race possibilities can be unfolded in the light of civilization and Christianity.

And it would be a far reaching economy to assist these people to enter a field suited to the widest employment and highest development of their energies. They would create new markets for American productions, and in pushing the enterprises of America to the heard of the vast Continent of Africa, would reflect undying glories upon the land of their bondage.

LIBERIA.

The present promising condition of Liberia is evidenced:

First. By the increased agricultural industry of the settlers, their extending cultivation of coffee, cocoa and sugar, which is placing them in a condition not only of comfort but of independence.

Second. By the growing commerce of the Republic, which is laying under cultivation all available products, spontaneous and cultivated.

Third. By the earnestness with which the people are turning their attention to the interior and pushing their settlements and agricultural labors to the healthy and fertile highlands in that direction.

Fourth. By the development among the Aborigines, especially the Kroo tribe, in imitation and through the teaching of the settlers, of the knowledge and practice of civilized arts, mechanical and agricultural; also, their increasing intelligence and capital for the conduct of foreign trade. They have begun to ship their own products directly to Europe, and import thence merchandise suited to their localities.

Fifth. The erection by the settlers of schools and churches by their own means for the benefit of themselves and the Aborigines without any prompting or pecuniary aid from the United States. Chief among the educational agencies recently established by the Liberians is the Rick's Institute, founded by the liberality of a Negro immigrant from Virginia, and supported by the Baptists with no aid from America. It is conducted by three ministers, one educated at Liberia College, one at Shaw University, Raleigh, N. C., and the other brought up in Liberia without any special school training. A Mohammedan convert from the interior has been employed to teach Arabic and the vernacular languages.

The Liberians are more than ever awake to their privileges and duties on that Continent. Their influence upon the natives is everywhere increasing, and instead of the settlers relapsing into barbarism, as it is sometimes asserted, they are making effective inroads upon the physical, intellectual and moral wilderness. The recaptive Congoes who were captured in slave ships by United States men of war and landed in Liberia thirty years ago, have learned the arts of civilization, embraced Christianity and become capable citizens, filling important offices in the Republic. Some of these people have been recently introduced into the Congo Free State, under the auspices of the authorities there, as elements of civilization, owing to their knowledge of agriculture and the trades.

Letters from Liberia give the following specific information of the efforts of individual settlers. The first refers to Mr. Solomon Hill, of Arthington, who emigrated from South Carolina in 1871:—

"His influence upon the Aborigines has been most wholesome. Two of the native youth trained by him (Pessehs) are now their own masters, and have their coffee farms and live in neat frame houses, cultivating from thirty to fifty acres of land. One of them has recently married a highly esteemed colonist, widow of one of the late prominent settlers."

The other describes Mr. Clement Irons, who went from Charleston, S. C., in the "Azor" in 1878:—

"I visited the workshop under the superintendence of Mr. Clement Irons, at the Muhlenberg Mission. The boys in this mission are trained in various handicrafts. They build carts and wheelbarrows, run steam engines, make farm implements, etc. Mr. Irons has constructed a steamboat for the St. Paul's river of native timber."

There are many other settlers who went to Liberia since the civil war, who are pushing with effect the enterprises of civilization. Liberia is not relapsing but advancing.

AFRICA.

Mr. Henry M. Stanley has again come within the limits of civilized life, having completed his extraordinary enterprize. His work in Africa is of higher value the more that is known of it. It appears that among the things he has settled are these: The Congo traced from the sea to its head: discovery of the water-shed of the Nile and the Congo: almost absolute proof that lake Victoria is the largest body of fresh water in the world: and that the highest peak of the "Mountains of the Moon" attain an altitude of 18,000 feet and to be entirely snow-capped for 1,200 feet. Mr. Stanley is the only white man who has crossed Africa from east to west and from west to east! He richly merits admiration and praise for his courage, his resolution and his achievements.

The Powers of Europe are parcelling out provinces in Africa for themselves and stationing representatives who will be ready to extend their supremacy. England, France, Germany, Italy and Portugal have each their "sphere," with centres of importance from which each is striving to dominate the country and the natives around them. Jealousies have already been aroused and the old nations of Europe find their colonial possessions in Africa sources of perplexity and discord.

It will be discovered, after years of fruitless trial and the expenditure of countless treasure, that the plan of The American Colonization Society is the most effectual one by which to plant the standard of enlightenment, freedom and redemption in the extensive regions of the "Dark Continent."

Liberia is a comprehensive missionary station. In the daily occupations of her people; in the processes essential to their life; in their religious organizations, and in their education methods, they are doing an unconscious but effective missionary work. Hundreds of Aborigines are coming into daily contact with the settlements and are learning, without friction, the ways of Christian society and of a civilized life. Liberia is America's gift to Africa—a genuine offshoot from the American Republic.

TREASURER'S REPORT.

Dr. *Receipts and Disbursements of the* AMERICAN COLONIZATION SOCIETY *in the year* 1889. **Cr.**

Received Donations,	$1,395 00		Paid Passage and settlement of Emigrants,	$8,873 06
" Legacies,	11,331 98		" Education in Liberia,	618 40
" Emigrants toward passage,	387 60		" Taxes and repairs of Colonization Building,	2,654 27
" Subscriptions to Repository,	8 25		" Paper and printing the African Repository,	361 47
" Rent of Colonization Building,	1,883 94		" Salary of Secretary and Treasurer, office expenses, printing, postages, expenses of meetings and of contested Will	2,719 05
" For Education in Liberia	453 52			
" Interest on temporary investments,	1,683 86		" Temporary Investment	2,200 00
Receipts,	$17,144 15		Disbursements,	$17,426 25
Balance January 1, 1889,	3,918 36		Balance December 31, 1889,	3,636 26
Total,	$21,062 51		Total,	$21,062 51

The Committee on Accounts have examined the Treasurer's Account for the year 1889 and the vouchers for the expenditures, and find the same correct.

REGINALD FENDALL.
JOHN MILLER, } *Committee.*
A. L. ELWYN.

Washington, D. C., *January 22, 1890.*

MINUTES OF THE AMERICAN COLONIZATION SOCIETY.

WASHINGTON, D. C., *January 19, 1890.*

The American Colonization Society held its Seventy-Third Anniversary this evening in the Church of the Covenant, Connecticut Avenue and N and 18th Streets.

Religious services were conducted by Rev. Teunis S. Hamlin, D. D., pastor of the church, who also presented the Seventy-Third Annual Report of the Society, stating that an abstract of the same had been printed and placed in the pews for acceptance by the audience.

The Annual Discourse was delivered by Professor Edward W. Blyden, LL. D., of Liberia, from the text, Acts 16, 9 : " And a vision appeared to Paul in the night; There stood a man of Macedonia and prayed him, saying, come over into Macedonia, and help us."

The benediction was pronounced by Prof. Blyden.

COLONIZATION ROOMS, JANUARY 21, 1890.

The Annual Meeting of The American Colonization Society was held to-day at 3 o'clock p. m., in the rooms of the Society.

In the absence of the President, Rev. Samuel E. Appleton, D.D., of Philadelphia, Pa., Senior Vice President in attendance, presided.

The Minutes of the anniversary on the 19th inst., were read, and with the Minutes of the annual meeting, January 15, 1889, were approved.

Arthur M. Burton, Esq., Rev. William E. Schenck, D. D,, and Rev. John Miller were appointed a committee to nominate officers for the ensuing year : and they reported, recommending the re-election of the present President and Vice Presidents, as follows:—

President.

1853. HON. JOHN H. B. LATROBE.

Vice-Presidents.

1851. Rev. Robert Ryland, D. D., Ky.	1878. Admiral Robert W. Shufeldt, U. S. N.
1851. Hon. Frederick P., Stanton, Va.	1880. Francis T. King, Esq., Maryland.
1859. Hon. Henry M. Schieffelin, N. Y.	1880. Rev. Samuel D. Alexander, D.D., N.Y.
1866. Hon. James R. Doolittle, Wis.	1881. Rev. Bishop H. W. Warren, D.D., Col.
1867. Samuel A. Crozer, Esq., Pa.	1882. Henry G. Marquand, Esq., N. Y.
1870. Robert Arthington, Esq., England.	1884. Rev. George D. Boardman, D.D., Pa.
1874. Rev. Bishop R.S. Foster, D.D., Mass.	1884. Rev. Bishop E.G. Andrews, D.D., N.Y.
1874. Rt. Rev. Gregory T. Bedell, D.D., O.	1884. Prof. Edw'd W. Blyden, LL.D., Liberia.
1875. Rt. Rev. M.A. DeW. Howe, D.D., Pa.	1884. Rev. Otis H. Tiffany, D. D., Minn.
1875. Samuel K. Wilson, Esq., N. J.	1884. Rt. Rev. Henry C. Potter, D.D., N.Y.
1876. Rev. Samuel E. Appleton, D. D., Pa.	1886. Hon. Alexander B. Hagner, D. C.
1876. Rev. H. M. Turner, D.D., LL.D., Ga.	1887. Hon. Robert S. Green, N. J.
1877. Rev. E. G. Robinson, D.D., R. I.	1888. Hon. William Strong, D. C.
1877. Rev. William E. Schenck, D. D., Pa.	1888. Rev. J. Aspinwall Hodge, D. D., Ct.
1878. Hon. Richard W. Thompson, Ind.	1888. Arthur M. Burton, Esq., Pa.

The figures before each name indicate the year of first election.

Whereupon, on motion,

Resolved, That the Report be accepted and approved, and that the Society elect the officers nominated by the Committee.

On motion,

Resolved, That the Society tenders its thanks to Prof. Edward W. Blyden, LL. D., for the very able, eloquent and instructive discourse before the Society on its Seventy-Third Anniversary, and that he be requested to furnish a copy of the same for publication.

Resolved, That the thanks of the Society are hereby tendered to the Pastor and Session of the Church of the Covenant for the use of their church on the occasion of our Seventy-Third Anniversary.

On motion, adjourned.

WM. COPPINGER,
Secretary.

MINUTES OF THE BOARD OF DIRECTORS.

WASHINGTON, D. C., *January 21, 1890.*

The Board of Directors of the American Colonization Society met this day at 12 o'clock M. in the rooms of the Society, No. 450 Pennsylvania Avenue, N. W.

In the absence of Hon. John H. B. Latrobe, President of the Society, Rev. Samuel E. Appleton, D. D., was, on motion, invited to preside, and took the chair.

Prayer was offered by Rev. William E. Schenck.

Mr. William Coppinger was, on motion, appointed Secretary of the Board.

Mr. Fendall and Rev. Drs. Addison and Sunderland were appointed a Committee on Credentials: and they reported the following named Delegates appointed for the year 1890 :

New Jersey Colonization Society. Gen. Clinton B. Fisk,* Samuel K. Wilson Esq."* Rev. John Miller.

Pennsylvania Colonization Society. Rev. Samuel E. Appleton, D. D., Rev. William E. Schenck D. D., Arthur M. Burton, Esq., Rev. Alfred L. Elwyn.

The following *Directors* were stated to be in attendance :

Executive Committee. Reginald Fendall Esq., Rev. Thomas G. Addison D.D., Rev. Byron Sunderland D. D., Dr. William W. Godding.

Whereupon, on motion,

Resolved, That the Report of the Committee on Credentials be accepted and approved, and the gentlemen named be received as members of the Board.

On motion,

Resolved, That Prof. Edward W. Blyden, LL D., and Mrs. Jane R. Roberts, of Liberia, be and are hereby invited to seats in the Board and to participate in its deliberations.

The unprinted portions of the Minutes of the meetings of January 15 and 16, 1889, were read; and the Minutes were, on motion, approved.

The Secretary presented and read the Seventy-Third Annual Report of the American Colonization Society.

Whereupon, on motion,

Resolved, That the Annual Report be approved and referred to the Standing Committees according to its several topics.

The Secretary presented and read the Statement of the Executive Committee for the past year and accompanying papers.

The Treasurer presented and read his report of Receipts and Disbursements for the past year, with the certificate of audit: Also, a Statement of the Property of the Society, and a Table of Receipts by States in the year 1889.

Whereupon, on motion,

Resolved, That the Statement of the Executive Committee and the Treasurer's Report, just read, with accompanying papers, be accepted, and that so much of them as relate to Foreign Relations, Finance, Auxiliary Societies, Agencies, Accounts, Emigration, and Education, be referred to the several Standing Committees in charge of those subjects respectively.

The Chairman appointed the *Standing Committees*, as follows:

Committee on Foreign Relations and on Education.—Rev. William E. Schenck D. D., Rev. Byron Sunderland, D. D., Hon. Charles C. Nott.

Committee on Finance and on Accounts.—Reginald Fendall, Esq. Rev. John Miller, Rev. Alfred L. Elwyn,

Committee on Auxiliary Societies and on Agencies.—Rev. Thomas G. Addison, D. D., Rev. Byron Sunderland, D. D., Arthur M. Burton, Esq.

Committee on Emigration.- Dr. William W. Godding, Arthur M. Burton, Esq., Rev. John Miller.

On motion,

Resolved, That a Committee be appointed to nominate the Executive Committee and the Secretary and Treasurer for the ensuing year.

Messrs. Burton, Miller and Elwyn were appointed the Committee.

Letters were read from the following named *Directors* presenting an excuse for absence, viz: William E. Guy, Esq., Dec. 10: Rt. Rev. H. C. Potter, D. D., Dec. 12: Edward Coles, Esq., Dec. 16: Rev. G.W. Samson, D. D., Jan. 7: and Rev. E.W. Appleton, D. D., Jan. 19: and from Hon. John H. B. Latrobe, President, Jan. 20.

On motion,

Resolved, That when the Board adjourn it be to meet to-morrow morning at 10 o'clock; and that at 11 o'clock, the members proceed to make their customary call upon the President of the United States to pay their respects.

The Board, on motion, adjourned.

WASHINGTON, D. C., *January 22, 1890,*

The Board of Directors met this morning at 10 o'clock, in the rooms of the Society, Rev. Dr. Appleton in the chair.

Prayer was offered by Professor Blyden.

The Minutes of the meeting of yesterday were read and approved.

Rev. Dr. Schenck, Chairman of the Standing Committee on Foreign Relations and on Education in Liberia, presented and read a Report: and it was approved.

Mr. Fendall, Chairman of the Standing Committee on Finance and on Accounts, presented and read the following Reports: and they were approved;

The Standing Committee on Finance respectfully report; that they have examined the evidences of property belonging to the Society and find that they agree with the statement of the Treasurer.

The Standing Committee on Accounts have examined the Treasurer's Account for the year 1889 and the vouchers for the expenditures, and find the same correct.

Rev. Dr. Addison, Chairman of the Standing Committee on Auxiliary Societies and on Agencies, read the following resolutions as their Report: whereupon they were adopted:

Resolved, That additional efforts be made to organize Auxiliary Societies in the States where they do not now exist.

Resolved, That the policy of the Society hitherto pursued, whenever practical, of employing agents to advocate its claims and collect funds, be continued.

Dr. Godding, Chairman of the Standing Committee on Emigration, read a Report; and the accompanying resolutions were adopted.

The Board took a recess to enable the Directors to call upon the President of the United States; and then resumed its session.

Mr. Burton, from the Special Committee on Nominations, recommended the election of the following:

Secretary and Treasurer—William Coppinger.

Executive Committee—Hon. Charles C. Nott, Reginald Fendall, Esq., Rev. Thomas G. Addison, D, D., Rev. Byron Sunderland, D. D., Dr. William W. Godding, Rev. Adoniram J. Huntington, D. D., Hon. J. C. Bancroft Davis.

Whereupon, on motion,

Resolved, That the report be accepted and approved, and that the Board elect the officers nominated by the Committee.

On motion,

Resolved, That the Annual Report of the Society be referred to the Executive Committee for publication.

Rev. Mr. Elwyn offered prayer, and the Board then, on motion, adjourned.

WM. COPPINGER, *Secretary*.

www.ingramcontent.com/pod-product-compliance
Lightning Source LLC
Chambersburg PA
CBHW032051230426
43672CB00009B/1561